Between 1918 and 1968, the forces of revolution and counter-revolution fought a ceaseless battle over Europe's history. In Germany and Spain, the Moscow-led communist parties led the revolutionary movements to disaster. In the decades after the Second World War, democracy was regularly threatened by right-wing movements which aimed to dramatically constrict democratic rights. This 'Bonapartism' continually threatened democracy in France until the 1968 worker- and student-revolt destroyed the foundations of Gaullism.

In this book a participant and political leader within the revolutionary movement gives his perspectives on those struggles. A biographical note by Ernest Mandel, which introduces this volume, explains how over six decades in the workers movement Pierre Frank became perhaps the best-known anti-Stalinist revolutionary in France. He was one of the first to be arrested during the crisis of 1968, when the French section of the Fourth International was banned.

Frank was secretary to Leon Trotsky in the 1930s, a central leader of the Fourth International from the 1940s and, until his death in 1984, editor of its French-language theoretical journal, *Quatrième Internationale*. His best-known books are *The Long March of the Trotskyists* and *Histoire de l'Internationale Communiste*, a chapter of which has been specially translated for this volume.

PIERRE FRANK

Revolution and Counter-revolution in Europe

From 1918 to 1968

REVOLUTION AND COUNTER-REVOLUTION IN EUROPE

PIERRE FRANK

Revolution and Counter-revolution in Europe

From 1918 to 1968

Pierre Frank

With a biographical introduction by Ernest Mandel

International Institute for Research & Education, Amsterdam
Resistance Books, London

Both the International Institute for Research and Education and Resistance would be glad to have readers' opinions of this book, its design and translations, and any suggestions you may have for future publications or wider distribution.

Our books are available at special quantity discounts to educational and non-profit organizations, and to bookstores.

To contact us, please write to: Socialist Resistance, PO Box 62732 London SW2 9GQ, Britain, email contact@socialistresistance.org or visit: www.socialistresistance.org

Published by Resistance Books, June 2011
Printed in Britain by Lightning Source
Design by Lauren Plum

The translations in this volume may be republished under
http://creativecommons.org/licenses/by-sa/2.0/

© International Institute for Research and Education, 2011.

Published as issue 49 of the Notebooks for Study and Research.
ISSN 0298-7902
ISBN 9780902869783

Contents

Pierre Frank (1905-1984) by Ernest Mandel	9
The German Revolution (1918-1923)	14
Summary of the course on the Spanish revolution	54
Democracy or Bonapartism in Europe?	61
Bonapartism in Europe	75
France under the Fourth Republic	80
A Study in French Centrism	92
Political Crisis in France	106
Evolution of Eastern Europe	110
Under Pressure of the Coming War	125
The politics of French Stalinism	141
A Review: Trotsky's Diary in Exile	154
Eighty Years Ago	162
The Workers' Parties and de Gaulle	167
The Algiers Putsch of April 22	185
Mr. X versus de Gaulle	194
The Transitional Program	205
"We Will Emerge Stronger Than Ever!"	215
May 1968: First Phase of the French Socialist Revolution	216
Otto Bauer, Representative Theoretician of Austro-Marxism	267

REVOLUTION AND COUNTER-REVOLUTION IN EUROPE

Pierre Frank (1905-1984)
Ernest Mandel

Comrade Pierre Frank died Wednesday April 18, 1984, in the morning.[1] He was 78 years old and had been active in the workers movement for over six decades. His comrades and friends paid him a last tribute at the time of his cremation at the Pere-Lachaise cemetery, in Paris, on April 27.

With the death of Pierre Frank, the Fourth International loses one of the very last survivors of the generation of revolutionary communists who joined the fight of the Soviet Left Opposition and Comrade Lev Davidovich Trotsky, at the time the Soviet bureaucracy exiled the Russian revolutionary leader to Turkey, in 1929. Trotsky had developed a substantial influence among the French Communist Left, partly because the relations he had established with trade unionists like Pierre Monatte and Alfred Rosmer and Communists like Boris Souvarine during and immediately after World War I.

As a result, beginning in 1923, the various organs of the French Communist Left gave wide coverage and support, albeit often critical, to the struggle waged by the Left Opposition and Leon Trotsky within the Communist Party of the Soviet Union and the Communist International.

But only a small nucleus grouped around the surrealist Pierre Naville, the trade unionist Alfred Rosmer and the young chemical engineer Pierre Frank fully identified with Trotsky's struggle. Pierre Frank joined Trotsky on the island of Prinkipo, near Istanbul, and became part of the secretariat formed round the old Russian revolutionary. These young secretaries were the team that helped Trotsky prepare the first conference of the International Left Opposition (ILO) in 1930 and draft the founding document of our world movement.

The 1929-1934 period was a period of initial growth for the Trotskyist movement in France. Pierre Frank actively participated in its leadership, with his friend Raymond Molinier. The magazine *Lutte de Classe* (Class Struggle) and the newspaper *La Verite* (The Truth) were launched. An intense propaganda campaign was waged against the rise of the Hitlerite fascist threat in Germany. Still more intense was the agitation campaign for the workers united front to stop

---

[1] Reprinted with permission from *International Viewpoint*, Issue No. 52, pp. 15-16.

fascism, first in Germany and then in France. This campaign failed in Germany, with well-known tragic consequences.

But in France, after the February 6, 1934 events, it succeeded and opened the way to a new rise of the workers movement in all Western Europe. But the very successes scored by Trotskyist agitation on the ground created considerable difficulties for the building of an organization.

The small Trotskyist organization of the time, the Communist League, was overwhelmingly outweighed by the two reformist apparatuses -- the social democratic apparatus of the SFIO (Socialist Party) and the Stalinist apparatus of the PCF (Communist Party) -- who collaborated closely to smother the revolutionary anticapitalist potential contained in the expansion of the working class struggles and mass organizations.

The French Trotskyists had to engage in a series of discussions to determine the correct tactical orientation in that complex situation. A series of grievous differences and splits ensued in which Pierre Frank and Raymond Molinier did not always pick the same side as Leon Trotsky. Still, there were some positive developments for the Trotskyist current during the 1935-1939 period: gains in the Socialist left and later in the centrist Socialist Workers and Peasants Party (PSOP) left, with the recruitment of people like Jean Rous, David Rousset and Daniel Guerin who stayed with the Trotskyist movement for a time, and Pierre Lambert and Marcel Hic who joined it to remain the rest of their lives. Nevertheless, the fundamental trajectory was not towards growth, but towards stagnation and setback. In addition, beginning in 1937 the weight of the Popular Front's defeat in France and of the defeats of the Civil War in Spain began to bear down and paved the way for World War II.

Pierre Frank, Raymond Molinier and their very small group, separated from the bulk of the forces that prepared the foundation of the Fourth International in 1938, were chiefly identified with a thorough-going preparation of antimilitarist and anti-imperialist work that earned them repression and persecution at the hands of the French imperialist government. This led Pierre to move to Great Britain where he was also persecuted by the British government, including being interned in a concentration camp. He was gladdened by the news of a beginning reconciliation with Trotsky shortly before the latter's assassination in August 1940.

In occupied France, the different Trotskyist organizations remained divided by tactical problems, but they all continued the struggle under the occupation and made no concessions at any time to either German imperialism, and its super-exploitation of the French working class, or French imperialism. The prominent role of these fighters in launching the massive workers' and people's resistance in France earned these organizations a new phase of growth, running from 1940 to 1948.

This is when the group connected to Pierre Frank in France, under the leadership of Jacques Grimblat and Rudolphe Prager, began to orient, after some mishaps, towards the reunification of the Trotskyist movement which was actually achieved in 1944, following the European conference of Trotskyist organizations that took place in February of that year, in the midst of the occupation. Pierre Frank had drawn all the lessons from his own misadventures in the late 1930s and rejected blind factionalism; he applauded the course towards unity with both hands.

As soon as World War II was over and he was allowed to return to France, he joined the united Internationalist Communist Party (PCI), became a part of its leadership and was assigned by the latter to the leadership of the Fourth International that had been reconstituted around Michel Raptis (Pablo). In this capacity, he actively prepared the Second World Congress of the Fourth International in 1948, as well as all the successive congresses of our organization up to and including the Eleventh World Congress in 1979. He was often the reporter on important political and theoretical questions at International Executive Committees (IEC) and World Congresses. He was also the editor in charge of the publication of the magazine *Quatrième Internationale* for several decades, and without his obstinacy that journal would not have the continuity that it enjoys today.

With the end of the post-World War II revolutionary upsurge in Western Europe, that is around 1948-1949, the French Trotskyist movement -- along with the Trotskyist movement in all Western Europe and North America -- went through a new period of stagnation and setback which were reflected by increasing internal problems and a series of splits. Pierre Frank participated in all these internal debates and understood they had a function beyond their negative aspects. The fact is, they served to maintain the programmatic and theoretical continuity of our movement through the inevitable readjustments necessitated by the new phenomena revolutionary Marxists had to grapple with, such as the victory of the Yugoslav, Chinese and Indochinese revolutions led by forces which originated in the international Stalinist movement but were led to break with it on key questions of revolutionary strategy to be able to lead the revolution to victory in their respective countries.

The small PCI survived during this period, led by Pierre Frank. Its main achievement was to understand the importance of the colonial revolution that continued to unfold in the world throughout the 1950s and 1960s. Because of this solidarity work, Pierre Frank was arrested in 1956. Thus, he had the honor of being the only leader of the French workers movement to be arrested for solidarity with the Algerian revolution.

Indeed, the PCI, spurred on mainly by Michel Raptis and Pierre Frank, committed itself to an active defense, including material and political aid, of the Algerian revolution, the Cuban revolution and the Vietnamese revolution. This enabled it to influence and then win over a broad current of Communist youth in the Union of Communist Students (*Union des Etudiants Communistes* -- UEC) that had spontaneously adopted the same orientation.

This led to the creation of the Revolutionary Communist Youth (*Jeunesse Communiste Revolutionnaire* -- JCR) and after the thunderbolt of May 1968, to the fusion of the JCR and PCI that gave birth to the Communist League, French section of the Fourth International, the first example in Europe of the transformation of one of the small original Trotskyist groups into a numerically stronger organization with more roots in the working class.

The resurgence of the world revolution in each of its three sectors, with the upsurge of the colonial revolution, the resumption of the workers struggle of prerevolutionary scope in a series of Western European countries, and the process that led to the Prague Spring, made it possible for the Fourth International to resolve, at least partially, the problem of its internal divisions and led to the reunification of our movement in 1962-1963.

For five years, the Fourth International had to work under conditions of extreme organizational and administrative weakness, with a day-to-day leadership reduced in fact to three people: Comrade Pierre Frank who was its organizational linchpin, Comrade Joseph Hansen, insofar as the reactionary Voorhis Act, forbidding U.S. organizations to affiliate internationally permitted, and myself. After the breakthrough and development of our organizations in 1968-1969, our movement was able to establish broader leadership structures in which Pierre Frank continued to occupy a prominent position.

His literary work includes many articles and brochures, but two of his books deserve particular mention: The History of the Fourth International and especially the monumental *Histoire de l'Internationale* Communiste (1919-1943) whose two volumes were published by La Breche Publishers in 1979. This book, which is the only scientific, Marxist work on this decisive topic illustrates the scope of the experience and lucidity that Pierre acquired in his nearly sixty years of activism. Likewise, it also reflects his fundamental concern for the continuity of communist theory and practice, that is, in the twentieth century, of revolutionary Marxist theory and practice.

Pierre Frank had a very deep sense of friendship, generosity and of the indispensable emotional ties that bind militants committed to the gigantic task of reconstructing the world on a socialist basis. Because our movement embodies an obstinate desire to maintain the continuity of the Communist movement, Pierre Frank attached particular importance to all manifestations of a rebirth of Leninism and Marxism in the Soviet Union and other bureaucratized workers states. The explosion of workers' struggles in Poland and around Solidarność, the appearance of Comrade Alexander Zimine's book *Le stalinisme et son "socialisme reel"* ("Stalinism and its 'Actually Existing Socialism'"), produced in the Soviet Union and published by La Breche in 1983, were a source of joy and satisfaction and marked the last years of his life. In all the conversations I had with him, these were the events, along with the need to give the utmost importance to the differentiations presently developing within the PCF, that occupied his attention.

Farewell dear comrade, dear friend, older brother. Your memory will live on in the Fourth International with whose existence and construction your entire life was identified. The growth and transformation of our movement, leading to the future mass communist International, will enable us to keep that memory alive in the entire international working class.

April 1984

The German Revolution (1918-1923)

Before 1914, Germany was in the eyes of the socialists all over the world, the first nation which would show humanity the way to socialism. Its industry had developed at an extraordinary speed, its capitalism had begun to dispute the hegemony of British capitalism, and its working class was both numerically the most powerful and the best organized in the world. It was the centre of gravity of the international worker's movement and constituted a "model" for all the socialist parties. Until then the German social-democratic party had dominated the 2nd International. But the bankruptcy of social-democracy in August 1914 threw a dark stain on that picture.[2]

In the very course of the war revolutionary minorities had covertly organized themselves condemning militarism. Strikes and rebellions had taken place. In 1918, the defeat of the German armies had been accompanied by revolutionary movements bringing about the fall of the Hohenzollern monarchy and the creation of *Räte*, the German word for soviets, i.e. councils. The audacious Russian revolution was in full swing, and with the triumph of the German revolution the victory of the socialist revolution would have been secured in Europe. One could not stress too strongly that the chief aim of the Communist International was precisely the victory of the socialist revolution in Germany.

This outlook, which had nothing of a utopia, was shared by the revolutionaries in the whole world. But even the most enthusiastic among them knew too well that the victory would not be won easily, that great difficulties existed in the very midst of the German working class. Lenin expressed this very clearly after the October victory in 1917.

The objective conditions in Germany were as ripe as possible. The theoretician of the social democracy, prior to 1914, Kautsky, who in 1909 had admitted this in his book The Way to Power (*Der Weg zur Macht*), however made every effort to attribute the attitude of the social democracy confronted with the war, amongst other causes, to the weaknesses of the working class in general and of the German

---

[2] © IIRE, 2010. Translated with permission of Editions La Breche by Hendrik Patroons from Chapter 2 of *Histoire de l'Internationale Communiste* (1919-1943), vol. I, 1979.

working class in particular. The latter assertion was belied by the history – left today almost completely in oblivion – of the revolutionary struggles during the years which followed the 1914-1918 war. Struggles to which hundred of thousands of workers took part, often arms in hand, lacking neither courage nor self-sacrifice. But it was obvious that, from the first 1918 revolutionary movements onwards and considering the tragic absence of a revolutionary leadership, that the question par excellence for the German revolution had to do with the relationship between the working masses and those who aimed at giving them a revolutionary outcome.

Set free from prison by the November 1918 revolution, Rosa Luxemburg and Karl Liebknecht had founded the German Communist Party from the *Spartakusbund* formed during the war. They had given it the name recommended by Lenin, following the bankruptcy of the 2nd International. Despite their popularity in the German working class, Karl and Rosa were however acknowledged as a leadership only by a minority in the very middle of the existing revolutionary vanguard: the Berlin *revolutionäre Obleute*, representing the factories of this city, did not support them in their majority. In their own party too, their existed strong ultra-left tendencies, and others too, liable to get involved in all kind of misjudged actions. Hence the weaknesses of the German Communist Party (KPD) confronted with the provocations of social democrats like Ebert and Noske in January 1919, and later on in March 1921.

The organization had gained considerable strength and had become a real mass party following the merger with the Independents[3] (USPD). There were in that party many outstanding "middle cadres", probably more than, in the other communist parties. But the question of the central revolutionary leadership, the head of the party, was far from having been solved. On its right, the party got rid, following the "March action", of Paul Levi, who had joined what was left of the Independents and was making his way towards the social democracy. On its left, the party had lost a substantial number of members for the benefit of the KAPD[4] which disintegrated. From the beginning of the year 1922, the KPD had largely made up for the losses following the "March action". The systematic practice of a united-front policy helped to strengthen it appreciably, not only in the regions of old socialist tradition, such as Saxony and Thuringia where there existed strong leftist socialist tendencies, but as well in Berlin where its influence was hegemonic in the workers' movement, in Hamburg, in the Ruhr, etc.

---

[3] The Unabhängliche Sozialistische Partei Deutschlands (USPD), a left-wing split from the social-democratic SPD.
[4] The *Kommunistische Arbeiterpartei Deutschlands*, a left-wing split from the KPD.

However, despite this progress, the KPD had not really found a steady central leadership. At the head of the leadership, there had been, since the end of January 1922, Heinrich Brandler, an extremely able militant of trade union origin; it included also competent Marxists like August Thalheimer, Paul Frölich, Ernst Meyer, experienced trade union militants such as Fritz Heckert and Jacob Walcher. The ability of that leadership, in concerning the day-to-day defence of the political and economic demands and propaganda, was undeniable; but it lacked self-confidence when confronted with the more general problems and the tasks implied by the latter. There were also militants in the party who, feeling in their heart of hearts the weakness of the Brandler leadership, aspired to a bolder policy and were harbouring a nostalgic yearning for bolder actions. Those tendencies could be found mainly in Berlin, Hamburg and the Ruhr, but they only had, to express themselves and lead them, persons as Maslow, Ruth Fischer, Scholem, Urbahns and so on, who were themselves afflicted with various weaknesses (lack of maturity for some, loose links with the working class for others) and above all, as far as the two main Berlin leaders were concerned, Maslow and Ruth Fischer, an often crude demagogy and a propensity in favour of internal manoeuvres in the party.

At the time of the 4th Congress of the Comintern, the KPD initial crises had been broadly overcome. The united front policy had been clarified. The party seemed to be on the way to the increasing strength and growth which had been experienced during the year 1922[5]. Exceptional events took place which confronted the party with much more demanding tasks than those which had occurred during its recovery and gradual progress.

The Occupation of the Ruhr

The Treaty of Versailles, signed in 1919, had imposed on Germany the payment of such a considerable amount of war reparations that they would have been completely illusory even if the German Government had wanted to honour the financial clauses of the treaty. The evidence of the extravagant character of those clauses

---

[5] The Austrian historian Arnold Reisberg, working at the Institute of Marxism-Leninism in the GDR, gives a very rich documentation about the way the united front policy was elaborated in the IC and in the KPD. The author does not hide the names of Trotsky, Radek and Zinoviev and does not distort the positions they defended (*Lenins Beziehungen zur deutschen Arbeiterbewegung.* Dietz, Berlin 1970; *An den Quellen der Einheitsfrontpolitik. Der Kampf der KPD um die Aktionseinheit der deutschen Arbeiterklasse in den Jahren 1921 und 1922. Ein Beitrag zur Erforschung der Hilfe Lenins und der Komintern für die KPD.* Dietz, Berlin 1971.)

from the point of view of the capitalist economy itself had been pointed out, during the drawing up of the treaty, by a young British economist, assigned to support the British delegation, who was later on to achieve a world fame: Keynes. The successive German governments, together with the German capitalists had no intention whatsoever to provide such reparations which, whatever the amount, hampered their aspirations for setting up again the economy of their country, in order to start again their march towards world hegemony. The signing of the Treaty of Versailles was followed by a number of international conferences, with the more realistic British Governments opposing, in the end, the French Governments. This opposition was encouraging Germany to resist the demands of the French government.

At the end of the year 1922, this situation came to a dead-lock. Taking a stand on some of the treaty clauses provided for the case of reparations being non-paid, the French Government backed the Belgian Government, ordered the military occupation of the Ruhr on the 11th January 1923, in order to procure the reparations through the work and resources of that region, one of the most industrialized and richest in Germany.

When considering that military occupation of a part of the German territory, not from the point of view of judicial claims put forward by the head of the French Government, the former President of the Republic Raymond Poincaré, but from the view of international relations between states, it practically meant an extension of the world war, a breaking down of peace. One should remember that there existed in the French political and military circles strong currents holding the opinion that the armistice of the 11th November 1918 had been signed prematurely, that the German territory should have been invaded and peace restored only after dismantling Germany. Independently from the fanciful character of such schemes, the occupation of the Ruhr was taking place at the time when the German political situation was very unstable and when revolutionary tensions remained just beneath the surface. The military intervention of French capitalism confronted all the German social classes with problems requiring exceptional solutions.

The German Government and the capitalists acted as if they were facing a state of war but, for the fact that being widely unarmed, they were unable to fight. The chancellor of the Reich and the Cuno Government, supported by the Reichstag, called the Ruhr population to "passive resistance". That meant refusing to obey the occupant's orders; the local authorities and the employers were to conform to the only directives of the German Government. As a result, heavy fines were imposed on towns, well known manufacturers, such as Thyssen, were arrested and condemned by the French authorities. In the Ruhr, nationalist organizations committed acts of sabotage, armed attacks, whilst the French Government which had declared martial law was encouraging autonomist groupings to create an independent Rhineland Republic. For the workers "passive resistance" meant most often strike during which they received help from their government, which did not solve at all their conditions of life, economically well as politically. That policy on the part of the German authorities, after few months, led to economic then political consequences which they had not foreseen when they opted for "passive resistance".

In the immediate, new problems arose inside the KPD. Obviously, it had to stand against the French occupation and take part in the strike with the Ruhr workers, but that was to be done without the supporting the Government and the capitalists. At the beginning, it did not associate with the official statements and declared one should fight both against "Poincaré in the Ruhr and Cuno on the Spree".

The Common Action of the French and German Communist Parties

The occupation of the Ruhr was actually an extension of the world war without armed struggle. During it, the Comintern had to show concretely how, unlike the social democrats, the communist parties led the fight against an imperialist war. As soon as the Ruhr was occupied, the leaderships of the French and German communist parties organized a Franco-German conference in Essen, supported by the French trade union CGTU, to which came delegations from the CPs of Belgium, Great Britain, Italy, Czechoslovakia and the Netherlands. That conference adopted a courageous position. The French Government reacted by putting in prison, charged of "plot", the French delegates Marcel Cachin, Albert Treint, the General Secretary of the Party, Gaston Monmousseau, the General Secretary of the CGTU and fifteen other leaders who were brought before the Senate invested with the power of High Justice Court. That "plot" was debunked a few months later.

Besides, the French Young Communist organization undertook an intense propaganda amongst the French occupation troops, giving out leaflets and papers written in French and German which called for fraternization between French and German soldiers and workers. The results of that propaganda and a few refusals to fire at the workers frightened the French authorities which proceeded to arrest many soldiers. The latter were brought before a court-martial. At the

Mayence trials, from June 1924 onwards, 37 French soldiers were sentenced to a total of more than 130 years of prison. The Ruhr events, the "plot", the action of fraternization occurred just after Frossard and a group which refused to adopt the resolutions of the 4th Congress of the Comintern had left. The action on the part of the French Communist Youth did not bring about great mass mobilizations, the working class having been for over a year under their employers' offensive. But the French PC which had just resolved long internal struggles had led the exemplary political struggle for a revolutionary minority; it was one of the first stages of the process of building a revolutionary party in France since 1914.

Under the impulse of the KPD, a commission of the Ruhr factory councils launched an appeal – the German trade union organizations led by the social democrats failing to act – to the various political internationals, to the trade unions and the social democratic parties with the aim of organizing a conference to discuss the question of the occupation of the Ruhr. That conference took place in Frankfurt in March, but with little success: the reformist political and trade union organizations did not attend.

With the extension of the occupation, incidents arose between the French occupation army and the German nationalist elements who were not at all native inhabitants of the Ruhr; former members of the "volunteer corpses" which in 1918, 1919 and 1920 had played a counter-revolutionary role were involved. The most notorious incident was an act of sabotage under the direction of a lieutenant one of those "volunteer corpses": Leo Schlageter. He was arrested, sentenced to death and shot by a Franc firing squad on the 26th May. The execution caused a considerable stir in the whole of Germany. At the same time, the Ruhr workers, reduced to struggle owing to their difficult situation, were subjected to the repression of both the French occupants and the German police who were very careful to see that the "passive resistance" should not endanger capitalist institutions and property. The German political situation was getting once again tense and taking a worrying turn, marked by the development of nationalist feelings, even inside the working class which was becoming more and more confused of the KPD's lack of determination.

At the end of January, the 8th Congress of that party, held in Leipzig had not put as the main item on its agenda the occupation of the Ruhr and had not worked out the possible perspectives. The discussion had been about the united front and the workers' government on account of the relationships with the Social Democratic Party which were taking shape in the Saxony. The Maslow-Fischer left wing had practically been almost continuously on the offensive since the 4th Congress of the Comintern, under any pretext. The tension increased in the KPD when in Saxony the Social Democratic Party of that *Land* decided at their convention held in March to break away from the bourgeois parties and to consider the possibility of a governmental coalition with the communist party. A meeting of the Presidium of the Comintern Executive held in April succeeded in reaching an organizational compromise amongst the leadership, but that precarious compromise did not meet the requirements of the political situation. A session of the enlarged Executive – the 3rd Plenum – was convoked for the month of May, but it was postponed until the 12th June, owing to the tense relationships which developed between Soviet Russia and Great Britain.

The Curzon Ultimatum

Important debates were taking place on the German situation when, the Soviet leadership had, all of a sudden, to concentrate on the question of the relationships between the Soviet Union and Great Britain. The Foreign Office was run by Lord Curzon, an ultra-reactionary conservative, who rapidly brought about the deterioration of the relationships established under the cabinet of Lloyd George. Within the tense international climate, brought about by the occupation of the Ruhr, the British *chargé d'affaires* in Moscow, handed the Soviet Government on the 8th of May, a 26 point note, referred to as the "Curzon ultimatum". It asked for the withdrawal of two Soviet notes written in the name of the Foreign Affairs Commissariat by the under-secretary of the Western Desk; that withdrawal was to take place within ten days failing which, the commercial agreement would be denounced and the *chargé d'affaires* recalled to London. Since May 2nd, Marshall Foch was in Poland reviewing the troops. On May 10th, the Soviet Ambassador in Rome, Vorovsky, was assassinated in Lausanne where he was on a mission for his Government. Those events, happening as it were simultaneously, looked ominous: war seemed near, even imminent to the Soviet leaders. They needed the whole of their diplomatic skill in order to, without lacking firmness, succeed in cooling the situation. But those events had diverted the attention of the Bolshevik leaders from the situation in Germany and had caused a postponement of the enlarged Executive 3rd session.

The Schlageter Affair

As a leading member of the Comintern, Radek's duty was to follow the German problems and the KPD policy. Left to himself, always watchful, supersensitive, impulsive, he could carry out sudden important political capers. The Plenum, starting on the 12th June had dealt with several items on its agenda when, on the 21st, during the discussion on the fight against fascism, Radek delivered a speech, the orientation of which was later on qualified as the "Schlageter line". During the previous months, discussions had taken place in Germany and in the Comintern on the position to be adopted towards the masses affected by nationalism. The KPD theoretician, Thalheimer had, in the party's theoretical review [referring to the Ruhr occupation], given himself up to disturbing distinctions when dealing with the policy of the German bourgeoisie.

Thalheimer made a distinction about the upper bourgeoisie, essentially counterrevolutionary domestically and objectively revolutionary abroad. He justified his judgment by putting forward examples dating from a time when the bourgeoisie in general still played a progressive role, but which were out of date now. The cowardice of the social democracy whose main leaders were turning towards the upper bourgeoisie could still less become an argument in favour of that thesis. The proletariat cannot accept, especially in an imperialist country the bourgeoisie as objectively revolutionary in its actions abroad, even if it brings about, through its policy, a revolutionary situation. The communist leadership could not disregard what was happening inside the petty-bourgeoisie for, in the relationship of forces between capital and the working class, the feelings of the various petty-bourgeois strata are an important component, sometimes even a decisive one. That problem was for a short time solved unfortunately by the "Schlageter line". In a speech at the 3rd Plenum, Radek could see in Germany "a great industrial nation thrown back to the rank of a colony", mistaking a country military occupied which was remaining in spite of that, one of the main imperialist countries in the world, with a colonial country essentially characterized by its economic structure and its dependence to imperialist countries.

It was not surprising that in a political situation as confused and as explosive as Germany's. The radicalisation of the masses should not present itself as a simple political phenomenon: the expanding anti-capitalist feelings were mixed with other feelings, resulting of old prejudices such as nationalist feelings, owing to the fact that foreign troops were occupying part of the national territory. Already in 1918-1920, the KPD and the KAPD had included tendencies in which bolshevism and nationalism mingled together. A revolution is never a "pure" political phenomenon. In the course of the First World War, the first European revolutionary uprising had been that of the Irish in

Dublin at Easter 1916 against British imperialism. During that uprising, workers' militias under the leadership of James Connolly had fought side by side with catholic formations (Connolly's socialist revolutionary convictions mingled with religious feelings). The fact had give rise to discussions amongst the anti-war and revolutionary minorities of that time. Some had condemned that political mixture. To which Lenin had answered very clearly:

"To imagine that social revolution is *conceivable* without revolts by small nations in the colonies and in Europe, without revolutionary outbursts by a section of the petty bourgeoisie *with all its prejudices,* without a movement of the politically non-conscious proletarian and semi-proletarian masses against oppression by the landowners, the church, and the monarchy, against national oppression, etc.-to imagine all this is to *repudiate social revolution.* So one army lines up in one place and says, "We are for socialism", and another, somewhere else and says, "We are for imperialism", and that will he a social revolution! Only those who hold such a ridiculously pedantic view could vilify the Irish rebellion by calling it a "putsch".

"Whoever expects a "pure" social revolution will *never* live to see it. Such a person pays lip-service to revolution without understanding what revolution is.

"The Russian Revolution of 1905 was a bourgeois-democratic revolution. It consisted of a series of battles in which *all* the discontented classes, groups and elements of the population participated. Among these there were masses imbued with the crudest *prejudices,* with the vaguest slid most fantastic aims of struggle; there were small groups which accepted Japanese money, there were speculators and adventurers, etc. But *objectively,* the mass movement was breaking the hack of tsarism and paving the way for democracy; for this reason the class-conscious workers led it.

"The socialist revolution in Europe *cannot* be anything other than an outburst of mass struggle on the part of all and sundry oppressed and discontented elements. Inevitably, sections of tile petty bourgeoisie and of the backward workers will participate in it— without such participation, *mass* struggle is *impossible,* without it no revolution is possible—and just as inevitably will they bring into the movement their prejudices, their reactionary fantasies, their weaknesses slid errors. But *objectively* they will attack *capital"*[6]

Lenin was frightened neither by words, nor by facts. Similar situations have occurred too when the greatest part of the European continent was occupied by the German armies during the Second World War.

---

[6] Lenin, Collected Works Volume 22. http://bit.ly/asIeVG

The KPD could not, of course, ignore the nationalist feelings displayed by the petty-bourgeoisie which was becoming more and more radical, nor by a part of the working class. One ought, by making use of the masse's anger, show them who the true enemies were, and where the solution laid. But between the "Schlageter speech" and its rectification, the KPD had proceeded to some "implementation" of that orientation. There had been meetings, discussions between the KPD and some nationalist leaders such as Count Reventlow. In a very short time a well-founded preoccupation led to a wrong course of action. One should not underestimate the consequences of that political swerve. (Later, during the "third period", the "Schlageterline" would cast its shadow on the politics of the party.) That occurred at a time when the German situation was climbing towards a paroxysm; it contributed to confusing, if only for a short time, the party members and still more, to divert their attention from the main orientation to be followed in such circumstances, from the aim on which all their strength should have been concentrated, that is to say, *the working class united-front in order to lead it towards the fight for power*. For the events took a surprisingly rapid turn.

The General Strike against the Cuno Government

The occupation of the Ruhr, that stronghold of German industry, created a kind of frontier in the middle of Germany; that fact, added to the "passive resistance" had a considerable adverse effect on the economy. Inflation developed in Germany to a level which has never been known since in a developed capitalist economy. A few figures can enable us to understand why the capitalists, and chiefly the German capitalists, have retained to this day an inexpressible fear of inflation.

In April 1922, a dollar was worth about 1,000 marks. During the course of 1923, the exchange value became[7]:

Mid-February	18,000 to 20,000 marks
May	48,000 marks
June	110,000 marks
July	349,000 marks
August	4,6000,000 marks

Those extraordinary figures are of course a rough estimate as they increased so rapidly. They can only give a small idea of what that inflation implied for the population. Prices did not mean anything anymore. The workers' wages, the civil servants' salaries, the

---

[7] W.T. Angress, *Die Kampfzeit des KPD, 1921-1923*, Dusseldorf 1973.

retirement or invalidity pensions could not keep up with the increase of the cost of living which, at a certain time, varied not only from day to day, but from hour to hour. No contract, no collective agreement, no statistical index could be a reference mark of any value whatsoever. With the exception of speculators and usurers demanding prohibitive interest rates, of factory owners exporting their goods in exchange for dollars or other stable currencies, the whole of the population was plunged at the end of the spring and at the beginning of summer into increasingly poverty and a general state of uncertainty.

The most affected by inflation were firstly those who only had a fixed income: retired people, pensioners. It was the case too, of small landlords who lived off the income provided by a few tenants: either the rents had lost their value or the sale of their property raised paper-money which lost its value immediately. The workers had been able to fight back for a while, but for only a short while, as the wages could not follow such an increase in prices. The workers' organizations were also struck in their activities in spite of the political possibilities which the situation offered; the value of membership dues lost all meaning and the wages of the trade union officers suffered the same fate as the wages in the factories.

That situation brought about an important radicalisation. The class struggle was spreading considerably. The working masses, seeing the lowering of their standard of living, engaged into actions which could not stay within the frame of bourgeois legality; they turned against their employers, the State and all authorities. As weeks were passing by strikes, demonstrations and street incidents multiplied. On the other hand, fascist forces were growing, more particularly in regions such as Bavaria, and turning to violence with the support of the military. A general state of anxiety prevailed. In that situation full of uncertainty, the KPD took the initiative in organizing an "anti-fascist day" on the 29th July. Except for Saxony and Thuringia, the state governments – starting with Prussia, its home secretary being the social democrat Severing – banned the demonstrations. The KPD leadership was divided on the response to that ban as it was not possible to ignore it without considering the means of standing up to armed intervention by the authorities. In the end it decided to hold only indoor meetings in the places where the demonstrations had been banned.

A few days later the situation took suddenly a turn for the worse, in a way which was also unexpected for the KPD leadership. The Reichstag had been convoked for the 8th August; the Cuno Government which had started the "passive resistance" at the beginning of the year, asked for a vote of confidence. It was the signal for strikes and demonstrations which multiplied. On 10th August, the

strike affected the Berlin underground and transport, then the printers, especially those working for the State Press producing paper money. This produced, together with the increase in prices and the fall of the mark, an inextricable situation. The strike was spreading in Berlin and in the whole of the country. Demonstrations multiplied, scuffles were taking place about everywhere and in many places the police proceeded to shootings resulting in deaths and casualties. On the 11the August, an assembly of the factory committees from the Berlin area drew up a platform with the following demands:
- Immediate resignation of the Cuno Government,
- Constitution a workers' and peasants' Government,
- Requisition of food supplies and a fare sharing under the supervision of the workers' organizations,
- Immediate recognition of the committees of workers' control,
- Lifting of the prohibition of the workers' militias (proletarische Hundertschaften),
- Immediate fixing of a minimum hourly wage of 60 gold pfennigs,
- Employment for all the unemployed in the production,
- Lifting of the state of emergency and the ban on demonstrations,
- Immediate release of working class political prisoners.

That platform was conveying the increased influence of the KPD in the factories. Negotiations took place between the trade unions, the Social Democratic Party and the Communist Party on the course to be taken, but in vain, since on this same 11th August, the Cuno Government, unable to find a solution to the situation, handed in its resignation and on the 12th August a government was formed in haste with on its head Stresemann. It was a wide coalition government – excluding the extreme right and of course the KPD – which had been contemplated for some time. The social democrats came back to the government from which they had been excluded since the fall of the Wirth ministry and the formation of the Cuno Government in November 1922. Stresemann was the leader of the *Volkspartei*, the party of the factory owners. It ordered at once the abandonment of the "passive resistance" which was a failure for German capitalism, in the same way as the occupation of the Ruhr was for the French.

As soon as he came to power, Stresemann promised too a kind a kind of wage expressed in gold to workers, tried to keep the fascists off, which although relatively weak in numbers were extremely aggressive, and above all to ward off the revolutionary unrest. He had to find at the same time longer term solutions in order to restore an economic situation in complete ruin. He could not succeed at that moment with only the help of German capitalism. It was then that American capitalism intervened under the form of the "Dawes Plan".

The Dawes Plan

The general strike which had caused the downfall of the Cuno Government was a warning for American capitalism as much as for German capitalism. At the end of the war, the U.S. Congress had refused to ratify the Treaty of Versailles, because it did not want to be bound by its decisions concerning Europe. A wave of isolationism went then through the United States. Isolationism was perhaps valid as part of an electoral platform, mainly with regard to the farmers of the Mid-West; but at a time when American imperialism was striving for world hegemony, isolationism – which besides had never really meant for the Pacific and Latin America – was not valid either with regard to Europe at a time when the ghost of the socialist revolution was standing up in the most industrialized country in that continent. The United States were bound to come to the help of the Stresemann Government in order avert a catastrophe in Germany.

During the year a Commission had been set up including representatives of the Allies and of the Germans under the presidency of an American General, Dawes, who acted formally "on his own account", but practically with the support of the U.S. Government. The Secretary of State Hughes went, also on his own account, in order to defend the conclusions of the Dawes Committee with the French and British Governments. That plan included a loan of 800 million marks-gold to the German Government to keep the German budget in balance and to stabilize the mark; at the same time, a device for transferring the German war reparations – the amount of which was reduced to a "reasonable" figure and set for several years – was designed. That gold-loan was drawn on Wall Street and also, for a non-negligible part on the City of London. The result of the French elections in May 1924 which gave the majority to the "left bloc" (a coalition mainly of radical-socialists and socialists) brought about the fall of the Poincaré Government, an intransigent champion of the Ruhr occupation, facilitating the acceptance of the Dawes plan. In the United States, the big banks which had covered the loan obtained a mortgage on German industry. The Dawes plan was approved too by the American Federation of Labor.

The Dawes plan was also part of a close diplomatic struggle started at Rapallo between, on one hand, Great Britain and France supported by the U.S. and, on the other hand, the Soviet Union. The Dawes plan was one of the first manifestations of the U.S. march towards world hegemony at the expense of Europe and more particularly the two powers, Great Britain and Germany, who had started in 1914 to fight each other for that hegemony. Great Britain had won a military victory, but it had been American imperialism's cat's-paw for the latter's greatest benefit. Europe had paid dearly for the war and the treaties which ended it, speeded up its decline: instead of victorious socialist revolutions joining forces with the Russian revolution in order to create a federation of Socialist Nations, 17 new States and so called independent territories were created as well as 7,000 kilometres of new frontiers which involved customs, armies etc. After the name of Dawes and other Americans, politicians, Generals, and so on (Young, Kellogg...) bearers of plans aiming at preventing capitalism from sinking, Balkanized Europe was to know a Second World War, followed by the Marshall plan.

The Dawes plan was not in itself able to right the situation in Germany. Its success depended necessarily on the political results that Stresemann Government would be able to achieve during the last term of 1923.

The Radicalization of the Working Class

In such desperate situation, the results of votes, the numbers of members joining organizations, and so on, can only give but a small idea of the political changes taking place within the masses. Those changes happened massively, so suddenly, that no statistics could register them correctly, unlike during the so called normal periods. Nevertheless the figures and changes in some organizations, the number of demonstrations, on condition not to accept them at absolute value, do give information on the changes which were taking place. A first sign of the radicalisation of the masses was seen trough the changes within the Social Democratic Party, particularly in the regions where it was firmly and of long standing established. Saxony and Thuringia were countries with an old social democratic tradition: Erfurt, Gotha, Weimar, Leipzig, Halle, Dresden, and Jena were towns which were part of the history of the SPD during its hours of glory. As early as March 4 1923, an extraordinary SPD Congress in Saxony won a victory for the left with a majority of three-quarters. The Congress decided to break the coalition with the Democratic Party and to enter into negotiations with the KPD. An agreement on the platform was not reached; the Government of the left wing social democrat Zeigner, nevertheless won a vote of confidence, thanks to the votes of the elected communists. The same thing happened in Thuringia. In the whole of Germany, the social democratic left wing was gathering strength; it went so far as forming a kind of faction within the party and obtained in the autumn a great success in the Berlin party organization.

In October, negotiations started again in Saxony and Thuringia between SPD and KPD.. On the 10th October, the Zeigner Government was reshuffled in order to include three communists: Brandler, Heckert and Böttcher. Similarly in Thuringia, on 16th October, communists Korsch, Neubauer and Tenner were appointed ministers. The agreement took place under a misunderstanding, Zeigner putting forward his team as a "ministry of republican and proletarian defence" which would act in favour of the impoverished masses. Later on the intentions of the KPD, or more precisely of the Comintern leadership, in favour of the entry in the Zeigner Government, will be appreciated. Owing to the inertia inherent in any organization, above all a reformist organization, the evolution of the SPD which brought Zeigner to reshuffle his government reflected *with delay and in a limited way*, a more important, deeper evolution within the masses. That evolution could hardly be seen at election time, for during that period, there was only one, that of the *Landtag* of Mecklenburg-Strelitz, in July. In that *Land* which was politically backward, whilst in 1920 the USPD had received 2,000 votes, the SPD 25,000 and the KPD none, the latter obtained 11,000 votes against 12,000 to the SPD.

The membership of the KPD and the Communist Youth increased considerably within a year (from 30,000 to 70,000 for the Youth). There was a very important increase in the number of printed daily communist papers. In Berlin, the circulation of *Die Rote Fahne* exceeded in number that of the daily social democrat *Vorwärts*.

Besides the few figures which can only show the trend of the events, there exists an abundance of testimonies of the prodigious development of the KPD's influence. Historians of all shades of opinions recognize it. Arthur Rosenberg stated categorically: "Without any doubt, the KPD had, during the summer of 1923 the majority of the German proletariat behind it."[8] Ossip Flechtheim, though being less positive, gives many facts to the same effect.[9]

Flechtheim's and Rosenberg's opinions (when Rosenberg was writing his book he had become an opponent of communism) are also supported by the socialist Braunthal[10] who was for a long time acquainted with Fritz Adler at the Secretariat of the Socialist International between the two wars: "The communist factory councillors were waiting for their party leadership to..." The more and more numerous demonstrations, struggles of variable importance were essentially led by the KPD members. At the 5th Congress, Brandler underlined the fact.

---

[8] A. Rosenberg, *Geschichte des Bolschewismus. Von Marx bis zur Gegenwart*, Berlin 1932.
[9] O.K. Flechtheim, *Die KPD in der Weimarer Republik*, Frankfurt a/M 1969
[10] J. Braunthal, *Geschichte der Internationale*, I & 2, 961-1963.

The factory councils were without any doubt at that epoch the organization most sensitive to the changes taking place inside the working class. The KPD successes at the elections to these councils, in many large, middle-sized or small towns were considerable: it had obtained the majority in about 2,000 factory committees, namely in two large factories. But – as Flechtheim underlined too – it made also an important advance inside the trade unions. During the meeting of the Comintern Executive in June 1923, that progress had prompted Walcher, the KPD leader in charge of the work in the trade unions, probably the most informed militant about the situation of the German trade union movement to say: "We are on the right course to take over the unions on the organisational level". We will come back to that question later on.

Since the beginning of the year, the KPD kept following the united front course, denouncing the occupation of the Ruhr and the policy of the German Government, and making considerable progress. However, at the same time, it was in a rut with regard to its activity. So that it was taken by surprise by the general strike which brought down the Cuno Government. It had not thought until then that the crisis which was deepening and the growing radicalisation of the masses would open up a situation in which the question of power would arise. From the June strike on, the IC having taken in the warning, intervened in a more direct, more urgent way in the policy and activity of the KPD.

The Comintern and the KPD

The KPD leadership, as I said, had not understood that the deep economic disorganization of the country would give rise to a revolutionary situation. At the beginning of the year 1923, Brandler had written in the theoretical KPD organ that the party needed some "small successes" to get the masses on its side.[11]

After the general strike which had brought about the Cuno's Government downfall, one could not talk any more of "small successes", but still the tone of the KPD leadership remained no less vague.

In a general way, during the first half of the year, the IC leadership, though it showed a deeper sensitivity than the German leadership, had not urged on the KPD leadership the necessity of getting itself and the party ready for a change of policy. After the general strike which brought about Cuno's downfall, Radek was still writing that he lacked information in order to estimate the importance

---

[11] I summarize; see *Die Internationale*, #1, 6th Jan. 1923 (H.P.).

and extent of the movement. He even anticipated a "relative lull" (*Correspondence Internationale*, #68, 29th Aug. 1923). But this generalized strike gave the warning to Moscow, where the situation was thought to be developing in a crucial way. The Comintern and the Red Trade Union International (RTI) launched an appeal to the workers of the world to support the German proletariat. They appealed once more to that effect, but in vain, to the Socialist International and the Amsterdam Trade Union International. The Executive Committee called to Moscow the KPD leadership and a delegation from the "left" of the party so that in such situation the party should be united in its action. The Political Bureau of the Soviet party started a campaign in order to alert the Soviet working class, gathered a gold and wheat reserve in order to come to the help of the German revolution, appointing a Commission in order to take all the necessary measures with regard to the situation (by sending Red Army Officers to Germany, military trained workers' militia and deploying propaganda inside the *Reichswehr* (the army) and the German police).[12]

The discussion in Moscow between the leadership of the Comintern and that of the KPD were protracted. Brandler, deep down, was more than undecided; he was opposed to heading towards the preparation for a struggle for power. On his arrival in Moscow he was surprised by the conclusions and the orientation of the Comintern leadership, in the end he let himself be persuaded, even acknowledged that that taking power would not be to difficult, that the difficulties would arise with the measures to be adopted in order to ensure afterwards, food supplies. But the resistance reappeared when Trotsky raised the problem of drawing a plan with a date for the uprising and defended his point of view even under the form of historical commentaries about various crises. Brandler obtained that the date should be left to a commission appointed by German leaders.

In the Soviet leadership, under the appearance of a unanimous position on that policy, there existed divergences on the necessity to go into action. But they were not expressed openly, even within the whole of the leadership. A few years later when the troika broke off, Zinoviev revealed a letter addressed to him by Stalin, dated 7th August 1923, in which the latter expressed his doubts of taking power in Germany without the help of the social democrats.

Stalin did not possess then the authority he was to exercise later on; his name was the last one mentioned amongst the triumvirs. But, given Zinoviev's undecided and often unstable character when important decisions had to be taken, one can have good reasons for

---

[12] See E.H. Carr, *A History of Soviet Russia. The Interegnum 1923-1924*, London 1954.

thinking that that Stalin's above opinion carried a great weight. It is possible that Stalin wrote that letter specifically in relation with the anti-fascist demonstration, engaged for the 29th July – more precise information has never been given – but that letter is typical of Stalin's fundamental position on the question and not a contingent one due to the circumstances: the German Communists must be held back, and not spurred on, we cannot supply them with anything, let the fascist be the first to attack, etc. In his capacity of General Secretary of the CPSU, Stalin sent, on the 10th October a telegram to the editor of *Die Rote Fahne*, Thalheimer, in which he saluted the coming German socialist revolution.

How far from "socialism in one country" Stalin showed himself in that telegram published in facsimile in *Die Rote Fahne*! But he blows hot in public and cold in private. And what he said in private was prevailing.

In all the measures which were taken at that time, the troika which was leading the Soviet Party and the Soviet Union was taking into consideration its concerns relating to the internal struggle it was leading in the Bolshevik party against Trotsky. Thus, Brandler, completely unaware of that struggle, had expressed the wish that Trotsky should come and help the German leadership. His request was changed, instead of Trotsky, Piatakov was sent, who was certainly fare from being a mere nobody, but he did not possess Trotsky's reliabilities, neither the authority which the latter would have had on the German communists. The troika did not want to give Trotsky any opportunity to increase his prestige and influence. Therefore it is not surprising that the KPD leadership, first of all Brandler, though acknowledging the plan which was worked out for the struggle, should have remained sceptical within himself. Trotsky, being more than anybody also convinced of the importance of the stake and the decisive character of the struggle, understood that state of mind and attempted to warn the Bolshevik Party Central Committee. In his book *The Third International after Lenin* Trotsky explained his position at that time clearly[13]:

"In the documents of the January 1928 conference, I am directly accused by the Political Bureau of a hostile and distrustful attitude towards the German Central Committee in the period prior to its capitulation. Here is what we find said there:

"'... Comrade Trotsky, before leaving the session of the Central Committee [September 1923 Plenum], made a speech which profoundly disturbed all the members of the Central Committee and in which he alleged that the leadership of the German Communist Party

---

[13] See pages 94-95 of the English edition, or pages 194-195 of the French edition

was worthless and that the Central Committee of the German CP was permeated with fatalism, sleepy-headedness, etc. Comrade Trotsky then declared that the German revolution was doomed to failure. This speech had a depressing effect on all those present. But the great majority of the comrades were of the opinion that this philippic was called forth by an episode [?!], in no way connected with the German revolution, which occurred during the Plenum of the Central Committee and that this speech *did not correspond to the objective state of affairs.*[14]"

"No matter how the members of the Central Committee may have sought to explain my warning, which was not the first one, it was dictated only by concern over the fate of the German revolution. Unfortunately, events fully confirmed my position; in part because the majority of the Central Committee of the leading party, according to their own admission, did not grasp in time that my warning fully "corresponded to the objective state of affairs." Of course, I did not propose hastily to replace Brandler's Central Committee by some other (on the eve of decisive events such a change would have been sheerest adventurism), but I did propose from the summer of 1923 that a much more timely and resolute position be taken on the question of the preparation of the armed insurrection and of the necessary mobilization of forces for the support of the German Central Committee."

The Chemnitz Conference

In order to start the fight for power, a plan had been drawn, based on a past hypothesis, that of the formation of SPD-KPD united-front governments in Saxony and Thuringia. These governments were not to submit to the authority of the Central Government but, on the contrary, help to establish workers' strongholds and ensure the arming of the proletariat. Such governments would unavoidably provoke on the part of the Central Government intervention which the whole of the German proletariat would be called to fight against. Circumstances looked favourably in Saxony and Thuringia, the Zeigner Government, which since the beginning of the year, had governed with the support of the communist votes at the Saxony *Landtag*, had continuously denounced the measures of the government in Berlin and seemed in favour of collaboration with the KPD.

The situation was, moreover, becoming more and more tense. On the 26th September, the Stresemann Government had officially interrupted the policy of "passive resistance and the nationalists

---

[14] *Documents of the Conference of the CPSU*, January 1929, p.14.

stormed at it, mainly in Bavaria where a putsch was obviously being prepared by the fascists. On that same day, the government declared martial law for the whole of Germany in response to Kahr, the Reich Commissary for Bavaria, who refused to obey orders given by the Berlin authorities. Then Stresemann appointed General Müller as *Reichswehr* Commandant for Saxony: making use of the rightist plots as a pretext to prepare an attack against the left is an old government trick everywhere.

The negotiations between Socialists and Communists in Saxony ended in an agreement on the 10th October. A Socialist-Communist Government was formed on the 12th, including three communist ministers, all members of the KPD central leadership: Fritz Heckert, Minister for the Economy, Paul Böttcher, Finance Minister, and Heinrich Brandler, Director of the *Land* Chancellery which controlled the police. The same thing was repeated four days later, in Thuringia where three communists entered the *Land* Government. On the other hand, in Berlin, talks were started between the SPD and the KPD local organizations; they lasted about a week but led to nothing.

The Saxony Government had hardly been formed when as early as the 13th October the *Reichswehr* Commandant for Saxony, General Alfred Müller, taking a pretext of a speech delivered by Böttcher, asked the Zeigner Government to break up the workers' militia. Müller did not receive any answer, but nothing was done either to provide the workers' militia with arms. On the 20th October, General Müller sent an ultimatum and on the same day the *Reichswehr* troops invaded Saxony under the pretext that it needed protection against an aggression from the Bavarian fascists!

General Müller's first letter to the head of the Saxony Government made a test of strength unavoidable. A Congress of all German factory councils had been prepared for the 9th November in Chemnitz, but the new situation created by General Müller's proceedings determined *de facto* the date when it was necessary either to start action or to capitulate. It was decided to limit the conference of the factory councils to those of Saxony only, in order to study questions such as food supplies, unemployment and so on. The plan was to enlarge its agenda to include the political situation created by the intervention of the *Reichswehr*, in order to, on the 21st October, call for a general strike against that intervention, the workers of the whole of Germany. The KPD sent messengers to Chemnitz from the whole of Germany who were to convey the decision, as soon as it was taken, back to all the regions to give a signal for action.

Chemnitz was a red town "*par excellence*"; the communists had played there, under the leadership of Brandler, an important revolutionary role, especially at the time of the Kapp putsch in March 1920. The Chemnitz socialists were also very left orientated. It seemed that all was set for the success of the prepared plan. On the eve of the conference, the communist faction held a meeting which decided that Brandler would propose a motion to the conference that it should launch an appeal for a general strike in the whole of Germany with the aim of defending the workers' government and the Saxony workers against the *Reichswehr*.

The conference opened on the 21st. Almost 500 delegates were in attendance, as follows: 140 factory councils, 122 trade unions, 79 control committees, 15 action committees, 16 unemployed committees, 66 KPD organizations, 7 SPD organizations, one USPD representative. But the assembly took a completely different turn from that which had been foreseen. After a few speeches, Brandler gave a report on the political situation and put forward to the conference to launch a call for a general strike. He asked for a vote to be taken at once. It was then that the Labour Minister Georg Graupe, a leftist social democrat, intervened, objecting that the assembly was not qualified to take such a decision, that the Saxony Government could not be put under the protection of that conference which would then substitute itself for the elected *Landtag* which had appointed the government. He threatened to leave the conference if the Brandler motion was put to the vote and put forward a countermotion consisting in the election of a parity commission of the two parties in order to study the question of the general strike, with the task of making a report to the conference before it ended. Brandler withdrew his motion and Graupe's was unanimously adopted. Later on, the commission put forward a motion according to which the conference would select a commission which would... and so on. It meant a pure and simple burial of the general strike. The KPD leadership, during a meeting on the same evening, giving up the prepared plan, renounced the general strike and insurrection, in other words, was capitulating without a struggle.

The messengers were sent back home in order to call of the instructions which had previously been given. Following an incident as to which there exist several versions, the demobilisation order did not reach Hamburg, so that in that city, the insurrection started on the 23rd October. Several hundreds of communists, with insufficient arms, carried for almost two days a struggle rather cleverly conducted from a military standpoint, despite their great technical weaknesses, but without being supported by the mass of the Hamburg workers. About twenty of the fighters died, about two hundred were wounded, a hundred made prisoners, among them the Hamburg communist leader, Urbahns, who took upon himself the whole responsibility for the action in court. During those days of armed struggle in Hamburg, there was no act of solidarity in the rest of Germany, not even in Berlin where the "left" led by Maslow and Fischer was predominant and with which Urbahns was politically in agreement. The German Government came out victorious, so to speak, without firing a shot. A few days later, it easily repressed a putsch attempted in Munich by Hitler and Ludendorff.

Thus, the Stresemann Government won the political victory which allowed the application of the Dawes plan for a few years to the greatest benefit of German capitalism. Thus was ending the revolutionary chapter opened by the 1917 Russian revolution.

The Different Tendencies in the KPD after Chemnitz

After the Chemnitz debacle, after the isolated Hamburg rising, the Berlin government took advantage of the situation. The KPD was declared illegal on the 23rd November and remained so until the 1st March; its return to legality from that date did not yet mean that its members were immune from legal prosecutions and arrests for the events which had taken place during 1923. But the KPD was more deeply affected by its failure than by the repression of the government. At a sitting, the Central Committee on the 3rd and 4th November had approved the leadership policy by 40 votes against 16. It was a short-lived vote. The events which had occurred and their literally shameful outcome soon gave rise to a deep dissatisfaction, an unspeakable anger in the whole party. Discussions and different political positions came to light. From the very beginning of December, three texts stood before the Central Committee, emanating from three factions set against each other at the Frankfurt Congress which had been held clandestinely in April 1924; although the KPD as such, had already been declared legal, some of its delegates, including some party leaders, were liable to be arrested. The faction texts and their explanations were published in a supplement to the party review *Die Internationale* in January 1924. The document put forward by Brandler and Thalheimer supported by Walcher and Clara Zetkin "On the October defeat and the present situation" included among others that the reasons of the defeat were objective in character and was not the result of essential tactic errors of the leadership, and that the leadership of the Comintern and the KPD not wrongly estimated the combativity of the working class.

The centre group which stood between Brandler's right wing and Maslow's left wing had gathered veteran leaders such as Remmele,

Koenen, Eberlein and said that the political situation had been a revolutionary one, and that the retreat of the party in October was mainly caused by tactical and strategic errors in the struggle for the unity of the proletariat, necessary to take power.

The Malsow-Fischer-Thälman left wing expressed its positions under the form of theses put forward by the leadership of the Berlin-Brandenburg district. It accused the leadership's refusal to organize the members for the final struggle, and its program of transitional democratic demands instead of a communist program.

As early as February, the Central Committee replaced the Brandler and Thalheimer leadership by a new permanent leadership (*die Zentrale*). The right was removed, the centre held five posts, the left two. The Comintern Presidium had held a session beforehand an account of which will be rendered further on. Discussions were taking place in the KPD which had lost a great many members. "The KPD membership had dropped from 267,000 in September 1923 to 121,394 in April 1924" Ruth Fisher wrote. 15 At the KPD April Congress in Frankfurt, the right was defeated (it hardly obtained any votes); the centre itself obtained only 35 mandates; the left won with 92 mandates. The elected Central Committee included eleven members from the left and four from the centre. Brandler and Thalheimer were never to come back to the KPD leadership. At that congress some incidents took place with the Comintern representation, in particular with Losovsky who was the Red Trade Union International's Secretary. Those incidents were to do more particularly with the trade union tactics: within the Left which had just triumphed, a tendency was developing which was in favour getting the trade unions out of the ADGB confederation, a tendency led by a man called Schumacher, a member of the Berlin organization.

In May, less than two months after the Frankfurt Congress, some elections took place at the Reichstag. The KPD henceforth completely legal, obtained about 700,000 votes. In December of the same year, it was only going to obtain 2,700,000 votes. Thus, the ebb of the working masses was expressing itself in the elections, following the zenith of October 1923 when the KPD had shown its deficiencies. The discussion about October 1923 events could not be limited to the KPD

---

[15] Ruth Fisher, *Stalin und der deutsche Kommunismus*, 1948, p. 476. This book contains a abundance of details that are rarely sustained and verifiable. It essentially aims to present by all means the Maslow-Fischer tendency's then-leadership as having had irreproachable positions and leadership; and having been victim of other people's manoeuvres. It contains no self-criticism of its leftist positions and of its own manoeuvres. It is very difficult to separate what is true and what is false in the numerous details and statements of this book.

which was not the only one which could be held responsible for the situation.

The German Discussion within the CI

The debates in the Comintern were opened on the 11th January at a meeting of the Executive Committee Presidium. There were present, besides the members of the EC, a strong German delegation with representatives of the three tendencies, and representatives of the Polish and the Bulgarian Parties.[16] Radek, as the Comintern representative to the KPD opened the debates with his report. It was followed by three other reports from the KPD tendencies. The divergences were deep, the antagonisms profound, but the debates were not as virulent as they had been, for example, following the "March action", about three years previously. Each one of the speakers was conscious that a grave defeat had been suffered, though it is evident with hindsight that none of them really grasped its real scope and consequences. The three German speakers repeated the essential points from the theses they had signed.

Like the other speakers, Brandler did not deal with perspectives, the divergences on that point being then very small: everybody was expecting new revolutionary crises at an early or not too long date. For Brandler, "we (that is to say the German leadership and the Executive Committee together) had overestimated our strength and underestimated that of the enemy. And we were thus compelled to retreat." The workers had been won to the KPD, as far as immediate demands were concerned, but not with regard to political problems – that conception was introducing an arbitrary division and evading the problem: was there or was there not a revolutionary situation. Brandler concluded that there was "no other possible policy". It was symptomatic that he should refer twice or three times to the "March action" when he had taken a courageous position and a share of responsibility. He concluded that there would have been in October 1923 a much greater defeat than in 1921 if an uprising had begun. Later on, Brandler and Thalheimer persisted in their opinions, even strengthening them.

Remmele, in the name of the centre, drew up a sketch of the general situation in some German regions during 1923, which was truly characteristic of a revolutionary situation.[17] He pointed out too

---

[16] The minutes of these debates have been published: *Die Lehre der deutschen Ereignisse*, with the mention: only for Comintern members. (Hamburg 1924.)

[17] "Often in the important districts on strike, the political power was in the hands of the workers; at the same time, the Länder governments were not in a position to carry out a policy directed against the worker's risings (...) In August (in central Germany) the

the wavering and the vacillations of the central Committee which, obviously, did not understand the nature of the situation. Compelled against its will to adopt a revolutionary path, the CC abandoned in the last weeks its propaganda and agitation activities, confining itself to a "technical" preparation, which added to the confusion. In the name of the majority of the Party, Remmele condemned the policy adopted in Saxony. He foresaw partial armed struggles in a relatively near future, advocated the maintenance of Brandler in the CC. He was in favour of Thälman (the left) taking part in the leadership because he represented a good tradition of proletarian struggle, but he denounced Maslow and Fischer as people elaborating their policy in ignorance of reality.

Ruth Fischer's report was for a good part, comparatively skilful: she easily brought to light the opportunist failure of the leadership, opposed Hamburg to Chemnitz, forgetting to mention Berlin where she had the leadership. She rejected the idea that the following weeks would see new revolutionary struggles, pointing out correctly that in the immediate, defensive economic struggles would take place. Feeling that Zinoviev was listening to her point of view, as he had never done before, she launched in abusive tirades, denouncing a crisis threatening to lead to the liquidation of the KPD and the Comintern too, stating that Brandler and Radek were carrying on with the policy formerly pursued by Paul Levi and Friesland, that the poison had not been eradicated, and that without an energetic intervention the right wing of the KPD would merge with the left wing of the SPD in order to create a centrist party. The future showed that Brandler, whose militant qualities were undeniable, even though he possessed an opportunist streak which proved disastrous in 1923, never returned to the social democracy and that he had nothing in common with Paul Levi. But Ruth Fischer's intervention did not come out of the blue, as will soon be seen.

As the Comintern representative to the KPD, Radek explained the policy he had carried through in agreement with Zinoviev. He defined at once the plan of struggle: to start in Saxony by defending the workers' government and from there to build a wall against the counter-revolution in the South, while mobilising the masses.

After the decision to draw back had been taken during his absence in Chemnitz, he strived to obtain from the KPD leadership that it should not be done without a fight, but he came up against a convergent refusal on the part of Brandler and Fischer at the very time when the Hamburg uprising was taking place. He agreed too, that he

---

situation was such that that the workers had complete control of the food supplies, they seized the lorries, went to the countryside to get food directly from the peasants (...)".

could not put forward truly precise proposals which would help towards the course he favoured; a common resolution was voted which remained a dead letter.

When studying the causes of the defeat, he mentioned the truly essential ones. Though he acknowledged the passivity of the masses, he could see its origin in the party policy, due to the sentiment they had that the party was not going to throw all its forces into the battle.

He pointed out the strange passivity of the KPD after the Cuno strike. "The German party declared (...) that it accepted the action platform (prepared by Zinoviev and Radek) (...) but the Party did not anything from August to October". Radek gave even a more fundamental explanation with regard to the CI. Coming back too the "March action" and the 3rd Congress turn with a view to winning over the masses, he observed that the situation had taken a new turn during the year 1923, and he added that both the KPD and the Comintern understand in time the coming of a second revolutionary wave. On the question of the perspectives, Radek was, rightly, prudent. The situation could lead to very different developments.

Radek did not put forward a firm position regarding the tendencies confronting one another in the German Party, but he fought openly Fischer's conceptions of a leadership becoming social democrat. The KPD, he said, was "still a communist party which was not ripe". Actually he was supporting Brandler's leadership though with some criticisms.

As the president of the Comintern, Zinoviev played an exceptional role in the development of the discussion. During the course of 1923, he had shared Radek's positions and had defended them publicly. It is necessary to study not only what he said at that Presidium meeting of January 1924, but his following interventions on the German question since October 1923 until the 5th Congress of the Comintern, in order to understand the cause of his variations and their consequences. He carried publicly all the responsibility for the policy followed until October, which brought upon him a misadventure. During the most decisive days in October, in order to mobilize the Soviet Party and the whole of the Comintern, he had written a pamphlet, *The Problem of the German Revolution*[18] in which he expounded the virtual power of that revolution, the essential problems to be faced and the ensuing policy. At the time of his writing, he anticipated the victory of the German revolution and wished, no doubt, through that pamphlet, to credit himself with the personal merit of having thought it out, explaining that the first task of the KPD

---

[18] G. Zinoviev, *Probleme der deutschen Revolution*, Hamburg 1923.

was to convince the masses that the leadership of the KPD could assume its duty to lead the working class to victory.

But between the time when he started to write that pamphlet, finished it, and left it at the printer's in Germany, the Chemnitz capitulation had taken place.[19] So that in the German edition he added a preface dated 2nd November and a postface in which he summed up the main conclusions he was drawing from the change in the situation. In that way, the variations and contradictions in his thought appear crudely in the German edition of that pamphlet. In the preface he forewarned against all panic, upheld the policy followed in Saxony and foresaw still victories. He was trying, besides to avoid internal struggles in the KPD.

In the postface, he set forward a different policy towards the social democracy, including its left-wing (rank and file united front; the left-wing of the social democrats at the present the main enemy) which will be referred to later on, and modifies his point of view too on the policy followed in Saxony, considering the entry of the KPD in the government as a military-political episode aiming at the formation of a fighting avant-garde, a policy that became a failure, since it was not accompanied by a massive armament of the workers.

But if Zinoviev was evolving at that time his judgement on the policy followed in Saxony, his ideas concerning the internal situation in the KPD seemed unchanged: unity was of the greatest importance considering the coming revolution.

When he intervened at the Presidium session, following Radek's reports and those of the KPD tendencies representatives, Zinoviev was far from definite; he even declared that concerning certain points, he might change his position during the two or three following months. Firstly, he did his best to dodge his responsibilities, but he could not conceal the fact that he himself had been urging on the KPD leadership the necessity of participating in the Saxony government. He claimed that the conception had been right, but not its realization. He refused to admit, under a futile pretext, that the German situation had only been understood tardily. On the other hand, he tried to bring confusion in the debate by referring back to the Comintern 4th Congress and to the discussion on the Workers' and Peasants' Government, synonymous or not with the dictatorship of the proletariat, on the united front, which, according to him was "a method of agitation and mobilization of the masses at a given time,

---

[19] He mentions the Chemnitz decision in this pamphlet: "When, on October 21, at the conference of factory councils held in Chemnitz, the communists, who foresaw the trap, proposed to declare forthwith the general strike, the 'left' social-democrats, with Zeigner at their head, sabotaged this proposal and thus opened definitively the road to General Seeckt".

against the social democracy, nothing more." In a general way he supported Fischer's positions on those questions. Going off the deep end in his analyses, he attacked Radek and a few others, who identified, in a mistaken belief, the military Seeckt regime in Saxony with fascism and talked about a November Republic defeat. But instead of rectifying those mistakes, he aggravated them by stating that the German Government was formed by a coalition between the social democrats and fascism.

That policy was relatively short-lived, and applied for a short time by Zinoviev. But his statement implied a complete misunderstanding of the nature of the social democracy and fascism; it contained, not only in a nutshell, the "theory" of "social fascism" which Stalin was to develop in practise less than ten years later, with all the disastrous consequences it engendered.

Zinoviev maintained that he did not want to intervene in order to make changes in the German leadership, but he was belied both by the tone of his interventions and by the pressure which was brought to bear on a party bewildered and thrown into confusion by defeat. Within the Central Committee, the centre tendency was for the time being, in the majority. It strongly criticized Brandler and the right wing tendency; of its own accord, it would not have expelled it from the leadership. The German centre and the right wing still exercised an appreciable influence at that Presidium meeting: a few amendments to the motion put forward by Pieck – who stood half way between those two tendencies – were only outvoted by 18 votes against 11. Zinoviev denounced a few "exaggerations" on the part of Fischer but, fundamentally, justified her policy. Finally he achieved a coalition between the centre and the left wing in order to create a new *Zentrale*. The motion he had adopted and which was put forward with a short introduction expressed that change, straight to the point. When the vote was taken on the policy, there occurred a kind of comedy which was to be the prelude to a system which contributed to the subsequent degeneration. For several reasons, the KPD right wing, Radek and a few other members of the Presidium stood against that motion. Nevertheless they delivered a statement which, tough it rejected some points or had reservations about others, concluded in favour of the vote of the motion. That Presidium was ending in a confusion which the following months did not clear up.

At the same time as the discussion on what had happened in October was going on some other discussions connected with the "Russian question" were taking place behind the scenes, which explains both, Zinoviev's attitude and what happened at the

Presidium. The "Russian question" was dealt with in private, as is shown by two speeches which appeared in the minutes. One the one hand, Remmele who was going to gain temporarily the KPD leadership stated at the time of the vote on the German question that the Russian Central Committee's position was the right one with regard to the German and Russian questions.

On the other hand, the Polish delegation made a statement attached to its vote for the motion answering an attack by Zinoviev against a letter sent by the Polish CC to the Soviet Party CC concerning Trotsky's condemnation, i.e. his removal from the leadership of the Party's and from the State.

Thus, the two questions, Russian and German had been arbitrarily linked – the German defeat was going to be used to fight against the opposition in the Soviet-Union. It is interesting to point out what, in a speech printed in the Leningrad Pravda on the 11th May 1924, Zinoviev stated with regard to the German events. Rejecting the opposition's accusations concerning the German events, Zinoviev stated, with a reference to Plekhanov, that the Party had on the contrary overestimated the revolutionary situation.

It's a surprising reference to Plekhanov, about a "premature" appreciation of the revolutionary situation, to a man who went bankrupt during the 1905 and 1917 revolutions!

Dodging Responsibilities

I study elsewhere[20] the whole of the Comintern 5th Congress proceedings, but it is impossible to end the chapter on the German revolution without including the discussions to which it gave rise at that same Congress. One must give a general outlook on that problem, as its consequences in respect to the Comintern and the future evolution in the Soviet Union will prove of capital importance.

At the 5th Congress, Zinoviev set the tune. He was then apparently the head of the troika which had just dealt Trotsky and the Moscow opposition their first great blows. He put forward to the Congress a description of the events in Germany skipping over their seriousness – as he had done in the article just mentioned above. He also skipped over the changes in positions – which he could have defended if they had been dictated by a deep analysis of the situation and not by his factional struggle in the Soviet Union. There existed a revolutionary situation, he stated in his long report to the Congress, during which the German leadership failed in its duty. He attacked Brandler, The KPD leader and Radek appointed by the Comintern to

---

[20] In *Histoire de l'Internationale Communiste*.

the German situation. But he added, the KPD had reacted strongly and had changed its leadership. There was now a new leadership and the German situation remained pregnant with revolutionary crises. As a conclusion, he put forward the idea that October 1923 would remain a mere episode in history. At the end of his report on the activity of the Executive Committee, he just stated that with his speech, the German subject was practically exhausted and that the agenda could be got on with.

But the Comintern and its sections, though already contaminated by the bureaucratisation had not yet reached the time of all-powerful Stalinism. A discussion took place. I shall not dwell on Fischer's intervention who, as the KPD leader, and speaking in its name, showed no restraint in her statements; she did not put forward an analysis of the events but aimed at crushing down Brandler and his tendency. On the other hand, a few speeches, such as Radek's, Brandler's and Zetkin's who expressed a different point of view, gave explanations with regard to the demagogy of Zinoviev and his temporary supporters with the same eagerness that many of them were going to apply two years later, abusing him.

Radek and Brandler did not deny that a revolutionary situation had existed. The pleaded guilty, but gave as an extenuating circumstance the fact that they had understood the situation too late and that the Party then had not had enough time to get ready for the struggle for power.

It is true that the nature of the situation in Germany in 1923 was understood by the KPD leadership and Radek only tardily, towards the end of July. But that is still far from being the deep reason of what happened three months later. If the whole of the KPD was also slow to move, sometimes without much conviction, the main cause was to be found amongst the leadership which had not been equal to its responsibilities. It was Zetkin's speech – in which she stood up for Brandler against those who wanted to use him as a scapegoat and in which she tried to win acceptance for a rightist trend against the ultra-leftism of the time – which laid an impressive charge against the leadership.

Some people maintained that during the crucial months, the masses had not shown the combativeness that they have had in 1918 at the end of the war. Those who drew the parallel were not going below the surface of things. In 1918, the uprising created by the sufferings engendered by the war had been enough to bring about the fall of the Hohenzollern monarchy, but it had left the bourgeois order untouched. In 1923 the problem of the seizure of power by the working class was set in a country where capitalism had still very strong forces. The "spontaneity" or more accurately, the very rising of the masses brought forth by history and the objective conditions, though it was very deep and powerful, was not enough to achieve that task on its own; it needed a leadership, able to take its bearings on that rising of the masses, to lay down a policy and determine the aims to be reached at the various stages of the struggle, to lead it up to the struggle for the seizure of power. It was wrong to expect the workers by themselves, without an organization to set forth the action to be achieved daily, more particularly in moments of crises when new initiatives were needed owing to a situation which was changing day after day, sometimes hour after hour. The "spontaneity" could only bring the mass movements to dispersion, owing to a lack of definite aims.

As far as the "lack of combativeness" was concerned, noted, it was stated, by some observers during the crucial October days in 1923, as far as that phenomenon existed, its origin was to be found in the relationship leadership-party-masses. The workers need organizations; but as they follow them, they are not passive with regard to them, in their action as well in their thought. At crucial times, they are very sensitive to the ability of the party leaderships, to their determination or the lack of it. That can be seen during the course of strikes, even partial or local ones; this is all the more evident during revolutionary times. The lack of fighting spirit within the German masses in October 1923 really reflected with lack of resolution within its leadership. They could see more or less clearly that something in the leadership was not equal to the events.

In the Comintern, the question of the "German October" was no longer ever seriously discussed after the 5th Congress; at the most it was used to fight against the German right wing (Brandler, Thalheimer). In so far as someone referred to it, he repeated word for word the official terms of the 5th Congress. The discussion developed in return, outside the CI. But as time was passing by, it dealt with the point of view which had never been in doubt during the year 1924, that is to say: had there been a revolutionary situation in Germany the previous year? In spite of all what has been said above, such a question is still worthy of a serious analysis.

Had There Been a Revolutionary Situation in Germany in 1923?

Most historians acknowledge that, rising violently during the war in 1917 in Tsarist Russia, the revolutionary wave, after having broken off capitalism at its weakest link, had swept over Central Europe from

1918 onwards, mainly in Germany. The revolutionary developments in the colonial and semi-colonial countries at that epoch, though not unimportant, were however still very limited, in comparison with those which followed the Second World War. The epicentre of the world socialist revolution was at that time in Germany; consequently the problems of the German revolution were at the centre of the debates of all the Comintern Congresses until the 5th inclusive. Each congress of the International was linked in a certain way to a stage of the German revolution. The 1st Congress followed the Spartakus uprising and the assassination of Karl Liebknecht and Rosa Luxemburg. The 2nd contributed to the birth of a German mass Communist Party, trough the merger of the Party and the USPD majority faction. The 3rd Congress dealt mostly with the "March action", condemned an ultra-leftist tactics, resulting of the impatience on the part of a Comintern tendency, and adopted the united front tactics; the 4th extended the united front tactics, dealing with the question of the worker's government. Until then, at the Comintern congresses, where the influence of Lenin and Trotsky had been prominent, the debates taking place had been clear and ardent in order to define precise lines of intervention. From one congress to the following one, one can appreciate the progress in the Comintern thought; mistakes were put right, even though with great difficulty. Starting from the German October 1923 events, things changed. The 5th Congress put forward an analysis of the 1923 events and perspectives for Europe which, rapidly, proved to be false; nevertheless no self-criticism, however restricted will ever be made in the future.

The leaders of a revolutionary party cannot create a revolutionary situation; they can only take full advantage of it when it exists to lead it to victory or miss the opportunity. The history of the struggles in which the working class in Europe set itself against the capitalist regime showed the existence of cycles, revolutionary periods of ebb and flow. The most prominent Marxists have not hesitated in drawing parallels – of course only valid within certain given limits – between those phenomena and some natural phenomena. It seems that the working class accumulates energy for years, then explosions of that energy take place during periods when gigantic demonstrations occur, monster strikes, when a will to fight rises from the whole class, including social layers which until then had shown very little combativeness relating to daily demands. Even though those cycles have been little studied, their existence is none the less certain. We have seen in Europe the one issued from the First World War, another more limited and weaker from 1935 to 1937, then the one which followed the Second World War (from 1943 to 1948), lastly the one which started in a spectacular way with May 1968 in France. In the very course of a period of ebb, one or several crises and revolutionary situations can arise as long as the energy stored within the masses has not been destroyed by defeats or wasted in struggles without issues.

Nobody can deny the existence of the revolutionary wave which started in Russia in 1917 and broke over Central and Eastern Europe. What happened to that revolutionary wave; how it spend itself and when did it disappear? After the great elementary rising of 1919 and of the first months of 1920 the bourgeoisie, which had been taken by surprise, recovered, but it had in no way vanquished the working class in all the Central and Eastern European countries, and chiefly in Germany. No doubt, the capitalist society still remained very shaky and the year 1923 was a year of great crisis. But after October 1923, European capitalism knew several years of economic prosperity and political stability. German capitalism, in particular knew an impressive revival. Before the crisis of 1929 the European mass struggles no longer extended beyond the frame of capitalist society, the democratic and pacifist illusions having gained strength. If in 1923, a revolutionary situation had not existed, the Chemnitz retreat would have had but a relative importance, other revolutionary situations should have arisen subsequently (as the 5th Congress was foreseeing it). On the other hand, faced by a revolutionary situation and missing the opportunity could only be fatal: a revolutionary party does not miss the coach with impunity and cannot escape the consequences of such a bankruptcy; to practice then, an ostrich policy can only but worsen them. That was the fate of the KPD.

The Comintern never really resumed the debates on the events of the year 1923. Those who did it were either opponents, expelled from the Comintern at different times or either historians. This E.H. Carr considers that what he calls quite appropriately the "German fiasco" was unavoidable, not so much, according to him, because of the policy of the Comintern and that of the KPD, than because of the existing military balance of power, chiefly the disproportion between the forces of the *Reichswehr* and those of the workers' militia. That disproportion was real, but to see the question under that light, meant seeing only one aspect of the question, the "technical" aspect, the working class being generally always very much at a disadvantage in comparison with the bourgeoisie. The fundamental question cannot be better dealt with than when studying the most elaborate and contradictory positions which have been put forward, on one hand by Trotsky during the years which followed the events, and on the other hand by Thalheimer in 1931. The first one started giving a general idea of the relationships between the German leadership and the masses and of the development of events since 1918, in a text dated from December 1923. He stated:

"If the Communist Party had abruptly changed the pace of its work and had profited by the five or six months that history accorded it for direct political, organizational, technical preparation for the seizure of power, the outcome of the events could have been quite different from the one we witnessed in November. There was the problem: the German party had entered the new, brief period of this crisis, perhaps without precedent in world history, with the ready methods of the two preceding years of propagandistic struggle for the establishment of its influence over the masses. Here a new orientation was needed, a new tone, a new way of approaching the masses, a new interpretation and application of the united front, new methods of organization and of technical preparation in a word, a brusque tactical change. The proletariat should have seen a revolutionary party at work, marching directly to the conquest of power.(...)

"If the party surrendered its exceptional positions without resistance, the main reason is that it proved unable to free itself, at the beginning of the new phase (May-July 1923), from the automatism of its preceding policy, established as if it was meant for years to come, and to put forward squarely in its agitation, action, organization, and tactics the problem of taking power."[21]

About a year later, Trotsky came back to the events of 1923 in *The Lessons of October*, in order to lay stress upon the exceptional role of the leadership during a revolutionary crisis. He also underlined two points upon which I shall come back further on, the question of the bourgeois military forces and the question of the workers' organizations capable of assuming the seizure of power. Lastly, in his letter to the Comintern 6th Congress (1928) Trotsky developed what he had written in *The New Course* and *The Lessons of October*; he was challenging the Comintern leadership, the KPD leadership and the conclusions of the 5th Congress on the world situation. He was taking up again the arguments developed above. He was stressing that there was no difference between the behaviour of the two tendencies which shared the German leadership, whose attitude to the revolution was fatalistic:

"Not only the Rights but also the Lefts, despite the fact that they had fought each other very bitterly, viewed rather fatalistically the process of revolutionary development up to September-October 1923."

In such a situation, he added, a few days are sometimes enough for a revolutionary situation to change and disappear for years:

---

[21] L. Trotsky, *New Course* (chapter 5 on Tradition and Revolutionary Policy), 1943 edition, pp 49-50

"[T]he danger arises that the policy of the party leadership and of the party as a whole does not correspond to the conduct of the class and the exigencies of the situation. During a relatively languid course of political life, such incongruities are remedied, even if with losses, but without a catastrophe. But in periods of acute revolutionary crisis, it is precisely *time* that is lacking to eliminate the incongruity and to redress the front, as it were, under fire. The periods of the maximum sharpening of a revolutionary crisis are by their very nature transitory. The incongruity between a revolutionary leadership (hesitation, vacillation, temporizing in the face of the furious assault of the bourgeoisie) and the objective tasks, can lead in the course of a few weeks and even days to a catastrophe and to a loss of what took years of work to prepare."[22]

Thalheimer who was, with Brandler, the main KPD leader at the time and its most famous theoretician, had been, with Brandler dismissed from the leadership after the Frankfurt Congress and later expelled from the Comintern, following differences with its Stalinist leadership. In 1931, he was again leading, with Brandler, an organization: the Kommunistische Partei (Opposition), a right wing opposition to the KPD leadership, which hoped to reach an agreement with Stalin (the internal policy of whom it approved until 1937). Some other groups and individuals had been expelled from the KPD and the Comintern, particularly the old left wing leaders such as Maslow and Fischer and the ultra-left wing member Scholem. Amongst the communists in opposition to the Stalinist policy of the "3rd period" the question of October 1923 was continually put back on the agenda. The criticisms put forward put forward by Brandler and Thalheimer against the ultra-left policy of the "3rd period" were shared by many, if not by all opponents. But the latter expressed reservations, not to say more, on the position of Brandler and Thalheimer because of their policy in 1923. Thus Thalheimer, being compelled to justify or explain that policy, wrote a pamphlet: *1923: Eine verpasste Revolution? Die deutsche Oktober legende und die wirkliche Geschichte von 1923* (A Missed Revolution? The legend of the German October and the true history of 1923.)

Written a few years after Trotsky had put forward his position, Thalheimer's pamphlet did not answer directly his main critic, but directed his argumentation against the contemporary policy of the KPD and the Comintern, that is to say against an ultra-left policy and he stated that it was the extension of that defended by the "left" of the KPD in 1923. There was a grain of truth in it. But the mistakes by Maslow and Fischer in 1923 and the ultra-left policy of the "3rd

---

[22] *The Third International Under Lenin*, pp 97.

period" could neither replace an analysis of the situation in 1923 nor justify the policy followed at that time by the German leadership. From the mistakes of some, (Maslow etc.) did not necessarily follow the correctness of the policy of the others (Brandler etc.). Trotsky had never defended the 1923 German "left" and he was not defending the policy of the "3rd period". Thalheimer asserted too that October 1923 had been a "legend" in order to create a diversion from the Russian question, from the divergences in the Bolshevik Party. It is true, as I have shown, that Zinoviev had first approved of the KPD activity, until and including Chemnitz, and that he had changed his position in connection with the internal struggle in the Bolshevik Party. It was quite fair for Thalheimer to recall those facts to Maslow and Fischer who had been strong supporters of Zinoviev at the 5th Congress. But Trotsky was not at all driven by such reasons in his assessment of the German leadership in 1923.

Therefore let us ignore those side-issues of Thalheimer's and look at his pamphlet essential argumentation. He first stated that, thanks to the correct policy of the party leadership, fascism had been beaten but that on the other hand the KPD victory had been prevented firstly, by concessions made by the bourgeoisie, and also by mistakes made by the leadership after August 1923, which it put right, in time, by sounding the retreat.

In reality, it meant that, for Thalheimer, it had been a mistake to strive towards the seizure of power in August, for there was no revolutionary situation at that time. In order to prove his point, Thalheimer referred to a text by Bukharin, in which the latter engaged in a polemic with Trotsky's *Lessons of October*, put forward the differences between the situation in Russia in 1917 and that of Germany in 1923: unlike in Russia, Germany did not have armed soldiers wanting peace, the strength of a slogan such as that of peace was lacking. There was neither a land question nor a question of nationalities. The *Reichswehr*, a class army, did not show, in opposition to what had been said at that time, signs of breaking up. The working class was divided following the division of Germany brought about by the occupation of the Ruhr.

He added also that there were no workers' councils, that the factory committees could not replace them and stressed that the policy followed until the Cuno strike was the correct policy.

The plan drawn up by the Comintern, he said, was a "speculative plan" which was rather imposed on Brandler and the "crucial mistake of the Party after the Cuno strike" was to "keep within the limits of a technical organizational preparation of that plan". Before dealing with the two other points in Thalheimer's pamphlet one must note that essentially the arguments put forward do not answer the question of knowing whether there existed or not a revolutionary situation. The comparison with 1917 Russia belongs to scholasticism: nobody can possibly think that the characteristics of the 1917 Russian situation must necessarily be found in other revolutionary situations, independently from the country and the time. It would be childish too, to think that a country must necessarily present a considerable degree of homogeneity in a revolutionary situation: the partition of Germany following the occupation of the Ruhr was then a cause of revolutionary situation, not an obstacle to it. The non-existence of councils (soviets) and the existence only of factory committees did not constitute an element which could modify, in a decisive way the nature of the situation. For someone who, like Thalheimer invoked the Russia of 1917, he should have known that at a certain time, Lenin gave up the slogan "all the power to the soviets" and considered the possibility of the seizure of power through the involvement of the factory councils. In a revolutionary situation, a leadership may be compelled, through the circumstances of the situation, to turn to other forms of organization (factory councils, militia, trade unions, rather than councils for the seizure of power; subsequently, it is a different matter to establish, through councils the foundation of the dictatorship of the proletariat. Finally if the KPD leadership confined itself, according to Thalheimer's words to an essentially "technical-organizational" preparation, to the detriment of the political preparation, that does not constitute the denial of the revolutionary character of the situation, but only a characteristic of the attitude of the leadership within that situation. The *Reichswehr* was not in the same situation as the Tsarist army in 1917, that cannot be denied; but contrary to Thalheimer's statement, many signs of political unrest had been reported within it; besides, it is extremely rare for an army to break up unless the masses have shown beforehand, through their uprising, that they are ready to take up the defence of the soldiers who would dare to question the military hierarchy.

Thalheimer's main argument was that the climax of the mass uprising took place during the general strike which got rid of the Cuno Government. He is in agreement on that question with the social democrat historian J. Braunthal, with the historian E.H. Carr and many others too. Thalheimer asserted too that the KPD had not won over the majority of the working class.

As far as the "apex" of the mass movement is concerned, Thalheimer, like all the historians who share his point of view, sees the events, in my opinion, under a static light which completely ignores the transformations which would have been brought about by a policy really centred on the struggle for the seizure of power. Because the

German leadership, overtaken by the general strike, did not draw at once any conclusion as to the revolutionary character of the situation and hardly did anything politically to advance the crisis to a higher level, one cannot come to the valid conclusion that August 1923 had been the "apex" and that afterwards, the movement, had surged back. The inefficiency of the KPD leadership had its logic, chiefly, consequences on the state of mind and the inclination of the workers to act. It is the same, as far as the united front is concerned. Thalheimer states especially that it had been achieved in Chemnitz, but that the workers would not have followed in the struggle for the seizure of power.

At the time when Thalheimer was writing those lines, that is to say during the rise of Nazism in Germany, his organization put forward, as did Trotsky, the necessity for a united front between the SPD and the KPD, in order to oppose the growing danger of Hitlerism. But if there was an agreement between Trotsky and the Brandler-Thalheimer rightist opposition upon an imperative necessity for a united front, they were in complete disagreement regarding the general conception of that united front. Brandler and Thalheimer, at that time, as they had done in 1923, raised the united front as a *strategy* which had to be pursued until the seizure of power – without moreover stating precisely whether it should include that supreme moment of the class struggle. For Trotsky, the united front was a *tactic* with the aim first and foremost of mobilizing large masses in order to set them into motion. Once that aim achieved, the revolutionary party had to go on pressing, whether there existed or not a united front with the reformist organizations, the movement of the masses, as far as possible towards the seizure of power. If the revolutionary party had to wait for the joint of the reformist party in the case of certain mass mobilizations, to consent to go beyond the set agreements, very likely, great opportunities to go further would be missed, and above all the opportunity to enter into the struggle for the seizure of power.

Thalheimer dissociates the Chemnitz Conference from what the *Zentrale* had decided before it was held; in fact it had opted for the decisive slogan without taking a real decision; it had to wait and know the state of mind of the masses which would emerge at that conference.

One cannot help but think of Lenin during the days prior to the October uprising when he feared that the decision would be depending from the meeting of the Soviet All-Russian Congress where possible, not to say unavoidable tergiversations within a large assembly would take place, on a question like the armed struggle for the seizure of power. Those hesitations and even some hostility were present within the leadership of the party. He thought it necessary to start the struggle prior to the opening of the Congress in order to draw the latter into the struggle. Had he acted as Brandler did, there would have been not one Russian Graupe but several threatening to withdraw from the Congress; moreover several delegates left the Congress at the time when the armed uprising was at its height.

The KPD had achieved during the year 1923, before and after the Cuno strike, "tremendous progress", to use Thalheimer's very words. I gave above, one of Walcher's statements, in which he said that the KPD was near to winning the majority in the trade unions. Such a statement deserves a few commentaries. The trade unions present some very clear characteristics: the working class constitutes their base, even tends to identify with them completely in some countries, as for example in Great Britain nowadays. But on the other hand the trade unions posses an enormous apparatus rising, like a pyramid, upon that base. The trade unions, at the workshop level are more or less the working class itself; but the more one gets towards the top, the more that apparatus tends to become interwoven with the State apparatus, to integrate in it, formally or not. The trade union apparatus has a great inertia; the top functionaries are almost unmovable. To say, as Walcher did, that the revolutionary party was near gaining the trade union leadership and at the same time, denying or ignoring that the question of State power was ipso facto on the order of the day in a country as industrialized as Germany, was truly misunderstanding the situation. The tactics of the united front should have served the KPD, whether the social democracy had accepted or not to maintain the organizational agreement, to take advantage of the progress already made in order to further it. Progress had to be made in order not to lose ground for certain. The relationship of forces is by no means statistical data to be weighed on a scale like goods; they are a function of the dynamics of the struggle. No leadership is able to create by itself a relationship of forces inexistent in a latent or virtual way. But the struggle transforms such a virtual relationship of forces to the advantage of the one who knows how to take the initiative, who dares to act. There is no need to ponder for a long time on Clausewitz's writing: what is true in the field of war is true in the field of the class struggle, especially when it reaches its highest levels. The eminent class struggle strategists and tacticians, Lenin and Trotsky, when they realized that the initial perspectives of the Comintern had vanished did not think out the united front just in order to take into consideration agreements between social democrat and communist organizations. For them, the united front could be of a defensive or offensive nature; it did not constitute a thing in itself: the united front could only be a tactic suitable to certain given circumstances with a view to go beyond them.

Involuntarily, Thalheimer in his pamphlet delivers judgment against the leadership of which he was the most qualified theoretician and against the wavering which characterized the Comintern policy in 1923.

All the rigid static thought of the German leadership in 1923 becomes apparent through those lines written eight years after the events. For a true revolutionary situation to be present after the Cuno strike, it would have been necessary for the German bourgeoisie to remain passive! But whereas it went into action, the KPD leadership remained passive. It seems there was a "plan of action" which did not foresee the reactions of the class enemy! There was a "leadership" which, confronted with an enemy who was taking initiatives, proved powerless while waiting to give the signal for retreat. It is hard to believe that Thalheimer could have been deeply convinced of what he was writing in his pamphlet. The latter rather seems an attempt to exorcize the torments of his revolutionary conscience on the 1923 failure.

Without any doubt, the situation in 1923 Germany did not present itself as that of Russia in 1917, though one must not think that the seizure of power by the Bolsheviks was an easy task. It is not certain that a socialist revolution would have triumphed in Germany in 1923. There never is any guarantee of success; but there existed beyond all doubt a revolutionary situation. The majority of the working class was following the KPD or turning towards it. The petty-bourgeoisie was in a disparate plight and turning towards those who would show determination and strength. It was precisely the revolutionary leadership which was lacking – the leadership, not in the general sense of the party – there existed a revolutionary party – but in the precise meaning of the leadership of the party. That leadership had shown itself to be blind with regard to the situation and wavering at the most decisive moment. Its failure had catastrophic consequences. The rising bureaucracy in the Soviet Union, at once grew stronger as a consequence of the retreat of the revolution in Germany which enabled it to be immediately successful at the expense of the forces which, in the Bolshevik Party were still putting their hopes in the world revolution. Within the Comintern, the repercussions of that failure will prove important as there did not then exist any national leadership with an adequate political maturity.

Summary of the course on the Spanish Revolution

1. After the ebb of the revolutionary wave following the first World War, there occurred in Europe two major social crises which, ending in defeats for the workers, led to the Second World War: 1933 in Germany, and the Spanish Revolution.[23]

2. The Spanish revolution, for the purposes of study, has an interest from various points of view
   a) from the objective point of view, Spain, like Russia in 1917, was midway between the position of a capitalist country (with some colonies) and that of an economically backward country--whence the complexity of the~ revolutionary tasks posed in Spanish society;
   b) from the subjective point of view, there was a whole gamut of varied political currents (reformists, anarchists, Stalinists, centrists, Trotskyists), without any overwhelming preponderance of one over the others, furthermore, as concerns Stalinism, we shall see the revolution beginning during 'Third Period' ultra leftism and ending with 'popular Front" opportunism.

3. Spanish society, as a result of its "slow and inglorious putrefaction" (Marx)
   — provincial particularism
   — decomposition of the old ruling classes (nobility)
   — role of the monarchy (tacking and centralization)
   — role of the Church
   — the peasantry
   — the army (frequent pronunciemientos[24] in the XIXth century)
   — the students and intelligenzia
   — the proletariat (1.5 out of 23 millions plus an equal number of rural laborers)
   — its history: 1909 Barcelona uprising; 1917 general strike.

---

[23] This guide to a course by Pierre Frank is from the summer 1959 International Cadre School organized by the International Secretariat of the Fourth International.
[24] In a *pronunciamiento*, a group of military officers *publicly* declare their opposition to the current government.

4. The beginning of the revolution.
- Fall of the dictatorship of Primo de Rivera (1930), as a result of municipal elections;
-14 April 1931. fall of the monarchy, proclamation of the republic.

5. The tasks of the revolution:
— the agrarian question (confiscation of the latifundia for the benefit of the poor peasants);
— national self-determination (the Catalans, the Basques),
— separation of Church and State, confiscation of the wealth of the Church for the benefit of the masses,
— programme of social legislation (social security, teaching, tax system)

Democratic tasks, within the framework of the conception of the permanent revolution, to add thereto transitional demands (nationalizations: railways, banks.., workers' control). Central political slogan; revolutionary constituent Cortes. At the same time, organization and arming of the workers, juntas (soviets) -- arming of the workers and peasants.

6. The trade-union and political formations of the working class in face the situation.

All affected by the traits of Spanish society.

Two trade-union federations the UGT (under the direction of the Socialists- Caballero) and, in Catalonia, the CNT (under the direction or the anarcho-syndicalists).

The Social Democracy tail-ending the bourgeois republicans (some had even collaborated with Primo de Rivera), no other goal than a bourgeois republic in which they could obtain elected representatives and even ministers.

The anarcho-syndicalists in the Federación Anarquista Ibérica (FAI), combative, but indifferent to the question of the state and to economic problems. Besides a rightist wing collaborated under cover with the petit-bourgeois Catalan separatists.

The Communists. numerical weakness and divisions aggravated by Stalinism (official party, Catalan Federation, Spanish Left). At the beginning of the revolution, first an incomprehension of its possibilities (declaration of Manuilsky), then official 'Third Period' policy (soviet the Socialists are "social-fascists," nothing about democratic slogans or on the constituent Cortes, and revival of the formula of a 'democratic dictatorship of the workers and peasants").

The Catalan Federation, more than rightist, localist. The "workers and peasants' bloc, negation of the party, democratic revolution without class analysis.

The Communist Left, numerically small, politically weak leadership (Nin, Lacroix, and Andrade),

7. The republic up till l935.
- August 1932 monarchist coup d'état attempted by Sanjurjo,
- 1934 uprising of the Asturian miners

8. Setting up of the Popular Front in 1935, in relation with the development of the international situation Bourgeoisie participants: Republican Left (Azana), Republican Union (Martinez Barrios), Esquerra Catalana (Companys), the Basque nationalists.
- Election victory of the Popular Front on 16 February 1936.

9. The government from February to 17 July 1936.
No social measures (no agrarian reform, no attainder of the Church, Morocco left in the hands of the army under the leadership of Franco. the other hand, repression of strikes, press censorship, closing of the Casa del Pueblo on the eve of the military uprising that was being openly organized.

The day of the army uprising, refusal to arm the workers, refusal of aid to the workers organizations (against the militarists' enterprise, described as 'absurd'), a two-day search for a rightist ministerial combination, offering the Ministry of War the General Mola, who was in command of the troops marching against Madrid.

From 19 July to 4 September, this government was no longer anything but a fiction, for the masses had intervened against the military *coup d'état*.

10. The revolution of July 1936
Uprising of the Barcelona workers, seizing the barracks; same initiatives at Madrid, Valencia, Malaga...

Formation of workers' militias, then of regiments based on these Militias, formation on 21 July of a 'Central Committee of 'Antifascist Militias.

Thus began the period of seven weeks when, faced by' the array led by the fascists, the bourgeois government was non-existent. Dual power existed.

In the rural regions, the land was taken by the antifascist committees of the villages, real-estate deeds, debts, and mortgages were destroyed,

In the cities, the committee organized production, transportation.

There was the basis for the creation of a workers' state, for that it would have been necessary that the workers' organizations collect and centralize power at the base.

But the committees were not in fact committees elected by the ranks, they were composed by mutual agreement of the organizations, which were headed toward an agreement with the bourgeoisie (or rather with what Trotsky called 'the shadow of the bourgeoisie').

11. The setting up of the government of Caballero (Left Socialist, leader of the UGT) was the result of this equivocal situation, to the advantage of the bourgeoisie.

Composition of the government 3 Left Socialists, 3 Right (Prieto) Socialists, who got on wonderfully with the Stalinists (2 ministers), end also 5 bourgeois ministers.

The programme of the Caballero government everything must be subordinated to the war against fascism, that is, in fact, the struggle was seen from an exclusively military angle with a renunciation of any political measure that might possibly have displeased the bourgeois ministers.

The land, confiscation only of that of known fascists.

The factories; collective contract

Morocco; nothing in reply to the proposition of Abd-el-Krim to cause Morocco to revolt if independence were granted it

Army: no soldiers' committees; reconstitution of a 'republican' army.

The Caballero government was completed, in Catalonia, by the formation of a government of the Generality (in which the POUM and members of the FAI and the CNT entered); no programme genuinely different from Caballero's.

12. The bourgeois state revived (September 1936-April 1937):

On 7 January, dissolution of the workers' committees ensuring supplies- -whence price increases, ration cards, and speculation

Dismantling of collective exploitations: Uribe, Stalinist Minister of Agriculture, named the former owners to be co-administrators of these lands.

Censorship imposed on the periodicals of the CNT, FAI, POUM public meetings forbidden.

Reconstruction of the police and the *guardia civil* (under the name of Republican National Guard), policemen forbidden to be members of a political party or a trade union, to be present at a workers' meeting.

Dissolution of the militias, arms to be turned in to the Interior

In addition, there was formed a GPU, which acted outside any legality.

13. The masses discontented, their pressure on their organizations

On 27 March, resignation of the CNT ministers from the Generality taken back on 16 April.

The POUM is hesitant, its leadership opposed to the setting up of soviets.

14. The May Days in Barcelona.

At the end of April, government provocations, arrests of anarchist leaders, disarming of workers. The workers answered by setting up barricades.

On 3 May, assault guards led by Salas (member of the PSUC) attacked the main telephone exchange in Barcelona, which the workers had had in their hands since 19 July. The attacks failed.

On 4 May the workers were the masters of Barcelona.

On the 6th, the C N T, then the POUM, orders that the barricades be evacuated. The government, which had promised to withdraw its troops, occupied the telephone exchange,

Repression began. Assassination of the Italian anarchist Berneri, Repression of the 'Friends of Durruti,' mass arrests...

15. Fall of the Caballero government:

The Stalinists presented to the government a project to dissolve the POUM. Caballero refused. Beaten by the Stalinists, the Prieto Socialists, and the bourgeois ministers, he resigned on 15 May.

16, The Negrín government, the 'government of victory' (Pasionaria dixit)

Purge of the courts, and installation of special courts for 'seditious acts', on 29 July, a trial announced against ten members of the Executive Committee of the POUM. On 7 August, suspension for a certain time of *Solidaridad Obrera*, organ of the CNT

Purge in the police of elements incorporated alter the events of July 1936.

In the UGT, a coalition of Right Socialists and Stalinists declared dissolved the Executive Committee of the UGT, whose majority was following Caballero, reconstitution of a new Executive Committee having the support of the government.

Factories: reduction of the rights of the factory committees to (control) working conditions and the stimulation of production; the Minister of Defense would grant orders only to those enterprises functioning "on the basis of their old owners."

Agriculture; breaking up of any collective enterprises that remained.

Illustration of this reactionary policy: the 1 October 1937 session of the Cortes: absence of Caballero, presence of Maura, reactionary ex-Minister of the Interior, and of Portela Valladares, ex-Governor General of Catalonia.

17. Repression in Catalonia and in Aragon:

On 28 May, prohibition of La Batalla, organ of the POUM. The "Friends of Durruti" outlawed. On 16 June, arrest of Nin; on the 17th, prohibition of the POUM.

In July 1937 'disappearances' by the dozens, and arrests by the hundreds. On 18 August, Companys had to give his resignation,

On 11 August, dissolution of the Council of Aragon (anarchist majority, dissolution of municipal councils.

18. The military struggle:

Before May 1937: the Catalan militias freed Aragon, warships attack Franco's troop transports. The workers beaten at Badajoz, and at Irun. (in the latter because of the French government, which stopped the munitions sent by Barcelona).

Nothing was done in Morocco (the 9 February note from the Minister of Foreign Affairs, the Socialist Alvarez del Vayo, to the French and English governments).

The republican government abandoned the fight on two fronts: the Zaragoza front (workers' movement under anarchist leadership) and the Basque front (evacuation of San Sebastian in September 1936 so as not to embarrass the Basque bourgeoisie).

Beginning with October 1936, Madrid was to become the main front.

After San Sebastian, abandonment without a tight of Bilbao (19 June 1937) and Gijón (21 October 1937).

This was already after the 1937 May Days. Beginning with this date, save for a few reactions by the republican troops, the initiative was to remain with Franco.

19. Non-intervention:

Germany and Italy were openly helping Franco (troops, materiel, torpedoing of ships in the Mediterranean by 'unknown" submarines).

The workers of all countries formed international brigades (after the 1937 May Days, a ferocious Stalinist control).

The Soviet government sold arms against gold and with political conditions.

The British and French (Blum) governments proclaimed "non-intervention" a diplomatic fiction that never had the slightest content. In January 1939, an agreement for the withdrawal of the volunteers.

20. Military defeat and political decomposition:

At the end of 1938, Franco's offensive in Catalonia. On 15 January 1939, the fall of Tarragona; on 26 January, entry into Barcelona without a fight. Thousands of men poured toward the French frontier On 6 February Franco's troops arrived at this frontier~

On 11 February, the Negrín government settled in Madrid. On 27 February, recognition of the Franco government by the governments of France and Great Britain. On the 28th, Azana resigned the presidency of the republic.

On 6 March, at Madrid, a pronunciamento against the Negrín government by the 'National Council Of Defense': Miaja, Casado, Basteiro, Carillo (UGT), San Andrés (Republican Left,) Vals and González Marín (CNT)

On 18 March, Besteiro proposed negotiations to Franco.

On 26 March, Franco renewed the offensive. Madrid capitulated the 28th.

Four months later, the Second World War began.

PIERRE FRANK

Democracy or Bonapartism in Europe?

The problems of the proletarian revolution are posed today[25] in Europe under the most varied aspects. It is not surprising therefore that differences on these questions are expressed in the ranks of the revolutionary vanguard. The comrades of the Socialist Workers Party in particular have discussed several questions concerning democratic demands and the possibilities of democratic regimes in Europe. If for some it were only a question of putting the emphasis on democratic demands while for others one of putting it on the slogans of Soviets and the Socialist United States of Europe, this difference would very likely be resolved in the daily activities of the parties, provided both tendencies knew how to connect dialectically the democratic slogans and the specific slogans of the proletarian revolution. On the other hand a question which must be treated with the greatest precision and which cannot be settled by daily activity is that of the nature of the present regimes in Europe. It is a theoretical problem of the first importance to know whether or not we have democratic regimes in Europe, for differences on this point must finally result — which is not necessarily the case with democratic slogans — in different policies, as happened on the question of the nature of the Soviet State which has so often been brought forward during the years of Stalinist degeneration and reaction.

Do Democratic Regimes Exist in "Liberated" Europe?

Our reply to this question obviously does not depend on the criteria required by the Foreign Office and the State Department for the diplomatic recognition of a government, any more than on those defined by Stalinist propaganda. Bourgeois democracy is a political form the analysis of which has been made by the most eminent

---

[25] These articles were written after the French elections, October 31, 1945, and were published in *Fourth International*, Vol.7 No.2, February 1946, pp.45-49 and Vol.7 No.3, March 1946, pp.93-94. The cabinet crisis which occurred several weeks afterwards seemed to confirm the main contention of this article, the Bonapartist character of the de Gaulle regime.

Marxists and it is their analysis which serves completely to guide us on this matter.

The principal problem of Europe is Germany. Unfortunately, under present conditions, the political forms and formations there are still only in an embryonic state; the military occupation governments stifle all political life capable of disturbing their own aims. Consequently, Germany scarcely affords us criteria concerning the political forms of the state in Europe.

Throughout that part of Europe occupied by the Red Army great overturns are taking place; but the Stalinist maneuvers completely distort the simplest bits of information. In any event we are not confronted with democratic governments far or near. These are governments based on capitalist property, under the control of the Moscow bureaucracy, and with a greater or lesser base in the worker and poor peasant masses. Only the presence of the Red Army assures their continuance.

But after all, the discussion among the American comrades has dealt, and moreover rightly so, with the countries of Western Europe, those which are in the "zone of influence" of American and British democratic imperialism.

Unquestionably, the most characteristic example in this zone is that of France, which once again constitutes the most appropriate subject for a Marxist study of specifically political questions. Let us say in the beginning that everything that is true for France is not necessarily true at present, for Italy, the Scandinavian countries, Belgium, etc., but it is certainly in France that the political tendencies manifest themselves with the greatest clarity and distinctness.

Do we have a democratic regime in France? Comrade Morrow, in an article aimed at summarizing the positions of his tendency in the discussion, replies in the affirmative in the following terms:

The struggle of the masses is limited by the fact that it still accepts the leadership of the reformist parties. The objective resultant is bourgeois democracy.

Another factor working for bourgeois democracy is the resistance of a section of the French capitalist class, led by de Gaulle, to US domination. There was much indignation at the plenum, notably from Comrade Cannon, when I defined the Gaullists as a bourgeois-democratic tendency. The majority could not understand this quite simple phenomena, that a section of the French capitalist class, first to resist German imperialism and then to resist US domination, was for a period basing itself on the masses through the mediation of the reformist parties. (*Fourth International*, May 1945).

We shall endeavor to show by an analysis of the class relations that this reasoning is faulty on a number of points. As one knows, it is always profitable not to examine a question solely by its appearance at a given moment, but to see it in its historical development over a longer period. This is very easy for us to do since the Fourth International has taken very clear positions on France over a period of many years.

In February 1934 a violent reactionary attack dealt a mortal blow to the democratic Third Republic. The new regime was defined by Trotsky as follows:

"... a preventive Bonapartist regime cloaking itself with the worn-out formulae of the parliamentary state and maneuvering between the insufficiently strong camp of the fascist regime and the insufficiently class conscious camp of the proletarian state" (August 1934).

The violent reactionary attack awakened the laboring masses. A strong surge to the left took place, which forced a leftward shift of the Bonapartist governments, at the same time that the Popular Front was created to check and mislead the revolutionary movement of the masses. The year 1936 saw the triumph of the Popular Front thanks to the exploitation of strong democratic illusions; but it also saw a strong surge of the workers (June 1936). The division of France into mortally hostile camps deepened. The regime of the Popular Front was not a democratic regime; it contained within itself numerous elements of Bonapartism as we shall see further on.

With Munich and the liquidation of the Popular Front, the governments of Daladier and Reynaud, resembling those of Doumergue and Flandin, prepared the Bordeaux transaction of June 1940 which served to install the Petain regime. Despite the support it received from German imperialism (it held power only with German support and went under as soon as the German Army had to quit French territory), this regime was not considered by us as fascist but rather as Bonapartist. In the notes he dictated for an article shortly before his assassination, which he did not have the time to write, Trotsky expressed himself as follows:

In France there is no fascism in the real sense of the term. The regime of the senile Marshal Petain represents a senile form of Bonapartism of the epoch of imperialist decline... Precisely because Petain's regime is senile Bonapartism it contains no element of stability and can be overthrown by a revolutionary mass uprising much sooner than a fascist regime. (*Fourth International*, October 1940).

Several months later a manifesto of the International Secretariat entitled *France Under Hitler and Petain* declares:

The swift invasion of the German troops has shattered the administrative system. The only group representing a certain relative solidity was the top layer of the Army. Around them rallied some Anglophobe politicians. This combination was crowned by the octogenarian Petain. The new Bonaparte did not even use cannon against parliament, which decided on its own hook to disappear...

The struggle for democracy under the flag of Britain and the United States will not lead to a noticeably different situation. General de Gaulle struggles against "slavery" at the head of colonial governors, that is to say, of slave masters. In his appeals this "leader" uses, just like Petain, the royal "we." The defense of democracy is in good hands! If Britain should install de Gaulle in France tomorrow, his regime would not in the least be distinguished from that of the Bonapartist government of Petain. (November 1940).

Thus our most responsible international body had predicted that a simple substitution of gangs following a victory of the Allies would not signify a change in the nature of the political regime. Have events verified this prediction or not? We find ourselves in the presence of an evaluation on the historical scale based on positions which were defended for many years by the Fourth International against all other theories and cheap labels spread by the other tendencies and formations of the labor movement. If an error was committed it would truly be a considerable one and we would be urgently obliged to seek the reasons for it and correct it. As for ourselves, we don't believe that our organization was in error on this point. We sought to define the regime of de Gaulle in 1944 at the moment when he had ceased being the leader of a military legion at London and had become the head of the government installed in Algeria as the step before becoming the head of the government at Paris. We gave only a personal evaluation which does not have the authority of the citations given above but one may well excuse us for reprinting it here, for it applies in large measure to the present regime in France.

The significance of the sentence pronounced by the Algiers tribunal goes far beyond the personality of Pucheu and of his judges. The sentence reveals the common nature of the Petain regime in France and the de Gaulle regime now established in North Africa which lays claim to the future government of France. At the same time, the sentence may serve to lay open some of the differences between the two regimes.

The Petain regime is the dictatorship of the army and the police in the service of big capital. This is Bonapartism, not fascism. It is Bonapartism propped up by the Gestapo and the German occupation troops.

The de Gaulle regime — especially since its establishment at Algiers — contains an ever increasing number of men from the army and the police who have deserted Vichy. This too is Bonapartism. It is

Bonapartism propped up by the Allied troops and the crumbs of Lease-Lend.

The differences between these two Bonapartist regimes are in no way exhausted by the fact that some of these French patriots have a marked preference for Basic British as opposed to the jargon of the *Völkischer Beobachter*.

In France, independent working class organizations are driven to illegality by Petain; in Algeria, where reaction still reigned supreme at the time of the proletarian offensive of 1936, the de Gaulle regime cannot help tolerating the open expression of trade unions and working class parties and must even seek their collaboration.

In France, Petain is constantly being spurred on by the agitation of the fascist organizations, in particular by Doriot's PPF. In Algeria, these same fascist organizations have been reduced to illegality and there actually appears to be no fascist movement in existence at Algiers. Obviously, one of these Bonapartist regimes leans essentially on fascist reaction, whereas the other leans more towards the exploited masses. This is nowise to the credit of one or other of the leading cliques, it is simply the resultant of the class forces in operation; but it is a fact of great importance for the future development of the class struggle. (*Fourth International*, June 1944).

We don't see that the "liberation" of France has brought fundamental changes in the above-mentioned characteristics of the de Gaulle regime. Unquestionably the weight of the worker masses is markedly heavier in France than in Algeria and the stronger democratic traditions are factors which contribute to weakening the regime and force it to drape itself in enough shapeless camouflage to hide its Bonapartist traits; but it doesn't change its nature.

Bonapartism

After having shown the continuity of our political analysis for more than ten years of French history and before proceeding to a more penetrating study of the de Gaulle regime, we believe it worthwhile to review some generalizations on Bonapartism at the cost of a new series of citations.

In *Origins of the Family, Private Property and the State* Engels explains how a Bonapartist form of state appears under certain circumstances:

At certain periods it occurs that the struggling classes balance each other so nearly that the public power gains a certain degree of independence by posing as the mediator between them. The absolute monarchy of the 17th and 18th century was in such a position balancing the nobles and the burghers against one another. So was the

Bonapartism of the first, and still more of the Second Empire, playing the proletariat against the bourgeoisie and vice versa. The latest performance of this kind, in which rulers and ruled appear equally ridiculous is the German Empire of Bismarckian make, in which capitalists and laborers are balanced against one another and equally cheated for the benefit of the degenerate Prussian cabbage junkers.

Limiting ourselves in this article to the Bonapartism of the capitalist regime we merely call to mind the definition of Bonapartism applied and explained on many occasions by Trotsky in reference to the Stalinist dictatorship. But Trotsky was very insistent in attributing this conception of Bonapartism to the von Papen and von Schleicher governments in the months preceding Hitler's coming to power; he did this in two pamphlets one of which The Only Road devotes itself mainly to this very question. He showed the same insistence concerning the Doumergue and Flandin ministries in France which had resulted from the violently reactionary attack of February 6, 1934. He showed the differences in the class relations between a democratic regime and a Bonapartist regime:

The passing over of the bourgeoisie from the parliamentary to the Bonapartist regime does not finally exclude Social-Democracy from that legal combination of forces upon which capitalist government bases itself. Schleicher, as is well known, sought in his time the aid of the trade unions. Through his friend Marquet, Doumergue has without doubt relations with Jouhaux and Co.... The essence of the democratic state consists, as is well known, in the fact that everyone has the right to say and write what he pleases but that the big capitalists retain the power of deciding all important questions. This result is obtained by means of a complicated system of partial concessions (reforms), of illusions, bribery, deceit and intimidation. When the economic possibility of partial concessions ("reforms") becomes exhausted, Social-Democracy ceases to be "the main political support of the bourgeoisie." This signifies: capital can no longer rely upon a lamed "public opinion"; it needs a state apparatus which is independent of the masses — i.e. Bonapartist.

In the one case, society turns almost in a circle about the big bourgeoisie as a pivot; the latter finds in the petty bourgeoisie and in a section of the working class a stable foundation; consequently the government and the state apparatus rest on these strata by means of a parliamentary majority. In the other case the big bourgeoisie does not find sufficient support in the masses which are polarised towards the camp of the revolution and the camp of the counter-revolution; under these conditions in order to save the social order the state apparatus, with the forces of repression in the forefront, tends to raise itself above society. *The state machine no longer rests on a mass base but maintains itself in unstable equilibrium between two camps*; these feats of social gymnastics come to a lamentable end the moment one of the camps takes the initiative in a decisive struggle.

The examples mentioned above for Germany of 1932 and France of 1934 are those of a weak Bonapartism in the period of capitalist decline; the qualification of Bonapartism in their case was not contested in our ranks probably because, as Trotsky wrote, it is still easy to recognize in an old man the characteristics which he possessed in his youth,

But the Bonapartism of declining capitalism can cloak itself in other costumes. In certain cases it is fairly difficult to recognize it, for example in the case of governments of the left, even very much to the left, notably of the Popular Front type. There Bonapartism is so outrageously varnished with a democratic sheen that many allow themselves to be taken in by it. The existence of Bonapartist elements in the Kerensky regime was the subject of a chapter of *The History of the Russian Revolution by* Trotsky who characterized Kerensky as "the mathematical center of Russian Bonapartism." This theoretical evaluation was in agreement with that of Lenin who, on September 23, 1917, wrote to the Central Committee of the Bolshevik Party: "We must give... a correct and clear slogan: to drive out the Bonapartist gang of Kerensky with its fake pre-parliament." There was no question there of an agitational formula. In *State and Revolution,* the greatest Marxist classic on the question of the state, Lenin, after having recalled the terms of Engels cited above with the same examples, adds the following phrase:

"Such, we add, is the present Kerensky government in Republican Russia since it began to persecute the revolutionary proletariat, at a moment when, thanks to the leadership of the petty bourgeois democrats, the Soviets had already become impotent while the bourgeoisie was not yet strong enough openly to disperse them."

Certain individuals may be surprised to see an idea applied to regimes so widely separated from one another and will doubt its usefulness. Many other ideas familiar to Marxists are applied to extremely wide fields and yet are no less correct and useful. For example centrism. Also, for example, the dictatorship of the proletariat, which is applied to the Paris Commune under its leadership of Proudhonists and Blanquists, as well as to Soviet Russia under the leadership of Lenin and Trotsky. The term "Bonapartism" does not completely exhaust the characterization of a regime, but it is indispensable to employ it in present day Europe, if one wishes to go forward with the least chance of error. Let us add finally that Marxism is not alone in the possession of such important general ideas; all the sciences do likewise. Thus chemists call bodies carbides which differ more widely from one another than the Bonapartism of Schleicher and that of Kerensky. And chemistry doesn't get along so badly either on that account. The contrary is true.

Let us note that the greatest theoreticians of Marxism did not at all define the political nature of a bourgeois regime by the positions which the latter held in the field of foreign policy but solely and simply by the position it occupied in relation to the classes composing the nation. Let us likewise observe that the limitation of the struggle of the masses because of the treacherous leaderships (according to the expression of Comrade Morrow) or, what amounts to the same, the paralysis or impotence of the mass organizations (to employ the terms of Lenin or Trotsky) does not give as "objective resultant" a bourgeois democracy, in the conditions of present day France, but rather a Bonapartism which possesses an apparent strength.

The de Gaulle Government

The conditions which dictate a Bonapartist regime to the bourgeoisie equally dictate a foreign policy which is in no way a policy of "resistance." The social crisis of France acquires a particularly acute character precisely because of the change of its world position. But to see French capitalism or part of it "resisting" American or German imperialism and becoming democratic by virtue of this is to fall into error.

France's crisis owes its extreme acuteness to the fact that a great power of the 19th century must accommodate itself to a second-rate position in the capitalist world of the twentieth century, because of the weakness of its economic base which has remained stagnant in the face of the development of new and younger powers. A retrogression of this type (like that occurring in Great Britain after its "victory" in the Second World War) does not only signify securing a camp stool in place of an armchair in the international conferences, but above all a considerable lowering of the national revenue, and therefore a considerable reduction in the standard of life, particularly for the working masses. The first luxury article that capitalism tries to eliminate under such circumstances is democracy. Well before 1939 big capital in France understood that it could no longer claim a seat of great power as in the past. It had to find a protector for a future full of threats. Inertia had more or less kept it trailing behind British imperialism; but it was easy to see that the latter was also in serious straits although it had more reserves to hold out longer. To resist the revolutionary movements it was necessary to look elsewhere than London and its ailing democracy. Besides, French heavy industry had some special business reasons for orienting French capital towards German imperialism, which, with the coming to power of the Nazis moved forward with seven-league boots.

But if French capitalism turned its eyes towards German imperialism and was guilty of counter-revolutionary defeatism in 1940 in the interests of its domestic politics, it none the less sought to prevent those few cards which remained in its hand from being completely taken away, knowing that German imperialism was still far from having consolidated its positions and that it had not been able to secure any better ally than Italy. On the other hand an important section of French capitalism (finished goods, industries, luxury articles, tourist trade) could not because of its special interests neglect the American continent where it had its principal customers. As a result, French imperialism, pulled from opposite sides, endeavored to play an intermediary role between Germany and the United States immediately after the debacle of June 1940, hoping to be able to earn a small commission for this work. It hasn't been forgotten that certain elements of American capitalism lent themselves for a time to this (Leahy mission). But when it became clear that the United States was intransigent toward German imperialism and the latter had no further chance of victory, this role of go-between was abandoned and the Bank of France and the *Comités des Forges*[26] themselves became "resistant," in their own fashion, of course. Billions were transferred to Algeria in the months preceding the occupation of North Africa by the Americans; the top French administration made contact with de Gaulle.

For a little more than a year, de Gaulle, as head of the government, while endeavoring from time to time to rattle his wooden sabre a bit, tried to reestablish this courtier's policy, adopting it to the new principal powers, that is to say, the US and the USSR, and ignoring Britain. De Gaulle quickly signed a treaty of alliance with the USSR, but this document soon proved to be worthless, for Stalin, having nothing to get from de Gaulle, let him down in all the international conferences which have been held since then. In his recent visit to Washington de Gaulle obtained some loans for French economy (in which sufficiently important American business interests are involved) but he returned empty-handed from the political point of view. It took him less than a year to learn that it is one thing to play the role of arbiter between two weaker states and another thing for a small state to wish to maneuver between two great powers. General de Gaulle would have been able to learn something about this without having to experience it if he had addressed himself to certain ancient

---

[26] The main federation for large employers in much of the 19th and 20th century.

Polish colonels. Finally, de Gaulle who was openly attacked by a section of the French bourgeoisie for his policy of isolation has taken a small step towards Britain and the countries of Western Europe by proposing to create an association resembling one for the blind and the paralyzed.

Any way one may examine it this foreign policy of French capitalism is in no way "resistant" and, besides, there is nothing in it which predisposes the "Gaullists" to democracy.

If one studies the class relations in France, the Bonapartist character of the de Gaulle government appears in the greatest clarity, since the day of "liberation" up to the elections of October 21, 1945 and to the conditions created by them.

The liberation of Paris was accomplished under the leadership of the *Comité National de la Resistance* (CNR), whose mass base was constituted by the workers' organizations (General Confederation of Labor, Communist Party, Socialist Party) and the militias composed in great part of worker members of these organizations. The CNR and more particularly the workers' organizations, would have been able at this time to establish themselves in power, supporting themselves on the militias and the local committees of resistance. (These last represented in a bureaucratic fashion, and not democratically, the proletariat and the exploited masses in general.) In this period de Gaulle personally had very few real forces and would not have been able to oppose the CNR. As for the reaction and the old capitalist forces they were completely demoralized and disorganized and were hiding themselves. To save the capitalist regime thus left stripped bare, it was necessary from the very beginning to find something to cover it again and to camouflage it for the eyes of the masses. For this desired effect the uniform of a resisting general was used and they raised him as the representative of the nation, above classes, parties and groupings. In many respects this operation resembled that which occurred in February 1917 when the conciliators of the Petrograd soviet yielded the power, surrendering without firing a shot, to a provisional government without any real base.

It goes without saying that the Bonapartism thus created has not at all the intention of leading too precarious an existence. It. seeks to create a base for itself while securing the complicity of the leadership of the political formations and others who, in the given period, canalize the class forces between which it tries to maintain itself.

PIERRE FRANK

Traitorous Working Class Leaders

From the very first de Gaulle had to obtain the collaboration of the leaders of the parties which included the working class in order to accomplish the dissolution of the militias, the submission of the local committees of resistance to the organizations of the old bourgeois states as well as a unification of all the armed forces under the control of the government artificially created by these leaders themselves. Despite the support of the traitorous leaders, this operation took several months to achieve.

Every Bonapartist government in France has tried to create a base for itself in the peasantry; the army having been for a very long time a sort of protector of the middle peasantry (see *The Eighteenth Brumaire* in particular where Marx wrote "The uniform was the holiday costume of the peasant.") In the new circumstances de Gaulle has remained faithful to the Bonapartist tradition. Shortly after the Second World War when the countryside suffered from the manpower shortage and it was necessary to resort to the employment of prisoners of war for the tasks of trained workers, especially in the mines, de Gaulle attempted to maintain an army of one million men, that is, a standing army superior to those which France had preceding the years of re-armament and direct preparation for the war. Promises have been made to the peasantry, higher prices have been allowed for their products, etc., without much being accomplished, however, in the way of results, since the peasants need manpower, materials, livestock, seeds, manufactured products; since there is a shortage of all these things; and since the profits they can make on the black market cannot be used to obtain these things.

The elections which have just taken place provide one of the most striking proofs of the Bonapartist character of the regime. Elections, a constituent, a parliament, a government responsible to an elected assembly, are so many disagreeable things for the general. He couldn't throw all this into the garbage can. What he was interested in above all was to wield stable power which would not be at the mercy of an assembly. Look, he said, at the history of the Third Republic with its cascades of falling ministries. Thus he decided that simultaneously with democratic elections to elect an assembly on the bases of program and parties, there should be held a referendum in the nature of a plebiscite designed to deprive the elected assembly of the greater part of its rights and to preserve, on the other hand, the greater part of the power in his own hands. Upon the announcement of this referendum a number of the democratic politicians of France shouted "Bonapartism." Surely it was not knowledge of Marxist literature on this question but very simply an elementary knowledge of the history of their country which led them to such declarations.

For a long time the French bourgeoisie has sought to resolve a problem that the years have made as insoluble as squaring the circle. It wanted "a strong state," in part to insure the defense of its frontiers, but mainly to hold in check the domestic enemy, the working class; but all the same, it did not wish this state to become too strong, for each time that it has permitted the state to entrench itself too strongly, it quickly found its own posterior in contact with the military boots. To assure themselves that the state would not be further disturbed by political conflicts, the generals evinced an intention to transform the whole country into a barracks and to deprive everyone, including the bourgeoisie themselves, of political rights. This is the essential reason why even the most reactionary and personally arbitrary democratic politicians of the Third Republic, notably Clemenceau and Poincaré, opposed and fought vigorously against the interference of the generals in politics. But that is already ancient history.

In the October 21 elections the end of the democratic regime was incontestably demonstrated by the inglorious foundering of the principal formation of the Third Republic, the Radical party, which had dominated and been maintained in every possible and imaginable way by that Republic. In *Whither France* Trotsky showed among other things that the policy of the Popular Front, the alliance of workers' organizations with the Radical party, was going in a direction directly contrary to the development of the situation, that is to say, to the decomposition of bourgeois democracy and of its principal party, that of the Radicals.

But the voting has created a situation in which Bonapartism is literally under one's nose. The double vote of October 21 — the democratic elections and the plebiscite — has resulted in the most desirable situation for a general of the *coup d'etat*.

Votes Almost Equally Divided

In the elections for the Constituent Assembly, the votes were pretty nearly equally divided between three parties: the Stalinist Party followed by a majority of the proletariat and by an important layer of the petty bourgeoisie of the towns and countryside; the Socialist Party, with a minority of the proletariat (without however losing its working class base in northern France) and a very great number of petty bourgeois votes. Finally the *Mouvement Republicain Populaire* (MRP), organized by Catholic politicians, who before the war flirted with the Popular Front and during the war participated in the resistance, but who were always solid pillars of the capitalist regime.

In return, they received on October 21 all the votes of the reactionaries who have realized that they had no chance at all under their old colors.

The plebiscite is such a model stratagem that you can say without fear of deception it could only have been conceived beneath the *kepi* of a general. A direct question for or against de Gaulle would never have given the desired result, for the present day Bonapartism is too weak to intimidate the voters.

Therefore guile was necessary. It was decided to pose two questions instead of one. (They even dreamt for a moment of posing three to do the job better.) To the first question there was no doubt that, save for a tiny minority of greybeards, everyone was going to reply *Yes*; the Third Republic is dead. To say *Yes* to the first question was to influence many voters to say *Yes* to the second question; besides it is easier to say *Yes* than *No* even in a referendum. It sufficed to wrap the second question in fine-spun language to finish the sowing of confusion. The result was a majority of about 60 percent of the votes for de Gaulle, who on the strength of this will receive the post of head of the government from the new assembly.

What is going to happen? De Gaulle, feeling strong with 13,000,000 votes behind him, does not have to share counsel with anyone. Before him is an assembly with three parties of practically equal numbers, and a perspective of new elections in nine months. They will all maneuver with each other. The Assembly and also the ministry in which the representatives will find each other again, will have to submit to the arbitration and will of General de Gaulle. All that resembles parliamentarism and democracy is going to be discredited in quarrels and in impotence; but there will always be a general to restore order!

At least for the most immediate future, the French government will be composed of representatives of the three parties. The Socialist party which cannot play the role of Bonapartism is in the most difficult position. It evidently does not wish to form a government with the Stalinists alone (the latter strongly indicated this possibility the day after the elections, because they were sure that the socialists would not take it into consideration; the Stalinists kept insisting strongly and will do nothing to realize it). The Socialist party can no more (under the present conditions) form a ministry with the MRP, leaving the Stalinists *in the opposition.*[27]

---

[27] Before the elections, Leon Blum, who couldn't fail to see the bonapartial danger, endeavored as is his custom to exercise it by sophisms. At first affirmed that a referendum is not necessarily a plebiscite — which is true; he added that the October 21 referendum would not be one — which was false, for its object was a vote of personal confidence and very large prerogatives to de Gaulle. Finally Blum, taking into account that the elected constituent would formally have the right to change, in very difficult

As for de Gaulle, it is evidently all to his advantage to make the ministry a nest of intrigues and disputes by introducing into it members of the three parties, which will contribute to discredit them and to reinforce his personal position. It is quite possible, as the Stalinists do not wish to conduct too "revolutionary" a policy and the MRP not being able to adopt too soon an openly reactionary attitude, that the crisis will not open in the very first days. But it is not the desire of the politicians — in or out of uniform — which regulates the development of events. The class conflicts will not fail at an early date to place the political problems on a razor's edge.

---

conditions, the head of the government, decided that for that reason he should remain at the disposition of this assembly. No more than de Gaulle did he present himself to the will of the voters, and tried to a certain degree to hold himself above the parties, including his own party.

PIERRE FRANK

Bonapartism in Europe

The importance of a correct definition of the European governments goes beyond the domain of theory. What Trotsky wrote in 1932 on the subject of Bonapartism in Germany preserves all its value *mutatis mutandis* for the bonpartism of 1945:

If we have insistently demanded that a distinction be made between Fascism and Bonapartism, it has been in no wise out of theoretical pedantry. Names are used to distinguish between concepts; concepts, in politics, in turn serve to distinguish among real forces. The smashing of Fascism would leave no room for Bonapartism, and. it is to be hoped, would mean the direct introduction to the social revolution.

Only – the proletariat is not aimed for the revolution. The reciprocal relations between Social Democracy and the Bonapartist government on the one hand, and between Bonapartism and Fascism on the other – while they do not decide the fundamental questions – distinguish by what roads and in what tempo the struggle between the proletariat and the Fascist counter-revolution will be prepared.

One must no more confuse the Bonapartism "of the right" with fascism than the Bonapartism "of the left" with democracy. We have seen that Bonapartism takes very different forms according to the conditions in which the two mortally opposed camps find themselves; we maintain also that the existence of democratic liberties, even of very great democratic liberties, does not suffice to make a regime democratic. The Bonapartists *à la* Kerensky, Popular Front... are even notorious for their flood of democratic liberty up to the point where capitalist society thereby even risks its balance and is in danger of capsizing. Democratic liberties do not proceed, as in a regime which one can correctly define as democratic, from the existence of a margin for reforms within capitalism, but on the contrary, from a situation of acute crisis, the result of the absence of all margin for reforms.

Precisely because we do not generally have in Europe at the present time democratic regimes, because there is literally no place for them and because the extension of democratic liberties can only undermine the Bonapartist regimes, we put forward the most extreme democratic demands, in connection of course with the transitional demands which prepare the duality of power.

The resolution of the recent national conference of the British section of the Fourth International ignores, alas, in a general fashion

Bonapartism for Europe, and employs the expression, devoid of content, "democratic counter-revolution" for the European governments. The resolution contains on the other hand a fairly good example for the future development of events in Europe, namely that of Spain in the period which extends from the fall of Primo de Rivera up to the civil war against the fascism of Franco. In all this period of the Spanish Republic there was no democratic regime properly speaking.

Bonapartism, as will probably be the case in all Europe, expressed itself through a series of epileptic convulsions, of great shifts to the right and to the left. The same phenomenon likewise occurred in France after 1934: 1934, violent reactionary attack; 1936, general strike and occupation of the factories; 1940, coup d'etat of Bordeaux; 1944, uprising against the Petain regime. These great leaps follow one another, accompanied by deepening division of the nation along with a political clarification on both sides in regard to the decisive struggle.[28]

The use of democratic slogans – combined with transitional slogans – is justified more precisely because the possibilities of a democratic regime are non-existent, because present-day Bonapartism is completely unstable and the struggle for the most extreme democratic demands can only end its existence. But again it is necessary for us to understand one another on the democratic slogans which we adopt and not to define slogans as democratic when they are not.

Let us merely recall in passing that the partisans of the *Three Theses* seriously propose to make a struggle for the freedom of religion – a democratic slogan, unquestionably – one of the most essential

---

[28] Since we here speak of the resolution of our British comrades let us note that it defines the new Labor government as "Kerenskyism". The Bonapartism, that they ignored, has found the means to insinuate itself into their document under a very special name. But we do not think that the present Attlee government is bonapartist à la Kerensky. Without questioning the coming to power of this government, that is to say, of a formation which rests on the working class but wishes to leave intact. The City and British capitalism, at the moment when the latter has only gained a victory at the price of its very substance, will accelerate the downfall of British imperialism. The oldest of democracies has, as a result of the last elections, reached a dead end. But the term "Kerenskyism" is not appropriate, for it already presupposes the accomplishment of the passage from democracy to this form of bonapartism. On the contrary, it is in the future, probably very soon, that this passage will occur and the British workers and their organizations will then have to face an important crisis. In Britain one can only observe features of bonapartism. For example the Labor government, under the pressure of capital and encouraged by the administrative apparatus, of which it hasn't harmed a hair, is inclined to play a role of referee above the parties, while a section of the Labor parliamentary group endeavors to continue representing in a reformist and parliamentary fashion the worker masses who have elected them

points in the struggle against fascism. For anyone who has not completely lost the use of his faculties in the course of these terrible years of reaction through which we have passed, it is clear that such a democratic slogan has nothing in common with us. It is on the contrary more and more evident that this slogan is today the property of a whole section of reaction which does not dare to show its true face.

But a great error, even a very dangerous error, has been committed in qualifying as democratic and in proposing to our organization the slogan of "the Republic" (cf. the article of Comrade Logan on Italy). We are completely in favor of the slogan "Down with the monarchy" in Italy, in Greece, and for all the countries where this institution inherited from feudalism exists. We are no less in favor of the slogan of the Assembly of a single chamber which is against the Senate, the House of Lords, etc.... But between these slogans and the "Republic" there is a deep moat which we cannot cross. In one case we endeavor to direct the masses against institutions of a profoundly reactionary character, which limit, even under the capitalist, regime, the possibility of democratic expression of the masses, and which, in moments of crisis become quasi-automatically the rallying point for the forces of the counter-revolution. In the other case, we would advance the slogan which, if we made the mistake of adopting it, would make us the promoters of a completely vague state form. "The Republic"? This slogan does not concern a partial objective but puts to the fore the very question of the state. What republic can we recommend in the current epoch? The Republic of Workers and Peasants Soviets alone, and not a bourgeois republic. The slogan of "the Republic" is absolutely silent on this point and can only, by its confusion, favor the class enemy.

It is evident that, despite our rejection of this slogan, we will not be neutral in the plebiscites which may be held in Europe on the question of the monarchy. We shall call the workers and peasants to vote against the monarchy, but clearly specifying that we do not have the choice as to the other term of the alternative, that we are voting against the monarchy but not in favor of the bourgeois republic.

It is almost twenty years ago that the Italian Social Democrats in one of their fits of theoretical audacity inscribed in their program of the struggle against fascism the slogan of "the democratic republic of the toilers" and, for a certain period, the Italian Communist Party, in one of its zig-zags to the right, had an equivocal position towards this slogan. When in 1930, a section of the leadership of the Italian CP broke with Stalinism, formed the New Italian Opposition and turned toward the Left Opposition, this slogan was the object of a clarification in the exchange of views which took place at that time. The old opposition, that of the Bordigists, had an absolutely negative attitude on democratic slogans; it was especially necessary that the new Italian comrades should not take for their part a position which could be exploited by the Bordigists and which would have been fatal in the struggle against fascism. In a letter to the comrades in the NOI Trotsky expressed himself as follows on the slogan of the Italian Social Democrats:

While advancing one or another set of democratic slogans we must irreconcilably fight against all forms of democratic charlatanism. Such low-grade charlatanism is represented by the slogan of the Italian Social Democracy: "The Democratic Republic of the Toilers". The "Toilers republic" can be only the class state of the proletariat. The "Democratic Republic" is only a masked rule of the bourgeoisie. The combination of the two is a naive petty bourgeois illusion of the Social Democratic rank and file (workers, peasants) and deliberate treachery on the part of the Social Democratic leaders (all these Turatis, Modiglianis and their ilk). Let me once again remark in passing that I was and remain opposed to the formula of a "National Assembly on the basis of worker-peasant committees" precisely because this formula approaches the Social Democratic slogan of the "Democratic Toilers Republic" and, consequently, can render extremely difficult for us the struggle against the Social Democrats. *May 14, 1930.*

The slogan of "the Republic" as such is also as erroneous and pernicious as that of "The Democratic Republic of the Toilers" although, we are persuaded, few comrades in our international organization would have at present an inclination to mix in the above fashion the forms of bourgeois power with the forms of proletarian power. But it is not the thoughts and intentions of this or that comrade which are under discussion but the slogan of "the Republic" itself. This is not a democratic slogan but, to employ the strong expression of Trotsky, democratic charlatanism.

The theoretical principles and positions which are a part of the accumulated capital of the Bolshevik-Leninists, gained in the course of their years of struggle against Stalinism, reformism and all the varieties of centrism in the workers' movement, and which we have called to mind in this article, obviously far from exhaust the questions which arise on the European situation. But it is indispensable to take them as a point of departure to permit our militants and our sections to orient themselves correctly despite the enormous confusion which rages and which, unhappily, will not fail to rage for the duration of a complete period, up to the point when the events and ourselves, in assisting events by a correct policy, consciously array an important fraction of the working class under the flag of the Fourth International.

France Under the Fourth Republic

Following the collapse of the Third Republic in 1940 and the termination of World War II, the year 1947 was supposed to inaugurate the definitive era of the Fourth Republic, with a Constitution adopted by referendum, with a Chamber elected by universal suffrage, with a Council of the Republic, a President of the Republic, a French Union embracing the colonies with or without their consent, and a Monnet four-year plan for the reconstruction of French economy.[29]

But this "definitive" era has had very precarious beginnings. It is much easier to elect Deputies and Councillors of the Republic than to form a government; the French Union is being realized in life by plunging the Viet Nam in fire and blood; the application of the Monnet Plan presupposes many conditions, none of which is present.

Where is France going? After the two world wars the economic situation is literally disastrous. The material losses are huge, as the most optimistic admit; and the setback cannot be recouped, for the day of small countries with limited national economies is over; the productive forces of the last century no longer suffice for the maintenance of colonial empires. There is no French solution.

Moreover, French capitalism, in assaying its own perspectives, entertains no illusions about its real capacities. The Monnet Plan — whether it will be realized or not — does not set high objectives; on the contrary, its goals are comparatively modest. In the report submitted by Blum to the United States in order to obtain a loan, it is stated:

France will devote all her efforts to modernize her industry and agriculture in order to attain by 1950 this level (25 per cent above that of 1929, if possible).

Even this will raise the consumption of energy, in terms of tons of coal per capita, only to 2.9 as compared with 4.15 for Great Britain and 5.1 for the United States. This would bring the per capita production of steel only to 240 kilograms as against 285 for Great Britain and 351 for the United States in the depression year 1937!

---

[29] France Under the Fourth Republic was originally published in *Quatrième Internationale*, January-February 1947. It was translated by Margaret Stewart for Fourth International, Vol.8 No.4, April 1947, pp.104-108.

In brief, French capitalism, feeling too old to plunge into adventures, clings to its "Maginot Line" mentality; it would be quite content if it is able to preserve the larger part of its inheritance from the previous generations, thanks to which is can keep an 'honourable' situation at the international level and justify a small folding chair alongside the large arm chairs of the "Big Three."

But even these modest ambitions are far from being assured. The year 1946 was supposed to be a special year, not included in the plan, during which the economy was to be reconverted on a peacetime basis and the levels of 1938 would be regained. (Let us recall that 1938 was a depression year for French economy.) But to obtain these results, a great deal is still required. In an article devoted to the importation of coal, *Le Monde*, November 16, 1946, arrives at the following conclusions:

... Despite a rather bad situation, which is undoubtedly temporary, our industry, while far from attaining the necessary rate of expansion, will nevertheless be able next year to stabilize itself at an average rate of approximately 80 per cent of 1938; but this effort can probably be sustained only by maintaining severe restrictions on home consumption and by utilizing in large measure the second-grade coal which is being extracted since the war from our mines.

The Monnet Plan pretends to ignore the international conjuncture. But in reality it is based on the hope that there will be no crisis in American or world economy before 1950, and that by that time French capitalism will be in a condition to sustain such a shock. But for several months the economists and business circles in both Britain and the United States have become rather dubious that American and world economy can avoid a crisis before 1950. There are various ominous signs (declines in commodities such as cotton, accumulation of inventories among manufacturers, wholesalers, and so on).

Monnet Plan

A few weeks ago the British Minister of Foreign Trade declared in the House of Commons that he expected a "crisis of readjustment" in 1947, which, according to him, would be like that of 1921, brief and of no great depth. The price-cutting experiment, introduced by Blum, which is a temporary measure primarily designed to divert the demands of the workers (for higher wages), is itself a speculation in part on an eventual decline of world prices sometime in 1947. But a drop in prices, bound up with a world "readjustment" crisis, would confront France with new problems and would probably entail the gravest consequences.

One of the conditions for the realization of the Monnet Plan is the stabilization of currency. The leaders of world finance, notably the directors of the International Monetary Fund set up at Bretton Woods, apparently consider the exchange rate of the franc as too high. About a week before it hailed Blum's experiment, *Le Monde* had the following to say both about prices and currency:

It appears that a rise in the rate exchange can be avoided only by the introduction of lower prices. But no matter from what angle we approach the question, the solution remains unclear. The prices of manufactured commodities, which are virtually the only ones concerned in exports, lag far behind agricultural prices, which are not permitted to decline out of political considerations and because of the impotence of economic controls. Any lowering of industrial prices, assuming this were technically possible, would therefore aggravate still further the imbalance of French economy... Finally, it ought not to be forgotten that the rise which we have been experiencing without interruption for 11 years and which has recently become accelerated, cannot be checked at a single stroke. A great deal of courage coupled with favorable circumstances is required to curb it little by little.

But the factor that dominates the whole situation in France, both as a consequence of the economic decline and as an element aggravating this decline, is the social and political condition of the country.

The patient's temperature can be easily charted. There was a succession of elections and referendums. More than a year after the "liberation" and a few weeks after the war ended, in October 1945, the first elections to the Constituent Assembly took place. The majority was gained by the Socialists and the Communists. As a parliamentary force, these two parties were practically equal. The old bourgeois parties had collapsed; the reaction did not dare show its face; the Radicals were in full retreat. In order to achieve the mobilization of all those who recoil from socialism and communism, big capital built the MRP, with any kind of material. This party masqueraded as socially minded (its leaders participated in the Resistance movement, accepted nationalization and announced their readiness to collaborate in the government with the workers' parties).

Electoral Fever Chart

By means of a referendum held on the same day and thanks to the compliance of the Socialists, the powers of the Assembly were limited in relation to the powers of the government. De Gaulle, still wearing the halo of "liberation," saw himself entrusted with the leadership of the government. But with the termination of the war, in the struggle between the tendencies of the bourgeoisie, toward a strong regime and the aspirations of the masses after all these years of suffering, the advantage was not on the side of the bourgeoisie. There was a growing clash between de Gaulle, who personifies the tendencies toward a strong regime, and the parties who distort and misdirect the aspirations of the masses. The parties did not bring their differences into the open; they issued no appeals to the country; they showed no militancy. But de Gaulle, finding no solid ground under his feet, walked out himself in January 1946, slammed the door behind him, bade farewell to politics, received the homage of all parties and retired to the provinces, there to wait and prepare, while the existing parties disintegrated, for a favorable moment to install the strong regime.

With the departure of de Gaulle, the three-party coalition continued under the leadership of the Socialist, Gouin. The Stalinists, who secured the disarmament of the militias and the dissolution of the committees, launched an appeal for increased production and extolled the wage-freeze, while the MRP started opposing any measure that might adversely affect capital in the slightest degree. To the right of the MRP there was constituted the avowedly and traditionally reactionary PRL, which is the culture medium for fascist elements, but which is not an actual party of fascism.

The friction within the three-party system kept growing, as the date for the Constituent Assembly drew closer. After obtaining numerous constitutional concessions from the SP and CP, the MRP — without leaving the coalition government or being forced by the other parties to leave it — repudiated the draft, and with the aid of the entire reaction succeeded in the May referendum in defeating the draft of a bourgeois constitution that had been already adopted by the Communist and Socialist deputies. Then came the June 2 elections for a second Constituent Assembly. Big capital, forcing the PRL to withdraw in many electoral districts, gave its backing to the MRP, which succeeded in taking the lead among the three major parties. The Socialist Party — which compromises itself on each occasion in its role as intermediary in the three-party coalition — lost as much on the right as it did on the left, despite the jingling dollars of the Blum loan. The CP made gains in the countryside, but stagnated or lost ground in the large industrial centers, although it came out in favor of removing wage controls three days before the elections.

Henceforward the formation of a government proved difficult. Workers' demonstrations multiplied and it was impossible to leave the CP out of the government. Following its defeat, the SP tried to make itself as inconspicuous as possible and left the direction of the government to the leader of the MRP, Bidault. The three-party regime was brought back again. In the interval between June 2 and November 10 the crisis of the three-party regime deepened. Prodded by the PRL, by the Gaullist Union and by de Gaulle himself, the MRP became more and more exacting in its demands. The SP and CP made more and more concessions on the Constitution (on the issues of the President of the Republic, Second Chamber, and so on), as well as on the workers' demands. The discontent of the masses found a pitiful expression at the Convention of the SP where the left wing did not know what to do with its majority. On the other hand, it found a virile expression in the mass movements that rolled over the heads of the trade union leadership (strikes of the postal and Treasury employes, and so on). The CP, while continuing to call for increased production and while continuing to engage in the most systematic class collaboration, resorted to all sorts of artifices in order to unload the responsibility for the three-party system on the Socialists and to pose as champion of the workers' demands (demonstrations for the 25 per cent wage increase, demonstrations against the high cost of living, and the like).

The Impasse

The draft Constitution, supported this time by the three major parties, was adopted only by a slim majority. In the November 10 elections, despite the repeated elections, the number of absentions, although on the increase, was not, however, very considerable. The polarization became accentuated. The center parties lost while the extremes benefited. In the bourgeois camp the MRP lost to parties on its right, while the leading political circles of French imperialism pushed the petty bourgeois masses toward the MRP.[30] We witnessed a shift of half a million petty bourgeois to the right, but at the same time we saw the inability of the big bourgeoisie to exploit this shift for the benefit of a more reactionary policy. On the other hand, the SP suffered a complete rout, losing about 750,000 votes and being literally ground to pieces between the MRP and the CP. The latter gained 250,000 votes, not only continuing to make further gains in the country as in June, but also regaining the lost ground in the great industrial centers. This is the way in which the desire of the working masses for a change finds its expression; they cast their votes for a party which under the existing conditions appears to them to be in the

---

[30] This became even more apparent two weeks later, when on the occasion of elections to the Council of the Republic, everything possible was done to regain for the MRP the position of "first party of France" which it lost to the CP during the November 10 elections.

best parliamentary and governmental position to satisfy their demands.

What have we witnessed since these elections? The party, which in its press and in the Parliament advances demands for the Presidency of the government, finds itself refused not only this post, but all other important functions in the new Republic. This party, whose capacity for action is so great, is made the target of a veto so far as key ministerial posts are concerned. The French bourgeoisie is not powerful enough to hold the working masses in check with its own forces. But since the November 10 elections, the CP has not dared to call upon the masses to intervene even in the same limited way, quite harmless to the bourgeoisie, as it did last June in connection with the decontrol of wages.

Post-Election Developments

The governmental crisis has unfolded solely within the framework of a struggle at the top. It has involved such grave political problems as the defense of the franc, cuts in the budget, new burdens, maintenance of the French Union in Indo-China. But on these questions there were no fundamental differences between the parties, including the Stalinist party. The government crisis, which is officially scheduled to reappear after the election of the President of the Republic, will not involve any basic differences in program. But the tension becomes obviously acute when it comes to permitting the Stalinists in the government and assigning portfolios to them. However, the French capitalists are aware that the presence of the Stalinists in the government has been a valuable asset to them during the last two years; they know that under the existing relation of forces, it would be impossible for them to govern in opposition to the CP and the CGT which is under CP control. Finally, they understand very well that the CP is no longer any threat at all to the capitalist system.

In the Chamber, Jacques Duclos — falsely identifying his party with the class he is betraying — complained that the workers were good enough to die in battle and to produce but not to govern. True enough, the bourgeoisie knows how to assay the ability of the CP to impel the workers to produce or to fight for them, but they will avoid, if they can, giving it places in the government, because they know that the CP leadership, while respecting private property and the capitalist regime, just as the traditional reformists do, is a tool of the ruling Kremlin bureaucracy. In the key international questions, the interests of the Moscow bureaucracy are placed by the CP leadership above the interests of French capitalism. A glance at the international situation suffices to understand how important this consideration is in connection with the composition of the French government. The fact that the CP holds the position of the most extreme chauvinism on the German question counts for little, inasmuch as there is no assurance of the constancy of these views. The SP which holds a much more moderate position toward Germany merits far greater confidence. Blum has just demonstrated that he will not hesitate to hold his own views while preparing the annexation of the Saar as a "loyal director" of French capitalism.

The preparations for the coming Moscow Conference unquestionably are a dominant consideration in the composition of the French government. While she lacks the authority of the three partners by whose side she sits, France can, by casting her vote either on the side of the United States and Britain or on the side of the Soviet Union, swing the compromise one way or the other. Let us recall how eagerly Thorez sought to reassure the Anglo-American capitalists by his statements in the press and to the British news agencies on the day after the elections when the CP advanced his candidacy for head of the government. Supporting this candidacy in the Chamber, Duclos pointed out that the comments in the British and American press were not "unfavorable." The United States and Great Britain who follow the developments in France very closely, did not fail to exert considerable pressure to eliminate or reduce the participation of the Stalinists in the government.

Despite the existing difficulties, "national unity" — in one guise or another — is excluded. It must be kept in reserve for much more serious situations. A government simultaneously in opposition to both the CP and SP is impossible; the MRP itself would not countenance this right now. An anti-Communist government with the Socialists participating is equally impossible, for the SP cannot allow the Stalinists to remain in the opposition. The three-party system or its extension through the inclusion of other "left" parties presents very great difficulties. So far as normal solutions are concerned, the Parliament that emerged from the November 10 elections cannot maintain a government. But if they do not wish to resort to the "strong state" (they cannot do so as yet), if they wish to avert troubles which may in one sense serve Bonapartist ends but which may also develop in just the opposite sense, then they must at all costs find a solution by which some time can be gained. The trick consisted in replacing an impossible coalition of the major parties by the weakest party, leaving nothing of the coalition except its hinge, already considerably worn out, and thus forming a government composed exclusively of the party which emerged the most enfeebled from the elections. This solution, in its own fashion "extra-parliamentary," presents some advantages for all.

A Tricky Solution

Blum is assuredly favorably regarded by Washington and London, who know that he will not lean internationally toward Moscow. From the domestic standpoint, it permits the two big parties, the MRP and the CP, to avoid the three-party system and all governmental collaboration and this is useful to both of them with regard to their respective clientele: they can offer Bidault without Thorez, and Thorez without Bidault. The bourgeoisie is enabled for a while to have a government *without* the Stalinists, without its being a government *against* the Stalinists. As touches the CP, despite its repeated declarations in favor of a "united" Republican government, the Blum solution does not displease it too much; for it is thus enabled all the more easily to pluck the Socialist fowl and to appease the malcontents within. It is likewise enabled the better to retain its control over the masses, by remaining, if not in the opposition then at least outside the government. This set-back may even permit it a little later on to return with even greater demands as the pressure of the masses increases.

But how do matters stand from the standpoint of Moscow's interests? In the first place, a party wielding such influence over the masses cannot follow the Kremlin's directives as automatically as a weaker party which is able to shift positions without any major repercussions. When Moscow executed a certain left turn among the Communist parties in 1945 and 1946, the French CP was actually the last one to engage in it and did so with greater reservations than any other. It is very difficult for it to move leftward, because behind it is the majority of the French working class and while it disposes of a rather large field for maneuvers, it cannot permit itself everything. However, since the end of November 1946 we have witnessed a retreat by Moscow on the international field. Beginning with Stalin's declaration, it became manifest during the last days of the conferences in New York. It was seized upon by the Turkish and Iranian governments who immediately employed repressive measures against Moscow's supporters in these countries.

Will this retreat have an effect upon the policy of the Stalinist parties? We have no exact indications as yet, but it is quite likely. Right now, it is already noticeable that while the question of the government is still being posed, how reluctant the CP leadership is — whether directly or indirectly through the CGT [Confederation of Labor] leadership — to put forward any workers' demands and how it abstains from any demonstrations to force the hand of the bourgeois parties.

As for the SP, up to the last minute of its existence it continues to show itself as the "loyal manager" of capitalism. Defeated at the last party Convention, Blum nevertheless retains the leadership and ignores the program that was adopted. Defeated in the elections, as they were inside their party, the leaders of the SFIO set what the left Seine Federation calls an "example of courage" by adopting the program of Schuman and creating a ministry that one journalist has described "as homogeneous as the SP." The post of Minister of State was entrusted to a leader of the "left" in order to associate him in all the services rendered to French capitalism.

Is Stabilization Possible?

Can the present unstable situation be ameliorated in the sense that there will be a marked increase in production, an improvement or even stabilization of the franc, and so on? Nobody really believes in such a development which would offer the SP a chance to save itself. On top of all the already existing difficulties has been added the Indo-China affair. It prevents cuts in the military budget, necessitates the use of transports, diverting ships from commerce with the rest of the world, to carry reinforcements and arms against Vietnam. And finally, it is not at all certain that French imperialism possesses sufficient military forces to enforce a compromise more favorable than the March 6 agreement, signed by people more compliant than Ho Chi Minh. The experience of the Blum "kiss" may defer for a while the working class actions which are threatening, as Tanguy-Prigent, the Minister of Agriculture, believes. But barring a miracle, conditions do not exist in France for even such temporary results as were obtained in Belgium; there are no stocks on hand and no possibilities of large-scale imports, the Belgian franc was not threatened, nor was the Belgian government at the same time constrained to undertake substantial increases in transport, gas, electricity, postal services and so on.

In spite of all the assistance afforded by the treacherous leaders, the bourgeoisie is in no condition to impose its solutions on the working masses. The bourgeois parties, especially the largest ones, are merely artificial structures doomed to fall apart under strong social tension. Their great man, de Gaulle, after a few brusque remarks, has confined himself to a short declaration in betaking himself to his winter headquarters. The three-party system has been cleverly exploited, the SP has been deflated and will not be reinflated again. But it is still necessary to utilize the Stalinist party and to exhaust the working class before the bourgeoisie, whose champion is de Gaulle, can dream of assuming the initiative.

PIERRE FRANK

Neither the bourgeois parties nor the SP nor the CP nor the CGT wish to pass through the experience of a government by the workers' organization. The leaders who flatter themselves as representing the working class dream only of combinations with bourgeois parties on the basis of bourgeois programs. The Stalinists have insisted in words on a government of "Republican Defense," a second edition of the People's Front. But the situation continues to develop in a direction different from the one they desire. They found themselves compelled to take up, and at the same time to distort, one slogan after another advanced by the French section of the Fourth International. After slandering the Trotskyists for months as agents of the corporations for their advocacy of wage raises, the Stalinists were forced on the eve of June 2nd to declare themselves in favor of lifting the wage controls. After shouting that a wage victory had been won, and after issuing appeals to struggle against price rises, they were driven to take up the slogan for a minimum living wage. They set this at a ridiculous figure of 84,000 francs, which, however, was accepted as reasonable by *Le Monde*. And they did so in face of the fact that the sum of 120,000 francs is far closer to the actual needs and corresponds even to the calculations of the CGT made in February 1945 and adjusted to the official rise in living costs since that time. The Stalinists have denounced the slogan of the sliding scale of wages, but they are now compelled to play cunningly with this slogan by declaring themselves in favor of "re-examining" the minimum living wage in view of changing living costs. For their fictitious "struggle against price rises," they have set up supervisory committees which have at the most embarrassed a few petty merchants in the local markets. After all the battles that have been waged and all the "victories" that have been won, the living conditions of the working class are such as make necessary the adoption of workers' control of production, as the Trotskyists advocate.

Two years after the "liberation," we are approaching an experience with Stalinism, stripped of those circumstances which have hitherto provided the Stalinist leaders with alibis. Parallel with this, or more accurately leading toward this experience, there impend struggles which will tend to pass over the heads of the Stalinist leadership. In 1946 we witnessed only skirmishes (printers, postal and treasury employees).

The traditional organizations and leaderships have been by-passed only to a very limited degree and in isolated instances. But these skirmishes have certainly not been without a profound effect. This is certainly true of the movement of postal employees, with its central and local strike committees, all elected in the course of the struggle, despite and against the official leadership of the Postal Federation.

Revolutionary Perspectives

If from the standpoint of world economy France lags lamentably, then her role in revolutionary politics can be of first-rate importance in Europe. Her working class movement, despite its glorious revolutionary traditions, has known the most abject opportunism. But since 1934 France has once again tended to become the classic country of political struggles, a country where these struggles are carried through to the very end.

Since the victory of the democracies, the European countries are confronted more than ever before with an alternative. They can choose to be engulfed by decaying capitalism, under a "strong state" installed to the detriment of the masses, amid an increasing Balkanization of Europe which would facilitate the outbreak of World War III, ending up literally in the annihilation of the continent. Or they can choose the victory of the masses who, despite their old treacherous leaderships, will smash the iron chains of capitalism and assure prosperity and peace through the establishment of the Socialist United States of Europe. Europe's choice will in large measure depend on the development of the class struggle in France and on the French proletariat's ability to reorient itself in the course of these battles around a new leadership, that of the Fourth International. However weak the PCI may still be, the encouraging indication is that the PCI has been able to make considerable progress during the last two years, in spite of the handicap of virtually having to renew its ranks during the war. The unification of the Bolshevik-Leninist ranks in France; the conquest of legality for the Party and its press, despite the Stalinist Ministers; its participation in almost one-fourth of the country in two electoral campaigns within the space of six months; the results gained which attest to the existence of a class-conscious revolutionary minority in the big industrial centers and even in the countryside; the rise of a revolutionary trade union minority that rallied the votes of 1,200 unions at the April 1946 Congress of the CGT; the steady progress recorded by the Party in recent months; the growth of an independent organization of International Communist Youth — all this is evidence that the maturing of the revolutionary crisis in France has not failed to find a conscious expression to a degree unknown in France as well as in other countries since the creation of the international faction of the Bolshevik-Leninists.

January 7 1947

P.S. After this article was already set up, news came of the formation of the Ramadier Ministry, which is predominantly Socialist, and into which the Stalinists, the MRP, the Radicals and independents have entered. The frailty of this combination and the reasons for it are given in the following comments of *Le Monde*, which at the same time confirm the importance of the international problems referred to in our article:

Everyone knows that one of the reasons, if not the main reason, for the creation of this government, as well as its chance for survival, if not the only chance, lies in the approaching Moscow Conference. The economic experiment could be carried out without the MRP, which, moreover, has great reservations on this score. It could be carried out with far greater difficulty without the Communist Party. But neither the latter nor the former wished or was able to retire from the scene at the hour when the future of Germany and Europe is to be decided.

A Study in French Centrism

The pre-war period was marked by an implacable struggle by the Fourth International against centrist organizations, particularly against the London Bureau, the international center which was the meeting ground for groupings which oscillated between Marxism on the one side and opportunism or Stalinism on the other. This side of our activity was limited in the postwar period; the London Bureau disappeared and most of the former centrist organizations went out of existence. (The Independent Labour Party, the oldest of these and the most deeply rooted in the British labor movement, came to the conclusion that it no longer was a factor on the political scene in Britain.)[31]

On the other hand, the postwar revolutionary crisis impelled the broad masses toward the old Social Democratic and Stalinist organizations. The problem of the building of revolutionary parties was posed at this stage in the form of the establishment of links between the Trotskyist organizations and the masses, so that as a result of common experiences they would be won over to the banner of the Fourth International.

The split between the masses and the leadership of the old organizations has begun in various ways but the Trotskyist organizations are still too weak to take full advantage of this development. Does that mean that there is room for centrist organizations? What would be their scope and their orientation? Such questions can only be answered by examining the situation concretely, country by country. The experiences on this point in France are quite specific, and while one must guard against drawing too generalized conclusions from them, they nevertheless are instructive in the building of a revolutionary party.

Following the "liberation" in 1944, the overwhelming majority of the working class and important sections of the middle class followed the Stalinist party. The remainder of the working class followed the Socialist Party which had wide influence among government employees and the middle class. As a result of the class-collaborationist policies carried on equally by the Social Democracy and by Stalinism, and then by the policy of the Stalinists after the formation of the Cominform and by the unbridled class-collaborationism of the SFIO (French Socialist Party), an important

---

[31] October 15, 1948. From *Fourth International*, Vol.10 no.6, June 1949, pp.180-185.

part of the middle class was thrown into the arms of de Gaullism and the old leadership began to lose its influence over sections of the workers and the middle class.

Confidence in the traditional parties has begun to wane. This process is quite advanced as far as the Social Democracy is concerned. It is less marked in the French Communist Party, the strongest of all Stalinist parties in Western Europe, which has at its disposal not only a huge" apparatus but a large number of worker-militants who have been associated with it over many years of struggle and who enjoy considerable authority in the factories.

In this process of disintegration, the transformation of centrist tendencies into centrist organizations tends to germinate at the weakest points of the old organizations. Moreover the workers' groupings are still far more inert than the petty bourgeoisie; they react more slowly but with far greater consistency.

This is being very clearly confirmed in France. The allegiance of members and sympathizers of the CP to that party has always been much stronger than that of SP members and sympathizers to Blum's party. Op to now the Stalinist party has suffered only minor losses among its worker-members. During the early part of 1947 when the CPF was still in the government and supported, the wage-freeze, some of its members went over to the Anarchists, specifically to the CNT, Anarcho-Syndicalist trade union federation, but the decomposition of this organization has been as rapid as its rise.

The bulk of the working class still follows the Stalinist party. One of the reasons for the absence of any broad development of a centrist organization was the "left turn" of the CP following the creation of the Cominform. Discontent with the policy of the CP is widespread and exists within the ranks of the party itself, where strong differences have been manifested to the position of Thorez, Duclos, Marty, etc. But these are widely diverse, politically and organizationally isolated from each other. Thus centrism assumes exceptional importance within the ranks of the CPF, embracing worker-militants who are under the pressure of a large rank and file but who, because of the policy of their leadership, are not permitted to carry on revolutionary activity corresponding to their own aspirations. Therein is posed the most important problem of centrism in France. Upon its solution depends the creation of a strong revolutionary party in France and at the same time the development of the class struggle in this country and therefore the development of class relations for an entire period in Western Europe.

What has already happened among the petty-bourgeois tendencies and in the ranks of the Social Democracy – while quite secondary to the above-mentioned phenomena: – is not a matter of indifference. In addition the evolution of a centrism, social democratic in origin and petty bourgeois in social composition, has been intimately connected with political developments in the *Parti Communiste Internationaliste* (French Trotskyists). As will be seen, the history of these groupings cannot be separated from the recent crisis of the French Section of the Fourth International, a crisis which is most clearly explained by the evolution of these centrist elements. It is a conclusive experience in this connection.

Before the Defeat of November-December 1947

Two closely associated tendencies took shape in the SP and split from it in 1947 – *Jeunesses Socialistes* (Socialist Youth – JS) and *Action Socialiste et Revolutionnaire* (Socialist and Revolutionary Action – ASR).

Deprived of political rights in the SFIO the *Jeunesses Socialistes* began an orientation toward a revolutionary program which was most marked at their 1947 convention at Montrouge a Paques. Six weeks later when the first Renault (auto) strike occurred, they solidarized themselves with the strikers and were expelled by the SP leadership. Their political evolution, continuing in an autonomous and somewhat devious way, led them to consider fusion with the PCI, and on December 13, 1947, their national committee resolved:

The National Committee of the JS notes that the discussion and actions carried on with the PCI have demonstrated that despite differences there is fundamental agreement on revolutionary program between the two organizations.

Therefore there can be no serious obstacle to the building of a revolutionary party uniting the JS and PCI.

The National Committee takes note that the resolution adopted by the ASR defines in essence a political orientation similar to that of the JS and the PCI and that therefore it now appears hopeful that after thorough political clarification and discussion, the three organizations will participate in the building of a united revolutionary party.

Special note should be taken that on December 13, 1947 "no serious obstacle" to unification of the JS and PCI existed.

Action Socialiste et Revolutionnaire was belatedly constituted in the SP around Dechezelles, co-secretary of the party, C. Just and members of the Lyons organization after a split with Rous, Boutbien and others to whom we shall return later. At the Lyons Convention of the SP held in August 1947, the ASR protested against the expulsion of the *Jeunesses* but it was not yet politically prepared to leave the party. It was only later, at the critical point of the 1947 general strike, that the ASR broke with the SP, adopting the following resolution on its position at its December 7th conference:

The only possible means for the abolition of the capitalist system and the institution of proletarian power and the building of socialism is the creation of a revolutionary party based on the class struggle.

Therefore the ASR sets as its goal the building of such a party and will issue an appeal for this purpose to all members and all organizations who agree on the following principles....

Under the impulse of the great workers' battle then in process both tendencies were evolving in the direction of a clear-cut revolutionary program. Unification with the PCI was on the agenda of both organizations; it was posed more concretely in the JS than in the ASR because of the more heterogeneous character of the latter, but the problem was clear enough to its leading elements.

The defeat of the November-December movement, the trade union split organized by Blum and Jouhaux (reformist trade union leader) and facilitated by (the Stalinist) Frachon, the capitalist and government offensive, the rise of de Gaullism, gave rise to the attempts of the socialists to find new ministerial combinations, and to the extremely complex policy of the Stalinists.

The Stalinists Intervene

The Stalinists were not inactive in this situation. Their agents in the SP, gathered around the paper *Bataille Socialiste*, who had said nothing against the expulsion of the JS and had not carried on any campaign against the anti-labor policy of the party leadership and the socialist cabinet ministers, came into violent conflict with the Managing Committee of the SP on the issue of its pro-American and anti-Russian policy. They courted expulsion for the purpose of chanelizing the discontent of the socialist-minded workers and of the left wing in the SP.

Soon after, what remained of the "left" in the SP, Rous, Boutbien and others – no longer able to remain silent or to freely desert to the leadership as was done by Marceau Pivert (leader of pre-war French centrism) – believed that it would be possible to circumvent the discipline of the SP by another device. In company with a number of journalists who proclaimed their independence from all organizations and with some figures from the literary world like Sartre and Rousset, they launched the *Rassemblement Democratique Revolutionnaire*, (Revolutionary Democratic Rally – RDR) a grouping without any programmatic basis, without any strict form of organization, without discipline, and above the parties. The aim of the operation was indicated in a pamphlet by Rous who advocated a policy of pushing the "third force" to the "left."

One would have thought that these two new "independent" groupings, one obviously pro-Stalinist and the ether a transparent appendage of the "third force," would not have been able to exercise any powerful attraction on the JS and ASR. These groups had the merit of breaking with the SP on a class basis. They knew from their own experience the exact worth of the leading figures of the *Bataille Socialiste* group as well as those of the RDR.

But a third element intervened in the situation which arrested the development of the JS and the ASR. This was the crisis in the PCI and the role played in it by the former right wing of the PCI, the Parisot-Demaziere faction which led the party from September 1946 to December 1947. Under the impact of the defeat of the workers' movement they cast aside the revolutionary program and broke with the Fourth International. Confronted with this split, the militants of the JS and the ASR, still either immature politically or confused, became disoriented and demoralized; Their progress stopped short and retrogression set in.

The Crisis in the PCI

How was it possible for this to happen to an old Trotskyist leadership?

The right-wing tendency in the PCI was not united by common political views (its members gave no evidence of precision in the formulation of their political positions and *La Verité*, under their editorship, manifested this, alas, only too often) but by a conception of building a revolutionary party which can be summarized as follows:

The Trotskyists have not grown in the past because of their "sectarianism" (meaning their attachment to a program which concretized the whole experience of the working class); it is necessary to be flexible; on occasion to put programmatic questions in the background; daily policy is not a question of principle; political skill is required to gain the leadership of a mass movement, which having been won can be directed toward certain ends. Some of them thought it possible to create this mass current by a vast superficial agitation, others by resorting to this or that conception or slogan which was popular on some occasion (such as the "Resistance"), others by creating a broad shapeless mass organization. (In essence, this conception is closely related to that of the Stalinists for whom the class is a malleable mass to be manipulated by an all-powerful apparatus.)

This is also the idea which pervaded the activity of the JS and the Dunoyer grouping in the SP. The left wing in the JS and the SP formed slowly, painfully and confusedly. But matters worsened after the split because of the substitution of a whole series of organizational maneuvers for genuine political struggle, resulting rapidly in mishaps, then in catastrophe.

Evolution of Socialist Youth

Jeunesses Socialistes, a very weak political organization, had an absolute need for an intense political life if it was to assimilate the program of the Fourth International. But instead and in place of that, at more or less regular intervals, Dunoyer gauged the "political consciousness" of the JS and set an organizational goal which according to him was to develop this consciousness. In the period which followed expulsion from the SFIO, a space of several weeks, there occurred a rapprochement with a Stalinist youth organization for the ostensible purpose of permitting the JS to have an experience with Stalinism; then activity oriented around the formation of "Committees of Revolutionary Regroupment" to give the JS an understanding of the need for a revolutionary party; and finally a rapprochement with the PCI in a joint electoral campaign in the municipal elections of October 1947 with a view toward fusion.

These youth, who should have been learning the revolutionary program by study and in actions other than an electoral campaign, were told to defend a program they did not understand by hook or by crook before the working class. Heavy damage to the JS was caused by these organizational gymnastics. Still one could hope toward the end of 1947 that with the adoption of the above-cited resolution by the National Committee of the JS, the worst would soon be over.

At that time, Dunoyer told us that there was "no serious block" in the "consciousness" of the JS to fusion with the PCI, and one could be thankful for that. But when the effects of the workers' defeat made themselves felt, Dunoyer, and with him the "consciousness" of the JS, began to evolve. The same evolution and the same zigzags were manifested by the defeated leadership at the 4th Convention of the PCI and in the leadership of the ASR.

Instead of the building of a revolutionary party by unification of the ASR, JS and PCI on a program which would be fundamentally if not formally that of the Fourth International, we saw first a new turn in the leaderships of the ASR and the JS in the direction of the Stalinist *Bataille Socialiste*. They told us that involved *in part* in this procedure was the unification of those elements with a socialist origin which would later serve as a stepping stone for the building of a revolutionary party[32].

This undertaking did not get very far because the leaders of *Bataille Socialiste* insisted upon an open attack against the PCI (which as was shown later would not perhaps have been unacceptable) and submission to the desires, big and little, of the leaders of the CP — which was hardly an attractive condition at a time when the wind had turned and was now blowing ever more strongly from the West.

The unification of the JS and the ASR which took place in 1948 was only a belated recognition of the existence of two leaderships over one and the same organization, or rather the vestiges of an organization. The ASR, thus unified, found itself on the horns of a dilemma; either to work for the building of a revolutionary party, as had been decided five months earlier and as was demanded by a tendency in its ranks grouped around comrades Dumont and Just — and that meant to seek a rapprochement with the PCI; or to abandon this perspective and, as inveterate centrists, to turn toward the RDR. The majority of the leadership, with the support of the ex-Trotskyists who betrayed their party and their program, adopted the latter solution and decided to enter the RDR[33].

Since then the ASR has virtually disappeared, its political disintegration proceeding apace. At a recent session of its central committee, after having expelled the tendency favoring the building of a revolutionary party in unity with the PCI, the majority divided into two sections, one for fusion with the Stalinist *Bataille Socialiste* in the

---

[32] At this point Demaziere sent a letter (July 31st) to the Political Bureau of the PCI in which he proposed:
"Review the question of organic unity with the JS and ASR, the tendencies closest to us. Such a unity, aside from its present uncertainty, no longer appears valid to me ...
"In its place we should favor and attempt to guide all partial regroupments: BS, JS and ASR for example, even on political and organic bases which would implicitly or explicitly exclude us."
Space is lacking to deal separately with the question of the unification of the JS and the PCI. At one time the right wing, feeling the ground slip from under at the 5th Convention of the PCI, wanted a spectacular unity with the JS in order to utilize them as a. pawn in the convention in order to retain the leadership of the party. The intervention of the International was required to prevent this maneuver against the PCI.

[33] Within the PCI, Demaziere penned another letter (March 4th) in which he touted the virtues and the future of the RDR in dithyrambic terms:
"The RDR slow in coming into the world seems to have quick success from its first days. My profound conviction is that it will experience considerable growth in the weeks to come and rapidly gain the adherence of several tens of thousands of members. It is a symbol, amidst the reigning confusion, attracting the bewildered millions of workers, intellectuals, petty bourgeois who do not want to choose between Truman and Stalin ..."
A decision of the top committee of the SP caused the departure from the RDR of Rous and Boutbien. The tens of thousands of members evidently did not come. The confusion remained

"Socialist Unity Party" and the other which no longer has any other hope than to be the spark plug of the RDR. It is noteworthy that Dumont who a few weeks later was to be the spokesman of the revolutionary opposition at the Congress of the CGT (French trade union federation) was expelled from the ASR by Sautery who was to vote with the Stalinists on all questions at the same trade union convention. This incident speaks volumes on those who wanted to teach the Trotskyists lessons in political flexibility.

The Free Men

To speak of the RDR as centrist is a little less than exact. Traditional centrism, mixture of Marxist phraseology and opportunist practice, is far superior to the positions taken by the RDR. The first manifesto announcing this social democratic offspring begins by amending Marx: Its motto is: "Proletarians and free men of all countries, Unite!" Being neither proletarians, who are specifically designated, nor capitalists, this expression can only refer to what we in our Marxist language and stubborn sectarianism call the middle classes, the petty bourgeoisie.

The concept of classes is abhorrent to the RDR. According to the "free men" of the RDR there are entities above the classes and their struggles, and the most important of these is "the Resistance." Only a malicious Marxist would point out that the "Resistance" was almost universally divided and engaged in mortal combat along class lines (Yugoslavia, Greece) or was rapidly dividing along sush class lines (France, Belgium).

Watching reactionary developments in France, a free man like David Rousset cries out: "No, the Resistance didn't want this!" One must have the brain of a free man to discover that one "of the errors of General de Gaulle... which has its roots in his social formation and in his political orientation... (is) to have understood the Resistance solely in the narrow framework of military action and intelligence." The capitalists and the militarists at their service are obliged to utilize the laboring masses in their wars in "the narrow framework of military action," to use the language of a "revolutionary democrat." This is no error on their part. The capitalists know what a class is and they know how to exploit petty-bourgeois intellectuals for their benefit.

"Freedom" Within the French Empire

The national problem is also tackled by the RDR from the point of view of "free men" and not from the class point of view. Lenin pointed out the role of the proletariat in the struggle of oppressed peoples for independence; he also demonstrated in his study on imperialism that this force subjugated, not only colonial countries but small modern capitalist countries as well to the yoke of the most powerful nations. This tendency has been tragically unfolded to the extent that we now see Europe put on rations by the United States. But Lenin did not depend upon free men, especially on the kind who could free themselves from Trotskyism. In his letter of March 4, 1948 which marked his break with Trotskyism, Demaziere discovered that "... along with scarcity there has arisen new exploiting and privileged groups (middle men, speculators) who are completely unconcerned with the independence of their country."

Is it any wonder that there are dissertations in *La Gauche* (the name of the RDR paper which in itself represents a program in France) on the guilt of the German people? Of course they do not speak of this guilt in any specific sense. But who doesn't know that the technique of these "left" personalities consists in finding progressive meanings for the ideas the ruling class utilizes for its reactionary policy?

International tension is now obliging the free men to take a position. David Rousset has discreetly abandoned the pro-Stalinist position he had on the morrow of the "liberation."[34] He sees only "the geographic extension of the Russian system whose state form does not respect all the freedoms." (The terms used to describe the GPU regime are very cautious because he does not wish to burn all his bridges.) And he also sees America whose "strategic advance is essentially aimed at safeguarding, wherever it is threatened, a moribund economic regime which, however, is indispensable for its economy."

The RDR proposes a "constructive struggle" against the Marshall Plan which consists in demanding from Wall Street an effective control over the utilization of American grants and credits by trade

---

[34] On the morrow of the "liberation," Rousset made three brief appearances in the PCI where, before vanishing completely, his activity was limited to defending a thesis before the Second Congress which he presented under the name of Leblanc. Here are the essential passages:

"To the degree that the Soviet bureaucracy today finds itself obliged to prepare its defenses in anticipation of a third war, it must pose and achieve the socialist revolution abroad. The liquidation of the Second World War has put an end to the theory and practise of the theory of socialism in one country in the eyes of the bureaucrats themselves.

"... Soviet economic forces intervene directly in world affairs in the political form of the Stalinist bureaucracy. In the new phase we have entered, they represent the only real and effective guarantee of the socialist revolution in the world."

Since then, friendship with the USSR is no longer in vogue. In the recent period Rousset, along with Sidney Hook and James T. Farrell, supporters of the Atlantic Pact, and leaders of the Catholic MRP, was an organizer of the "anti-Stalinist," "peace" conference in Paris.

union organizations. To whom is Washington to give control over American funds granted to capitalist states? To Jouhaux or to Frachon? And for what purpose? Perhaps to build socialism? The free men are especially free in using any kind of formula which does not tie them down to anything concrete.

There is no lack of denunciation of "the old colonialism" by these personalities on the "left." They favor the right of the people to self-determination but within limits, that is within the French Union, or, to be more precise, within a genuine, democratic, revolutionary French Union. Provided that they take care to keep within these limits, the Vietnamese, the people of Madagascar and the Algerians will be entitled to complete self-determination. In other words, in place of the "old colonialism" our free men propose a new colonialism, democratic and revolutionary, which we suppose is to be enforced by the good capitalist Republicans.

Centrists and the Problems of the Class Struggle

The petty-bourgeois character of the centrist tendencies manifest themselves in many ways toward domestic problems. In ***Drapeau Rouge***, organ of the JS, as in *La Gauche*, workers' demands far from occupying a primary position are only the object of afterthoughts. Only during the second half of 1947 was there a momentary effort in *Drapeau Rouge* to give more consideration to specifically workers' problems. The demands which they do put forward vary from issue to issue according to the editor of the moment. In June 1948, the RDR was at one and the same time in favor of the sliding scale of wages and for an increase in wages proportionate to the increase in productivity. Are they trying in this manner to satisfy all tendencies in the labor movement?

The centrism of the former right wing of the PCI and the leaders of the ASR and the JS is most completely revealed on the question of the united front. There was an entire period when the two old leaderships – Social Democratic and Stalinist – were united in opposing strikes, and when the initiative was in the hands of the working class which was restrained only with the greatest difficulty by these leaderships. The problem of the split in the workers' movement was not a practical question but, on the contrary, it was the slogan of the general strike which embodied the highest form of the unity of the workers' front. During this entire period our centrists, on every occasion and out of all contact with reality, agitated for the united front, going so far as to propose a "united electoral front" to the CP and SP in the November 1946 elections.

Following the defeat of the general strike, the initiative passed over into the hands of the bourgeoisie and it became necessary to rebuild the unity of the workers' front, to organize a working-class resistance which could be transformed into a victorious counteroffensive. Thus when the united front should have become the central axis of the policy of a revolutionary party concerned with elaborating a perspective for the working class, this slogan virtually disappeared from the platform of the centrists.

There has never been any lack of ambiguity on the character of the RDR, judging even from the conceptions of its supporters themselves. For some it is a formation based on a more or less precise program in competition with the existing parties. For others the RDR pretends to be a rally above parties for the purpose of opposing the other rally (de Gaulle) and, because of this, realizes within itself a united front of the masses. But since the masses have not decided to follow this kind of organization, the RDR cannot be anything else but a political formation, a sub-party without a precise program. It will neither achieve the united front nor contribute to its achievement. To the degree that it hinders the formation of the revolutionary party, it hinders the realization of the united front.

At a time when everyone knows that the dominant question in France is that of power, when de Gaulle and the Stalinists who influence three-fourths of the country, campaigning on the one side for a "strong state" and on the other side for a government of "democratic unity," the free men have nothing to say to the laboring masses on this question. Their approach to this question is possibly embodied in the proposal by (George) Altman [a social democrat] who, proclaiming his loyalty to the Republic (it is really touching), calls for "a rally of all the left forces in the country... with formal guarantees for the free expression of differences." This may, appear somewhat complicated, this "revolutionary, democratic rally" which is itself enclosed within a "rally of all the left forces," seasoned with unrestrained rights for everyone to say everything and to do nothing, the total result being the well known old tale which is entitled: left bloc, popular front, tripartitism.

That is the essence of the program of the centrists. And for this purpose Demaziere proposed to the PCI that:

"The revolutionary vanguard of which the PCI is a part should enter the RDR and play the game intelligently and thoroughly. In the prevailing state of disintegration and bewilderment in the workers' vanguard, some key values will help our militants find their way again. As for the rest we should withhold our views until there is sufficiently widespread activity which would permit us to make ourselves better known than in the past."

Free Men of All Countries, Unite!

The centrists have their peculiar way of being internationalists. Before the war, the "London Bureau" was the center for a number of political formations which met from time to time, exchanged fraternal greetings, adopted vague resolutions, but otherwise felt no common bond whatever. The war put an end to this Bureau and most of its affiliates.

The split of the right wing from the PCI occurred on the eve of the Second World Congress of the Fourth International. They parted company with the Bolshevik Leninists in more than 30 countries in order to unite with the free men of the editorial board of *Franc Tireur* and the Flore cafe. This done, Demaziere, Dunoyer and company announced that they were prepared to remain within the Fourth International on the condition that the latter would be content to receive occasional reports of their activity in the RDR – in other words on the condition that the Fourth International would take the place of the defunct "London Bureau."

But since there were Ceylonese, Uruguayan and even French Bolshevik-Leninists who had no stomach for this international with the "new look," it became necessary for the ex-Trotskyists and their associates to clear their conscience by devising some form of internationalism. This did not prove to be difficult. "A movement not bound to any system, any regime, any doctrine" (Altman pontificated) should have no trouble finding other free men beyond the frontiers and the oceans who are similarly free and similarly uninhibited by doctrine.

If rumors are correct the ex-Trotskyists are assured of the help of Shachtman and the POUM, a Spanish party, in the publication of a periodical (The magazine has since appeared under the name *Confrontation Internationale*). International alliances are very helpful for politically characterizing a movement.

Trotsky designated the POUM as having been the most serious of the centrist organizations. It had a workers' base in Catalonia and a certain revolutionary tradition. Although some of the leaders of the POUM pretend to have leanings toward the Fourth International, they never lose an opportunity to assist the opponents of the Trotskyists or to display sympathy for them. It has become a standard practice to be sympathetic to the Fourth International while coming to an agreement with those who are trying to betray it.

La Batalla, organ of the POUM, was preoccupied with the presidential elections in the US. They were aware that our comrades in the SWP were carrying on a vigorous campaign for their nominee, Farrell Dobbs. They were equally aware that Shachtman's organization had advised American voters to take their pick among the "socialist candidates," that is, to vote either for the SWP candidate, or for Norman Thomas, or for the candidate of the archaic grouping, the SLP. It is noteworthy that the most decisive elements in Shachtman's group (James T. Farrell, Albert Goldman) who were sympathetic to Norman Thomas, left the organization on this question. Referring to Shachtman's vague position, *La Batalla* (September 18, 1948) wrote:

"It would have been more correct to come out publicly and officially in favor of the Socialist Party candidate and even participate actively in his behalf in the election campaign."

Thus as between Trotskyism, whose candidate was a militant worker with a record of struggle and who was imprisoned for his activities during the war, and American "socialism," whose candidate was a former preacher who supported the imperialist war and has nothing in common with socialist thought, the sympathies of the POUM are on the side of social democracy.

We have no doubt that Shachtman is well able to cover the pages of a magazine with his scribbling. But on the basis of what program? The word program itself is rare enough in his writings. And what are his perspectives? Having returned to his country after a visit to Europe, he found a completely demoralized organization. This is the opening observation of all the articles in the *Internal Bulletin* of the Workers Party and of some of the articles in its public organs. The Second World Congress of the Fourth International, the strongest international gathering of Trotskyists, to use Shachtman's own words, made no impression upon him. He voluntarily closed the door upon it. He sees no solution except to renounce the name "Workers Party" in favor of a study and discussion circle. And as for the rest of the Marxists in the world, he recommends that they plunge into the mass movement without a program – this movement being represented in France not by the Stalinist party but by the RDR! Shachtman joins hands with Demaziere on every point. Without doctrine, without principles, no one is held responsible for anything by anyone. What a remarkable magazine will emerge from such an ideological vacuum!

It is with considerable disgust that we watch this wretched comedy in which ex-Trotskyists are the chief actors. But it throws considerable light on the struggle which took place over the years in the PCI, a struggle between the supporters of the Trotskyist program and a petty-bourgeois wing which was attempting to free itself from the Trotskyist program and organization.

PIERRE FRANK

The future of centrism, originating in petty-bourgeois and social democratic groupings is unquestionably very circumscribed in France. The struggle of the Trotskyists against this tendency should now permit them to turn their attention to the other centrism, that of the workers breaking with Stalinism, with all the necessary theoretical clarity as well as with all the indispensable flexibility needed to advance on the basis of the program of the Fourth International.

Political Crisis in France

The importance of a correct definition of the European governments goes beyond the domain of theory.35 What Trotsky wrote in 1932 on the subject of Bonapartism in Germany preserves all its value *mutatis mutandis* for the Bonapartism of 1945:

If we have insistently demanded that a distinction be made between Fascism and Bonapartism, it has been in no wise out of theoretical pedantry. Names are used to distinguish between concepts; concepts, in politics, in turn serve to distinguish among real forces. The smashing of Fascism would leave no room for Bonapartism, and. it is to be hoped, would mean the direct introduction to the social revolution.

Only — the proletariat is not aimed for the revolution. The reciprocal relations between Social Democracy and the Bonapartist government on the one hand, and between Bonapartism and Fascism on the other — while they do not decide the fundamental questions — distinguish by what roads and in what tempo the struggle between the proletariat and the Fascist counter-revolution will be prepared.

One must no more confuse the Bonapartism "of the right" with fascism than the Bonapartism "of the left" with democracy. We have seen that Bonapartism takes very different forms according to the conditions in which the two mortally opposed camps find themselves; we maintain also that the existence of democratic liberties, even of very great democratic liberties, does not suffice to make a regime democratic. The Bonapartists *à la* Kerensky, Popular Front... are even notorious for their flood of democratic liberty up to the point where capitalist society thereby even risks its balance and is in danger of capsizing. Democratic liberties do not proceed, as in a regime which one can correctly define as democratic, from the existence of a margin for reforms within capitalism, but on the contrary, from a situation of acute crisis, the result of the absence of all margin for reforms.

Precisely because we do not generally have in Europe at the present time democratic regimes, because there is literally no place for them and because the extension of democratic liberties can only undermine the Bonapartist regimes, we put forward the most extreme democratic demands, in connection of course with the transitional demands which prepare the duality of power.

The resolution of the recent national conference of the British section of the Fourth International ignores, alas, in a general fashion

---

35 From Fourth International, Vol.11 No.1, January-February 1950, pp.15-18.

Bonapartism for Europe, and employs the expression, devoid of content, "democratic counter-revolution" for the European governments. The resolution contains on the other hand a fairly good example for the future development of events in Europe, namely that of Spain in the period which extends from the fall of Primo de Rivera up to the civil war against the fascism of Franco. In all this period of the Spanish Republic there was no democratic regime properly speaking.

Bonapartism, as will probably be the case in all Europe, expressed itself through a series of epileptic convulsions, of great shifts to the right and to the left. The same phenomenon likewise occurred in France after 1934: 1934, violent reactionary attack; 1936, general strike and occupation of the factories; 1940, coup d'etat of Bordeaux; 1944, uprising against the Petain regime. These great leaps follow one another, accompanied by deepening division of the nation along with a political clarification on both sides in regard to the decisive struggle[36].

More precisely, the use of democratic slogans, combined with transitional slogans is justified because the possibilities of a democratic regime are non-existent, because present-day Bonapartism is completely unstable and the struggle for the most extreme democratic demands can only end its existence. But again it is necessary for us to understand each other on the democratic slogans which we adopt and not to define slogans as democratic when they are not.

Let us merely recall in passing that the partisans of the *Three Theses* seriously propose to make a struggle for the freedom of religion — a democratic slogan, unquestionably — one of the most essential points in the struggle against fascism. For anyone who has not

---

[36] Since we here speak of the resolution of our British comrades let us note that it defines the new Labor government as "Kerenskyism". The Bonapartism, that they ignored, has found the means to insinuate itself into their document under a very special name. But we do not think that the present Attlee government is Bonapartist *à la* Kerensky. Without questioning the coming to power of this government, that is to say, of a formation which rests on the working class but wishes to leave intact. The City and British capitalism, at the moment when the latter has only gained a victory at the price of its very substance, will accelerate the downfall of British imperialism. The oldest of democracies has, as a result of the last elections, reached a dead end. But the term "Kerenskyism" is not appropriate, for it already presupposes the accomplishment of the passage from democracy to this form of Bonapartism. On the contrary, it is in the future, probably very soon, that this passage will occur and the British workers and their organizations will then have to face an important crisis. In Britain one can only observe features of Bonapartism. For example the Labor government, under the pressure of capital and encouraged by the administrative apparatus, of which it hasn't harmed a hair, is inclined to play a role of referee above the parties, while a section of the Labor parliamentary group endeavors to continue representing in a reformist and parliamentary fashion the worker masses who have elected them.

completely lost the use of his faculties in the course of these terrible years of reaction through which we have passed, it is clear that such a democratic slogan has nothing in common with us. It is on the contrary more and more evident that this slogan is today the property of a whole section of reaction which does not dare to show its true face.

But a great error, even a very dangerous error, has been committed in qualifying as democratic and in proposing to our organization the slogan of "the Republic" (cf. the article of Comrade Logan on Italy). We are completely in favor of the slogan "Down with the monarchy" in Italy, in Greece, and for all the countries where this institution inherited from feudalism exists. We are no less in favor of the slogan of the Assembly of a single chamber which is against the Senate, the House of Lords, etc.... But between these slogans and the "Republic" there is a deep moat which we cannot cross. In one case we endeavor to direct the masses against institutions of a profoundly reactionary character, which limit, even under the capitalist, regime, the possibility of democratic expression of the masses, and which, in moments of crisis become quasi-automatically the rallying point for the forces of the counter-revolution. In the other case, we would advance the slogan which, if we made the mistake of adopting it, would make us the promoters of a completely vague state form. "The Republic"? This slogan does not concern a partial objective but puts to the fore the very question of the state. What republic can we recommend in the current epoch? The Republic of Workers and Peasants Soviets alone, and not a bourgeois republic. The slogan of "the Republic" is absolutely silent on this point and can only, by its confusion, favor the class enemy.

It is evident that, despite our rejection of this slogan, we will not be neutral in the plebiscites which may be held in Europe on the question of the monarchy. We shall call the workers and peasants to vote against the monarchy, but clearly specifying that we do not have the choice as to the other term of the alternative, that we are voting against the monarchy but not in favor of the bourgeois republic.

It is almost twenty years ago that the Italian Social Democrats in one of their fits of theoretical audacity inscribed in their program of the struggle against fascism the slogan of "the democratic republic of the toilers" and, for a certain period, the Italian Communist Party, in one of its zig-zags to the right, had an equivocal position towards this slogan. When in 1930, a section of the leadership of the Italian CP broke with Stalinism, formed the New Italian Opposition and turned toward the Left Opposition, this slogan was the object of a clarification in the exchange of views which took place at that time. The old opposition, that of the Bordigists, had an absolutely negative attitude on democratic slogans; it was especially necessary that the new Italian comrades should not take for their part a position which could be exploited by the Bordigists and which would have been fatal in the struggle against fascism. In a letter to the comrades in the NOI Trotsky expressed himself as follows on the slogan of the Italian Social Democrats:

While advancing one or another set of democratic slogans we must irreconcilably fight against all forms of democratic charlatanism. Such low-grade charlatanism is represented by the slogan of the Italian Social Democracy: "The Democratic Republic of the Toilers". The "Toilers republic" can be only the class state of the proletariat. The "Democratic Republic" is only a masked rule of the bourgeoisie. The combination of the two is a naive petty bourgeois illusion of the Social Democratic rank and file (workers, peasants) and deliberate treachery on the part of the Social Democratic leaders (all these Turatis, Modiglianis and their ilk). Let me once again remark in passing that I was and remain opposed to the formula of a "National Assembly on the basis of worker-peasant committees" precisely because this formula approaches the Social Democratic slogan of the "Democratic Toilers Republic" and, consequently, can render extremely difficult for us the struggle against the Social Democrats. *May 14, 1930.*

The slogan of "the Republic" as such is also as erroneous and pernicious as that of "The Democratic Republic of the Toilers" although, we are persuaded, few comrades in our international organization would have at present an inclination to mix in the above fashion the forms of bourgeois power with the forms of proletarian power. But it is not the thoughts and intentions of this or that comrade which are under discussion but the slogan of "the Republic" itself. This is not a democratic slogan but, to employ the strong expression of Trotsky, democratic charlatanism.

The theoretical principles and positions which are a part of the accumulated capital of the Bolshevik-Leninists, gained in the course of their years of struggle against Stalinism, reformism and all the varieties of centrism in the workers' movement, and which we have called to mind in this article, obviously far from exhaust the questions which arise on the European situation. But it is indispensable to take them as a point of departure to permit our militants and our sections to orient themselves correctly despite the enormous confusion which rages and which, unhappily, will not fail to rage for the duration of a complete period, up to the point when the events and ourselves, in assisting events by a correct policy, consciously array an important fraction of the working class under the flag of the Fourth International.

Evolution of Eastern Europe

The Soviet buffer zone of Eastern Europe, which came into being after the Second World War, has aroused lively discussions in and around our ranks. Our opinions have evolved and we have rectified errors committed on this question in the past years.[37] Today the evolution of the buffer zone countries on a number of fundamentals has been completed in an irreversible manner. Our ideas have been clarified on several important questions such as the nature of these states and the conclusions to be derived therefrom. The resolution submitted to the Congress registers our progress in this matter. It is not without value to view this problem from as broad a viewpoint as possible, to first of all retrace the road we have traveled.

The History of the Buffer Zone Question

At the end of the Second World War, as a result of the Potsdam agreements, the entire world was confronted with a zone of influence of the Soviet Union in Eastern Europe. The Russian state – which we considered a degenerated workers' state – dominated a series of capitalist states militarily and politically; coalition governments between Stalinists and bourgeois politicians were constituted; the capitalist economies were not fundamentally uprooted, although important changes had been introduced.

Molotov had declared at the first occasion, in the name of the Soviet government, when Russian troops entered Rumanian territory, that his government had no intention of altering the social system of these countries. The only and avowed desire of the Kremlin in these countries was to replace the hostile governments of the past (the *cordon sanitaire* at the end of the First World War) by governments friendly to the USSR. But we understood at that time that what was involved was not the desires of the Kremlin bureaucracy. The workers' state, and not only the bureaucracy, would have its influence on the new territories. What, could this lead to?

On the theoretical plane we took as our point of departure our definition of the USSR and Trotsky's succinct remarks in *In Defense of Marxism* on the question of territories occupied by the USSR and susceptible to integration within it. These remarks have been cited

---

[37] Report to the Third World Congress of the Fourth International. (August 1951), from *Fourth International*, Vol.12 No.6, November-December 1951, pp.176, 213-218.

many times in our discussions and are certainly known to all the comrades present here. Let us only refer to this one:

"Let us for a moment conceive that in accordance with the treaty with Hitler, the Moscow government leaves untouched the rights of private property in the occupied areas and limits itself to 'control' after the fascist pattern. Such a concession would have a deep-going principled character and might become the starting point for a new chapter in the history of the Soviet regime; and consequently a starting point for a new appraisal on our part of the nature of the Soviet state."

These lines prove how important the evolution of the buffer zone was for us and for the world workers' movement. Developments in the buffer zone also were of decisive importance for the Soviet Union.

We followed these developments passionately, meticulously. If you assemble everything that has been written in our ranks since 1946 on this question, it can be stated that we have never sinned in the domain of the concrete study of the events. We may have committed errors in theoretical interpretation and in perspectives but our study of the events was always very rigorous. No one ever contested the facts presented by the International as the basis of our discussions. All the discussions took these facts as their point of departure.

We must confine ourselves here to a reference for historical reasons only to the discussions we have had with those who had a different definition of the USSR than ours. These discussions with the theoreticians of "state capitalism" or of "bureaucratic collectivism" never had any bearing on the buffer zone, properly speaking; they were simply appendices to the discussion on the Russian question. Neither the supporters of the theory of "state capitalism" nor those of the theory of "bureaucratic collectivism" contested the facts assembled by the International. The facts had only a minor importance for them. Later on we will mention the discussions between comrades sharing our common theoretical basis.

Our movement took a position on the question of the buffer zone for the first time at the Preconference (March 1946) and at the 1st Plenum (June 1946). The resolution adopted by the Preconference noted:

"The introduction of a series of militarily and politically controlled countries into the economic sphere (of the USSR);

"The plundering and politically reactionary, conservative and capitulatory nature of the Soviet bureaucracy...

"The granting of governmental powers to the leaders of the Communist Parties regardless of their real strength;

"The elimination of oppositionist elements, the expropriation of foreign concessions, the acceleration of economic reforms by encouraging organs of dual power (committees of control of production, trade committees of poor peasants which carry out the agrarian reform)."

This resolution declared itself in favor of the progressive reforms, for the right of the peoples to self-determination, for the free development of the workers' movement.

The 1st Plenum dealt especially with the occupation of numerous territories by the victor armies. The resolution said the following concerning the territories occupied by the Soviet armies:

"The Fourth International demands the withdrawal of all foreign armies, including the Soviet army, from all occupied territories...

"The Fourth International does not in any way abandon its slogan of the unconditional defense of the USSR. The Fourth International is likewise for the defense of the progressive measures which have been realized in the territories occupied by the Red Army...

"Wherever reactionary movements appear and, with the support of the imperialists, attempt to overthrow the more or less statified economy and to re-establish landed private property... we will oppose these movements and fight on the side of the Red Army for the defeat of the imperialists and their agents until the workers of these countries are strong enough to confront the bourgeois counter-revolution alone.

"In all the occupation zones our militants should defend our policy in such a manner so that it cannot be utilized against the Soviet Union to the advantage of imperialism."

We see then that in the first two positions, we clearly formulated our position on the defense of the USSR and the reforms carried out in the buffer zone against imperialism, and on the defense of the workers' movement of these countries against the bureaucracy, but that there is not a word on the nature of these states and their economies, nor on the tendencies of their development.

The first general theoretical position taken was formulated in the theses written by comrade Germain [Ernest Mandel] on *The USSR on the Morrow of the War* which appeared in the *International Bulletin*, September 1946. It was said that in a general way this study expressed the position of the International Secretariat, and it opened the discussion on the USSR, the buffer zone and Stalinism for the 2nd World Congress. Here is its essential part concerning the buffer zone question:

"Inherent in the system of production brought into being by the October Revolution is the tendency to break out of the frontiers of the USSR especially because the productive forces on a world scale cry out for collectivization...

"Taking as our point of departure the tendency of the bureaucracy to 'structurally assimilate' the countries where it maintains its occupation over a whole period and which it wants to integrate into its economic system; taking likewise as our point of departure the impossibility of achieving this assimilation without the action of the working mosses, it can be stated that the countries occupied by the Soviet bureaucracy can be divided into three zones:

"a)... all the territories incorporated into the USSR, there structural assimilation has been completed...

"b) In Poland, in occupied Germany, in Yugoslavia and in Czechoslovakia, the beginnings of structural assimilation correspond to a very strong revolutionary impulsion or to an exceptional situation involving the physical disappearance of the propertied classes... The nature of the economy and of the state remains bourgeois in these countries. However, the relationship of forces are such that for the moment the bourgeoisie is at the mercy of an action of the proletariat. It is only the bureaucracy's fear of the proletariat of these countries as well as of imperialism which keeps it from delivering a coup de grace to the native capitalists.

"c) In Finland, Austria, Hungary, Rumania and Bulgaria the state and the economy remain fundamentally bourgeois."

This long quotation needs no comment. In the discussion which occurred at the time, Marcoux, who had assembled a very important documentation on the question, examined the question in a static manner and even denied the existence of a tendency to structural assimilation; his point of view was rapidly outmoded by the march of events. On the other hand, comrade E.R. Frank, who was in agreement with the analysis, defined what was developing in the buffer zone as a tendency toward the establishment of a "state capitalism" based on a mixed economy (state capitalism and private properly) and not toward the installation of a workers' state[38].

At the 2nd World Congress (April 1948) which took place some weeks after the Prague coup, the discussion did not go beyond the positions previously taken by the International in 1946. In the *Theses* adopted by this Congress, the part dealing with the buffer zone describes the policy of the bureaucracy, there also verifying its dual character; it shows that due to the development of the international situation the bureaucracy despite itself found itself obliged to adopt a series of economic and political measures against the native

---

[38] It should be pointed out, however, that when the discussion resumed at a later stage E.R. Frank was one of the first to make clear that capitalist property relations had been destroyed in the buffer zone, the process of "structural assimilation" having been completed.

bourgeoisie. It underscored the sharpening of the tendency toward total structural assimilation, but viewed this as possible only through a revolutionary mobilization of the masses in opposition to the bureaucracy. The *Theses of the 2nd World Congress* declared that the situation was transitory, but also that the economy of these countries remained capitalist and that the state remained a bourgeois state in its structure as well as in its function.

Politically the Congress confirmed our position of struggle against the restorationist tendencies and our support of the struggle of the masses for which it formulated a program of transitional demands. Finally, the state and the economy being characterized as capitalist, the *Theses* came out in favor of revolutionary defeatism in these countries in the event of war.

Viewed with hindsight, the discussion then was marking time as a result of the situation itself. It was necessary that the situation itself become further clarified for us to make further progress.

Some months after the 2nd World Congress, the split between the Yugoslav CP and the Cominform occurred. In the period which followed, important economic and also political developments began to occur in the buffer zone countries which transformed them considerably. All these events renewed the discussion and placed it on a new plane. On the other hand, the events in China were also to contribute in the clarification of our thoughts on a whole series of problems, including those of the buffer zone.

The 1949 Resolution

The discussion led to the adoption of a resolution by the 7th Plenum in April 1949.

The 7th Plenum resolution described the developments which had occurred in the buffer zone since 1945, namely the period of agreements between Washington and the Kremlin, marked by agreements with what remained of the native bourgeoisie in the buffer zone countries, and then the period of "cold war" marked by a struggle against the economic and political positions of the native bourgeoisie, which was waged primarily with bureaucratic methods.

The 7th Plenum resolution concluded with a study of the theoretical significance of the evolution of the buffer zone countries. This latter part explains the transition regimes of.the buffer zone countries as the resultant of the action of several factors: the decomposition of capitalism having attained a very advanced stage in these countries, the belatedness of the world revolution, and the role of the USSR as a workers' state but acting tinder the leadership of the bureaucracy with the methods peculiar to this caste. We have nothing essential to change on this point and that is why we have incorporated this part of the 7th Plenum resolution in the resolution submitted for adoption to the 3rd World Congress.

But a part of this same 7th Plenum resolution showed itself to be inadequate or ambiguous or false and the discussion immediately reopened. It was the part of the resolution dealing with the social nature of the buffer zone states which reactivated the debate. The resolution recognized that structural assimilation had reached a very advanced stage, it noted that the bourgeoisie was no longer in power as the ruling class. But it refused to say that the "leap" to workers' states had been made. The resolution considered these states as bourgeois states of a special type, something like "degenerated bourgeois states" although their structure – in the words of the resolution itself – was closer to that of the USSR than that of normal capitalist states. As a reason for this definition the resolution mentioned "the historic origins of the present situation and... the still indecisive social physiognomy" of the buffer zone countries. It indicated "the elimination of national frontiers between the buffer zone countries" as the "decisive and fundamental" factor for the completion of structural assimilation.

One year later, at the 8th Plenum, the discussion still continued in our ranks, and besides the adoption of a brief resolution on the class nature of Yugoslavia, two resolutions were submitted for a consultative vote of the Plenum, one by comrade Pablo, the other by comrade Germain, differing in the premises on which they based their definition of the Yugoslav state and in which the problem of the nature of the buffer zone countries was in fact inferred.

The developments which have occurred in the buffer zone since then have enabled us to overcome the differences which existed at the time and to evolve a very precise position, with an equally clear understanding of the reasons which caused the delay and the errors of our movement on the question of the buffer zone.

The Social Nature of the Buffer Zone States

We believe that the buffer zone states are no longer capitalist states and that, like the USSR, they are fundamentally, i.e. in the domain of the relations of production and property, workers' states. The changes which were made in their economies, the extension of nationalization and planning to all spheres of the economy, fundamentally distinguishes them from capitalist states.

What has happened in these countries *is not a quantitative increase* in nationalizations as has taken place in certain capitalist countries, *but a qualitative transformation of the economy*. It is not only heavy and light industry which is nationalized and planned but also the banks, all of transportation and all trade, foreign and domestic, wholesale as well as retail (in large part at least).

It is true that the land is not formally nationalized. This is not a negligible question, but it is not fundamental from the standpoint of a sociological characterization, in view of the considerable restrictions on the purchase and sale of land, and the introduction of collectivization on the countryside.

The relationships of production and property have been upset from top to bottom in these countries, and this transformation is continuing and involving spheres which have not as yet been affected (with the exception of agriculture with which we have already dealt). A return of these countries to a capitalist type structure will only be possible through a counter-revolution, which is obviously linked to the outcome of the coming war.

These are the fundamental changes of the economic structure which make us characterize these states as workers' states. There are, to be sure, important differences on the political and even on the economic plane among these states and between them and the USSR. That is not surprising. The evolution of varied human societies, among them workers' states, toward socialism cannot help but be affected by a whole series of factors. The march from capitalism to socialism will certainly give rise to very diverse social forms.

What is happening in the buffer zone countries is rather the obverse. The reactionary intervention of the Moscow bureaucracy tends to impose forms approximating those in the USSR upon these countries and also to Russify an important part of their state apparatuses for the purpose of assuring Kremlin control.

We are also witnessing on the plane of social relations in the buffer zone countries the imposition of a policy modeled on that of the Soviet bureaucracy which is directed towards the creation of an apparatus and socially privileged stratum in relation to the mass of the workers.

But all of these elements, which have a very great importance in determining our policy in these countries, are not decisive so far as the sociological characterization of these states is concerned.

Exception is made, in the resolution submitted to this Congress, in this sociological characterisation of the buffer zone countries, for the Soviet zone in Austria which has not undergone any of these fundamental transformations.

PIERRE FRANK

Deformed and Degenerated Workers' States

The resolution submitted to the Congress designates the buffer zone states as deformed workers' states. What do we mean by this designation?

We did not use the term degenerated workers' states because of the fact that this designation should only be applied (as in the case of the USSR) to a workers' state which was born in the revolutionary struggle of the masses and which subsequently deteriorated as a result of the bureaucratic seizure of power to the detriment of the working masses.

The buffer zone states are not the product of the revolutionary action of the masses but of the action of the bureaucracy, to which question we will return later. The defects they now have were present from the beginning. We do not mean "deformed" in the sense of workers' states marred by bureaucratic deformations as was the case with the USSR, in the first years of its existence. In this context the word deformed means that these states have primarily the same fundamental defect as the USSR, i.e., the complete elimination of the proletariat, on the economic as well as the political plane, from the leadership of these countries.

In saying that we have been belated in characterizing these states as workers' states, we do not believe that we were wrong on this point in 1946 and at the time of the Second World Congress. We still believe that up to 1949 these states still retained a fundamentally capitalist structure, although it was considerably damaged from the capitalist point of view. The descriptions and analyses made by our movement up to 1949 were correct as a whole. We had correctly emphasized the principal tendencies of development. We were hesitant on the possibility of the realization of these tendencies under existing conditions or at least as we interpreted these conditions.

The transformation of bourgeois states (decayed) into deformed workers' states under the conditions it has occurred has raised a series of theoretical problems which should be dealt with.

For us, the norm in such a transformation is the revolutionary action of the masses, their armed struggle destroying the old apparatus of the bourgeois state and substituting a new state for it. The manner of the transformation in the buffer zone countries does not correspond to the norm. Essentially it was the result of the action of the bureaucracy of the USSR and its agents. Does this call for a revision of Marxism? We do not think so at all.

From what happened at the beginning of the Second World War and from the deductions Trotsky had drawn from these events, we were ready to grasp the tendency toward structural assimilation, to understand these phenomena as they occurred. But we hesitated in our theoretical generalizations. Why?

The bureaucracy is not a class, it has no fundamental role in history, it does not make history, on the contrary it seeks only to cheat history. But it has demonstrated an undeniable power, for reasons we well know, to deform and disfigure the march of the historic process. Stalinism falsifies past history, but it employs the same methods – and they are not without their consequences – on the present. We have seen Stalinism distort fundamental ideas in the minds of communist workers; we have seen it manipulate workers' organizations and their policy. The Kremlin bureaucracy, with all the material and political power it derives from the Soviet state, has been able to manipulate phenomena to the point of rendering them momentarily more or less unrecognizable, without however derailing the fundamental social forces and the laws of history. One of our primary weaknesses was that of not always being able to rapidly disentangle the profound nature, of phenomena from the disfiguration they had suffered at the hands of the bureaucracy.

On the other hand, we ourselves did not exactly appreciate the conditions under which the bureaucracy had to operate. It is true that it acted in quite an empirical manner; in the beginning it did not dream of going beyond its agreements with imperialism. It merely wanted to convert the buffer zone states into zones of military protection and not into a belt of workers' states on the borders of the USSR. Molotov's declaration when Soviet troops entered the territory of a capitalist state for the first time, the theory of people's democracy (1st edition), was not (contrived to deceive the bourgeoisie. The Kremlin bureaucracy had been obliged to go further than it intended. But we have only recently begun to appreciate more exactly the conditions under which the Kremlin acted. It is only approximately one year ago that we have begun to appreciate the grandeur of the revolutionary forces in all their scope let loose by the decomposition of capitalism. The discussion on the political report at this Congress has permitted an understanding of the full scope of these forces.

It is the decomposition of capitalism which has spoiled all the calculations of the bureaucracy as well as of imperialism in their search for a compromise which was also to include the buffer zone countries. We were especially cognizant of the bureaucratic character of the measures taken by the Kremlin but we were insufficiently appreciative of the forces which impelled the bureaucracy to reluctantly take the measures which in turn more and more barred the road to a compromise with imperialism and created a fundamentally different situation particularly in the buffer zone countries.

Among the causes of error on our part was the absolute juxtaposition of the action of the masses and that of the bureaucracy. We said: A workers' state is not the creation of bureaucratic action, but only of the revolutionary action of the masses. The bureaucracy, as we well know, never or almost never eliminates the action of the masses in its interventions; what it seeks to suppress is the action of the masses which it cannot rigorously control; but it is very well able to utilize the action of the masses which it can control in order to attain its own objectives at, a given moment.

That was also true in the buffer zone countries. It placed the workers' movement there under its tutelage, it proceeded from purge to purge, it destroyed all initiative of the masses, all independent action to a considerable degree, but it nevertheless mobilized these masses in a form it completely controlled for the purpose of being able to proceed to the important changes it deemed necessary in the buffer zone countries. We did not believe that it could carry out an operation of such scope in the buffer zone countries without losing control of the mass movement.

Because we were not always capable of analyzing the deformative effects of bureaucratic action on the historic process, because we did not have an extremely precise estimation of the forces let loose by the decomposition of capitalism and because we did not always understand the utilization of the masses by the bureaucracy, we committed errors on the buffer zone question; and we became involved in a problem which was not the real one, because there was no real solution for it, namely that of the criterion which determines the moment when the "leap" takes place. We were not faced with a relatively normal process. History had gone through bureaucratic channels in these countries and the endeavor to apply rigorous norms there was not without its dangers.

It goes without saying that in recognizing the character of the bureaucratic action in the buffer zone countries we not only do not attribute any progressive character to it, not only do we continue to consider it as counterrevolutionary as a whole, but we underscore the limits of bureaucratic possibilities. They were brought to bear on bourgeois countries in full decomposition where social relations had already been very unstable before the war and where the bourgeoisie had been considerably undermined during the war.

ft also goes without saying that the evolution of the buffer zone countries since 1945 does not provide the slightest justification for the theory of "people's democracy" (1st edition) which imitated the old social democratic revisionist conception of a possible gradual passage from capitalism to socialism. This theory has been a lamentable failure in Western European capitalist countries. In Eastern Europe, the bureaucratic intervention which was substituted for the revolutionary action of the masses had nothing whatever in common with gradual, organic evolution.

The buffer zone situation has also demonstrated several facts to us which lead to important theoretical or political conclusions.

The buffer zone situation demonstrated that the coming to power of Stalinist parties under bureaucratic conditions (contrary to those in Yugoslavia or China) had similar although less marked consequences on these parties. The contradictions of society were reflected in these parties with growing acuteness. The pressure of the masses made itself strongly felt in opposition to the demands of the Muscovite bureaucracy. The apparatus, even the leadership itself of these parties, is sensitive to this pressure. Thus far the tendencies expressing or reflecting this pressure have shown themselves extremely weak in face of the GPU apparatus, but one cannot exclude a different development in objectively different conditions.

Another very important point. The buffer zone experience has revealed — and even bourgeois observers have testified to this — that the working masses of these countries, although very hostile to the bureaucracy, are very attached to the transformations in the system even though they were achieved bureaucratically. Trotsky wrote in the definition of the USSR which he gave in *Revolution Betrayed*:

"*The social revolution betrayed by the government party still lives in the property relations and in the consciousness of the toilers.*"

In the buffer zone countries as well, the social transformations not only live in the existing property relations but also in the consciousness of the toilers although these social relations occurred not in a revolutionary but in a bureaucratic way. That is a very important element for a proper appreciation of the buffer zone countries.

What we have learned on this point from the Ukrainian independence movement is also very significant. As a result of the division of the Ukraine before the Second World War, the Ukrainian nationalist movement in Poland had contributed in bringing independence tendencies into being in the Soviet Ukraine. But on the other hand, the difference in social system between these two sections of the Ukraine had led to the evolution of the Ukrainian nationalists in Poland toward the adoption of the social forms of property of the Soviet Ukraine. This is a phenomenon which should not be forgotten, especially in the case of present-day Germany.

PIERRE FRANK

Policy Toward the Buffer Zone Countries

Our policy for the buffer zone countries, given the conclusion we have arrived at on their class nature and also the place they will have in the coming war, does not raise any moot problems. The discussion on the political resolution has clarified the problems posed by the buffer zone countries.

We are for the unconditional defense of these workers' states against imperialism in the war now being prepared. It is fundamentally the same problem as that of the defense of the USSR. We defend these states as working class conquests, regardless of the bureaucratic means which were used to bring them into being and regardless of the policy followed by their governments. Our defense of these states in no case, at no time, implies a limitation of our criticism of the policy followed by the governments of these states.

We have designated these states as deformed workers' states specifying that their deformation has been identical to that of the USSR principally in the expropriation of the proletariat from the administration of these states. It follows therefore that, as for the USSR, *our political program for these countries is that of political revolution* having as its aim the elimination of the bureaucracy from power and its resumption by the working masses. This point does not raise especially different problems from those of the USSR. Let us merely observe that there is not a native bureaucracy in these countries possessing strength comparable to that of the Soviet bureaucracy; in truth, it is the Soviet bureaucracy which constitutes the principal prop, the principal strength of the native bureaucracies.

As in the case of the USSR, it is obvious that the defense of these countries does not exclude but on the contrary implies our support to movements of the worker and poor peasant masses against the bureaucracy. In the case of these countries, as in that of the' national minorities in the USSR, we are also in favor of supporting mass movements for national independence from the yoke of the Soviet bureaucracy. In the buffer zone countries we are for the independence of these countries and their organization into a voluntarily organized federation.

All these points present no difficulties. They have long been the common property of our movement acquired on the question of the USSR in the past years by following step by step the evolution of the first workers' state. The only difference is that these countries suffer even more severely from their unequal relations with Moscow than do the nationalities of the USSR. Over the decades the national question has always been a very sensitive point in these countries. Finally the question of their federation has had a long tradition in the workers' movements of these countries, it having figured in the programs of socialist parties of these countries even before 1914.

In conclusion, we see that the buffer zone question has, in fact, been the extension of the Russian question which has so often been discussed in our movement, and not the point of departure for a new chapter in the history of the Soviet regime. But it is an extension which has taken its own peculiar course.

Our definition of the USSR, our comprehension of the dual role of the Soviet bureaucracy has permitted us to orient ourselves in a generally correct manner in the study of what has happened in the buffer zone countries and in understanding their fundamental tendencies. At bottom this was decisive.

But on the other hand, various inadequacies on our part have made us mark time, have led us into secondary problems and even into error. Today the situation has largely contributed in permitting us to overcome our weaknesses without great internal difficulties. It permits us to basically understand the buffer zone countries, their development, their contradictions.

We believe that the discussion based on the resolution presented by the International Secretariat will enable our movement to acquire all necessary clarity on this question and to seriously arm our militants for the political problems they will be faced with in the coming years.

Summary Speech by Reporter

After speeches by 15 delegates, the reporter made the following points:

The buffer zone was a relatively new phenomenon for which our only terms of reference were the occupation of territories by the Soviet army at the beginning of the Second World War. The term we employed in 1946, that of "structural assimilation," corresponded to our comprehension of this phenomenon at the time and of the perspectives of development we were then able to envisage. In light of what has occurred, a definition more closely approximating the phenomenon might possibly have been contrived. However, that did not appear necessary to us then, provided that more was not read into these words than was actually intended.

The words "structural assimilation" in the resolution do not mean that the buffer zone states have been incorporated in one or another form into the USSR or that their economies no longer have any independence in relation to that of the USSR. This term simply means that these states have fundamentally the same structure, the same fundamental relations of property and production as that of the first workers' state, the USSR. It is true, as the resolution points out, that the economic relations of these states with the USSR have been extended but that does not mean "structural assimilation" to us.

We live in a period of uninterrupted convulsions and that is why our theory should more than ever be a guide to action and not be transformed into rules which become abstractions when confronted with the reality. As is indicated in the report, one cannot apply the "norm," i.e. in this case, to demand to know the date on which the "leap" occurred. We will not repeat the explanation given in the resolution on this point. Let us only add that in a number of countries one would seek in vain for the "date" on which they passed over from feudalism to capitalism.

A comrade has mentioned the absence of nationalization on the land to prove the formation of new bourgeois strata in the country, thus creating dual power and an accumulation of dangers for these countries. We have pointed out in the report that the absence of nationalization of the land was an important question but not at all decisive for a characterization of the sociological nature of these countries.

It is true that tendencies toward the restoration of capitalism manifest themselves on the countryside in these countries because of their economic backwardness. But to proceed from there and to speak of new bourgeois strata is stretching the point too much; it is even less valid to speak of dual power. The facts do not support such statements. Tendencies are not yet a bourgeois class or dual power.

It is true that there are dangers to the non-capitalist structure of these states in possible developments on the countryside. That was the case with the USSR from the NEP up to 1928; although in this instance it must also be recognized that the danger was in nowise removed by nationalization of the land. The danger is also to be seen in Yugoslavia, which will be discussed on the next point of the agenda. But it is already possible to say that what makes these phenomena on the countryside dangerous in Yugoslavia is the considerable pressure now being brought to bear by imperialism on the country. The dominant pressure on the buffer zone countries at the present time comes from the opposite direction.

A comrade has raised the question of the application of the term "exploitation" to the Soviet bureaucracy. It is not a class, he says, and therefore its role in production is not that of exploitation in the Marxist sense of the term. Agreed. But if I am not mistaken the 2nd World Congress used the term "exploitation" for the mixed companies which the USSR had then imposed on the buffer zone countries. The Soviet state, in fact, played a capitalist role in these companies as is also the case with certain workers' organizations which engage in businesses associated with their general activity. The Soviet state acted as a capitalist in the case of the mixed companies and thus we have actually a case of exploitation.

The more complex question with which comrade Pablo has dealt is the one raised by several comrades on the completion of structural assimilation. We noted tendencies to structural assimilation beginning with 1945-46. From that time on, there existed potentially the possibilities of transformation which subsequently occurred. But its completion was the result of national and international factors.

The scope of nationalizations is not enough for an appreciation of the developments in the buffer zone countries. In 1946, there remained not only a capitalist economic structure, but the reconstructed states also had a capitalist political structure. With a different relationship of forces, another situation might have resulted in some of the buffer zone countries.

As a consequence of the "cold war," the Soviet bureaucracy was not only obliged to adopt a series of economic measures fundamentally transforming the economic structure of these states, but it also had to embark on a series of measures fundamentally transforming their political structure in order to align them with the structure of the USSR. The period in which these transformations occurred, bringing to completion the tendencies to structural assimilation which had existed from the beginning, dates clearly from the start of 1949, extends through that year and into 1950.

We also have to rectify what is erroneous in the draft document on the question of Albania. It is quite accurate that during the Second World War a development very much like that of Yugoslavia occurred in that country.

The question of the buffer zone has not only served to better arm us politically on the subject of Eastern Europe and of Asia but in general to help us better understand the period of transition from capitalism to socialism as we know it in its first stages.

PIERRE FRANK

Under Pressure of the Coming War, Imperialism Beckons "Third Camp"

The preparations for the third world war do not consist only in an enormous *material* arms production. In order to mobilize the greatest possible mass of people in the service of imperialism, the most varied ideas and arguments are set to work, reflecting the extraordinary material and ideological pressures bearing down upon individuals and organizations.[39]

A few dreamers are still able to muse about impossible neutrality. The capitalists of Western Europe are beside themselves because they have to follow the directives of Washington, but they have no other choice. The conflict in preparation is developing such scope that it is already smashing century-old traditions. The idea of the bourgeois fatherland – for which millions of men went to their death in the course of two preceding world wars – can no longer serve to deceive very many people in Europe. More subtle ideologies are required. The simple booby-trap of "Stalinist totalitarianism" also serves the same end.

In any event, from now on every one is taking his place more or less openly in the struggle. The Kravchenkos have chosen "freedom" in order to don the American uniform with the hope of re-establishing private property in the USSR. At the same time the bourgeois world finds itself abandoned not only by the greater pant of the laboring masses in a growing number of countries, but also by wide layers of intellectuals. Even bourgeois are deserting their class. Can there be a more striking symptom of the decline of the bourgeoisie than the case of those officials of the British Foreign Office, one of the most selectively staffed of institutions, deserting their world? But in the milieus of the working class and the revolutionary vanguard, or where claim is made to a place in this vanguard, the struggle is similarly going on, the class pressures are likewise in motion.

---

[39] Under Pressure of the Coming War, Imperialism Beckons "Third Camp" (December 15, 1951) comes from *Fourth International*, Vol.12 No.2, March-April 1952, pp.57-63.

We Are "Buried" Once More...

The Third World Congress of the Trotskyists has clearly drawn the positions of our movement in the coming war. We are in the camp of the USSR, of China, of the people's democracies against the camp of imperialism. This position has not emerged unexpectedly. It is the traditional line of our movement. It was ours during the course of the Second World War. It has been particularly emphasized and more precisely defined since the beginning of the war in Korea and since the preparations for the third world war have taken on an intensive character.

This position has caused a great hue and cry. It has brought us once more the accusation launched almost periodically against us: We are capitulating to Stalinism! For some we are even tools of the Cominform. For others, good souls, the Fourth international which might have played such a great role in history has taken the fatal road leading to its ruin. Once again we are being buried, with or without flowers. To tell the truth, Stalin and his gang, who have had other means to employ against us, have so often boasted of slaying us that we are no longer awed by hearing such funeral orations. We are periodically "buried" because periodically certain people experience the need to bury Marxism.

We will say nothing here of those within the working class who have openly and without circumlocutions placed themselves in the camp of American imperialism, as in France the collaborators in that magazine which is still mockingly entitled *The Proletarian Revolution*[40] We want to deal with those who have defended, and with those who, still defend, the so-called position of a "Third Camp" or of a "Third Front," with those who advocate equal independence of the two camps facing each other and a struggle directed simultaneously against the one and the other of these camps.

Various Types of "Independence"

The idea of "independence" of the two camps or the two blocs exists not only in the ranks claiming to be part of the working class, but in certain bourgeois groups as well. Even certain bourgeois governments claim to follow an international policy based on such a consideration. We will deal only with organizations of individuals claiming to belong to the working class. Among them we can observe these ideas in tendencies that move in various directions. Recently a common statement was signed by the Socialist Parties of Japan and India in favor of a policy independent of the two blocs. These

---

[40] Organ of the Syndicalists led by Pierre Monatte. – Ed.

organizations, as is evident to those who have followed their evolution, have not at all reached the stage of crystallization on the basis of clearly defined positions. They have broken, or are on the road to breaking, with the bourgeoisie and with the right wings which directly expressed the pressure of the bourgeoisie within their organizations.

We must neither pass judgment on these parties on the basis of these statements nor accept these positions as conclusive for these parties. The signing of such a statement by these parties expressed a stage in a progressive evolution which is, however, inadequate, incomplete, and replete with dangers. We must turn elsewhere in order to see the inherent dangers in this position of the "Third Camp." Either toward such organizations as the Yugoslav CP which, after an excursion to the left, passed through this position in its evolution to the right; or to such organizations or tendencies relatively crystalized politically, such as the POUM ("Marxist Party of Workers Unity," in Spain) and the Shachtmanites, who have been and still are the most systematic defenders of the "Third Camp."

The Yugoslav Case

There is not much to be gained in pursuing this subject on the Yugoslav side. Immediately following their break with the Cominform, the Yugoslavs made an obvious theoretical effort toward a political orientation. Then, when the pressure of the international situation became too strong and they saw their sole hope in important material assistance from the West, they remembered what they had learned at the Stalinist school: that principles were made to be scoffed at and that there were always theoreticians available to justify the worst compromises in the name of Marxism. Tito discovered the blessings of the West, concluded a military agreement with the USA, and now condemns every idea of a "Third Camp."

For the Yugoslav communists whose uneasiness requires some theoretical explanations, Djilas proclaims the bureaucracy a new class and the USSR as state capitalism. If that isn't enough, the Yugoslav State, which is "on the road to withering away," certainly possesses some more powerful arguments in the person of Rankovitch, the Minister of Internal Security. But the practical evolution in Yugoslav diplomacy is most striking. Breaking with Stalin, the Yugoslavs first claimed, and justly so, the right to decide for themselves what their policy shall be within the anti-imperialist camp. As pressure of the Soviet government and of its satellites became increasingly onerous, they declared for an "independent" position, and for a period walked upon this tightrope. Unquestionably their situation was a very difficult one.

But refusing to turn toward the workers of the world, and having far more confidence in the jet planes which might come to them from Washington, they sold their principles along with their merchandise. They abandoned Korea to American aggression. They came to the last session of the United Nations to deny even their principle of the equality of all nations, large and small, for which they had dared rebel against Stalin. In his speech Kardelj, for the first time, took a position for a Pact of the Big Powers... in order to insure peace. Up to then the Yugoslavs had denounced this kind of agreement as made at the expense of the small nations, and as not aiding.the cause of peace. However, the Yugoslavs are now ready to accept not just any kind of a pact among any combination of "big powers." Kardelj favors a "Four Power Pact" such as Washington might perhaps allow, but not a "Five Power Pact" such as Moscow, desiring to associate China in its game, is demanding. In this current Yugoslav policy, principles play a very small part. An "independent" position, a "Third Camp", is a very difficult position to hold when there is a State to run... Shall we have better luck when we turn to those who only have slighter responsibilities or no responsibilities at all on their shoulders?

With Whom Can a United Front Be Made?

In fairness to the POUM, let us note that of all the centrist organizations born between the first two world wars it is the only one to survive. Burnt by its experiences with the London Bureau, the International Workers Front, and other ephemeral creations which the POUM supported, the leadership of this organization had practically abandoned the idea of being an integral part of an international movement and was content with attending all possible meetings in the role of "observer." Violent debates may have taken place at these meetings but the POUM "observers" remained silent. *La Batalla* subsequently published reports with the minimum of political comment, the leadership of the POUM appearing to exist above all the difficulties which beset working class and would-be socialist organizations.

But the approach of war has brought about some changes. On the Third World Congress of the Fourth International, *La Batalla* expressed itself unequivocally:

"The three adopted resolutions and in general all the decisions taken confirm that the Trotskyist movement has radically changed the line followed for some months and is orienting towards a policy of capitulation to Stalinism." (October 10, 1951).

Capitulate to Stalinism? The accusation could have grave consequences not for the Trotskyists, at whom it has already been repeatedly leveled, but for those hurling it. For it is self-evident that, not to be politically inconsistent, one must adopt the same attitude towards those who capitulate to Stalinism as towards the Stalinists, and we will see further on that the POUM has a well defined attitude on this last point.

A national conference of the POUM recently held in Spain took a certain number of positions. On the coming war the conference took a position simultaneously against Washington and Moscow. According to this conference the third world war will not be what the Trotskyists call it, namely an international civil war, but "a struggle for world domination" between Yankee imperialism and the Russian bureaucracy. In the working class movement

"the socialists who have gained strength at the expense of the Stalinists in certain countries (Belgium, Germany, Scandinavian countries) are acting almost without exception as a wing of Western capitalism. On their side, the Communist parties are behaving like what they are, instruments of the political and military strategy of the Kremlin."

As for the POUM, it sets itself the following tasks:

"1) To intervene actively in all actions and all independent movements against war. 2) Collaborate closely with all forces independent of capitalism and of Stalinism. 3) Support the unification of all revolutionary socialist tendencies and organizations."

We find no theoretical basis in the document of the POUM sustaining this position, and we do not want to quibble over the "active intervention" of POUM observers in "independent" movements which the POUM will have ever increasing difficulty in finding, judging by its attitude toward us. But for a better evaluation of the position of the POUM, let us see how it is applied on the national scale. For the "Marxists" of the POUM will certainly not dispute with us over the fact that there is a connection between the international policies and the national policies of an organization as well as of a State. The resolution of this conference on the Spanish situation contains this directive:

"To establish an organ for united action with all working class and republican organizations with the single exception of the Stalinists."

With the single exception of the Stalinists! An impassable barrier is raised – which, moreover, will render the greatest service to the Spanish Stalinists. But in the same number of *La Batalla* in which the resolutions of this conference are published is to be found an article criticizing the Spanish social-democrats for having made a pact with the monarchists, and in which we read:

"(The monarchists) forged the military uprising of July 1936, supported Franco with the greatest energy, have mingled and even identified themselves with Franco fascism. Nevertheless, one might for the moment put this aside, while never forgetting it, with the object of constituting a common front of struggle with them against Franco and his regime, hoping that the progressive forces would later go beyond the objectives of the monarchists: But all the monarchists, from the pretender and down the line, have never shown the slightest desire to struggle, to act, to want to overthrow Franco fascism."

Thus, according to the leadership of the POUM, a united front which must include all working class and republican organizations (with the sole exception of the Stalinists) could even be considered with the monarchists if there were even the slightest leaning toward struggle among the latter. Why? Because – one might hope "that the progressive forces would later go beyond the objectives of the monarchists." But we, who are for a united front with the Stalinists (whose objectives may be condemned, but of whom it cannot be said that they are not struggling), "hoping that the progressive forces (mainly the workers) would later go beyond the objectives" of the Stalinist leaders, we vulgar Trotskyists, are on that account capitulating to Stalinism. You can point to the examples of Yugoslavia and of China where the class struggle under the leadership of the Stalinist chiefs went beyond the plans of the Kremlin. It will be of no use, for the leadership of the POUM, shut up in its national boundaries, does not recognize the Spanish CP as a working class party...

Why is the leadership of the POUM so flexible toward the bourgeois camp and so intransigent toward the Stalinists *where Spain is concerned*, and why does it manifest an equal hostility to both the camps on the *international plane?* (The political friends of the POUM, notably Shachtman as we will see later on, are far from being so "equidistant" on the international plane.) It is necessary not to forget that Washington persists in supporting Franco, and not those with whom the leadership of the POUM is bent upon agreement. For the moment there is an insurmountable wall, just as on the Stalinist side – but it is Washington and not the POUM which has erected it.

Shachtman Studies Lenin

The "Third Camp" in the pure state, if one may use the phrase, is Shachtman himself. Ever since he broke with Trotskyism, he has constructed innumerable theories on innumerable subjects. He has abandoned the idea of building a broad organization embracing "all tendencies in revolutionary thought" for the far more modest role of an educator of the working class without political ambitions. In addition, he also dispenses priceless advice to working class militants and others throughout the world, but his advice is of precious little use to them. In all his flip-flops over more than ten years we must concede his consistency on one point: he has remained loyal to the "Third Camp" (although the latter has undergone several variations in the process of aging). He has, moreover, had to defend this idea tenaciously against his own followers, who at fairly regular intervals have deserted him and gone over openly to the camp of imperialism, abandoning forever the building of the "Third Camp" in order to struggle against their enemy number one, Stalinism.

In the course of the Second World War, Shachtman took an attitude which we condemned on the question of the defense of the USSR and of the colonial countries entangled in this war. For him the war made an indivisible whole: the USSR, China and India were fighting for the imperialist cause. As a logical consequence he was a defeatist for these countries. But in spite of this error and although he could not build a hypothetical "Third Front," he did display an intransigent hostility to the bourgeoisie of his own country, and that was unquestionably something to his credit. It is always hardest to be a revolutionary in one's own country.

Unfortunately for him, the pressures bearing down today are incomparably stronger than those which prevailed all the way through the Second World War. This cannot surprise those who understand that this time we are facing primarily an international civil war and that this is something different from the inter-imperialist war into which the USSR was drawn...

Subjected to far greater pressures today, the champion of the "Third Camp" is, as a consequence of his ideological weakness, slipping so fast as to foreshadow only the worst for the future. In the May-June and July-August 1951 issues of his magazine *New International* he has revealed his positions in a 22-page long article entitled *Socialist Policy and the War*. The article is more than a significant retreat from his previous positions, more than a continuation of the backward march he has been pursuing. Capitulation to imperialism is virtually inscribed therein.

Like all of Shachtman's outpourings, the article twists and turns dizzily all over the landscape. It is painful to follow the author's train of thought. First observation: He quotes Lenin in these terms: "To be a Marxist, one must appraise each war separately and concretely." But Shachtman himself at no point undertakes more than the most superficial analysis of the social character of the forces and movements confronting one another. The question is treated at times as if it had already been settled once and for all, at times by some brief remarks which carry little weight in the article as a whole. More than half the article is devoted to historical precedents. More particularly, Shachtman pounces upon the First World War and recalls the positions supported by Lenin in that period. From there he makes a prodigious leap to the third world war, completely forgetting that there has been a second world war and that at the beginning of the latter he was somewhat at odds with Trotsky on the attitude toward the USSR and on the question of the "Third Camp." Shachtman's historical recollections are capricious.

Lenin "Abandons" a Slogan

But let us return to Lenin and to the First World War. After all, it is not bad to delve into *Against the Stream*, into those articles which have been basic in the education of the revolutionary generations after 1920. Shachtman, at the end of wearisome dissertations, recalls the main political conclusions of Lenin in this first inter-imperialist war: revolutionary defeatism, transformation of the imperialist war into civil war. But having said that, Shachtman suddenly launches out into a very long disquisition on the theme: Lenin abandoned transforming the imperialist war into civil war. Shachtman indicates, without learning anything therefrom at all, that Lenin did not thereby make any concessions whatever to the so-called "revolutionary defensists."

Those alleged socialists called upon the masses to continue to get themselves massacred in order to "defend" democracy', while – as Lenin relentlessly emphasized – the provisional government was continuing to serve the same imperialist interests as were defended up to then by overthrown czarism. What Lenin did was to show that the problem had to be posed in another form for the masses. The masses had themselves begun to execute the Leninist strategy, that is to say, to "transform the imperialist war into civil war." Shachtman writes as though he is unaware of this in his article. But it was because of this fact, that Lenin's strategy required a formulation suited to the new conditions.

In the former empire of the czars a "dual power" had been set up, that of the bourgeoisie (the provisional government) and that of the masses (the Soviets, under a leadership of Mensheviks and S-Rs anxious to collaborate with the bourgeoisie). These two powers went through a highly unstable coexistence at the beginnings of the revolution. The task of the revolutionists consisted in aiding the masses to go through their own experience with this dual power on the plane of domestic policies as well as on that of the war (which the bourgeoisie wanted to continue, whereas the masses longed for peace).

It was necessary to aid this experience until such a time as it became possible to pass over to a new stage of the revolution, in which the dual power would be liquidated by the rise of a workers', peasants' and soldiers' power.

But Shachtman, who quoted the sentence of Lenin on "concreteness," no longer remembers it, any more than he bothers with the very special characteristics of this dual power. He has brought out this example only to retain one thing: Lenin modified his tactic, abandoning the transformation of the imperialist war into civil war[41]. Only later on in his article will we understand why Shachtman has been on the hunt for this example. With history thus clear in our minds, let us follow Shachtman as he passes to the third world war. He defines this war as follows:

A Definition of World War III

"The powers that will dominate and direct the Third World War are those that are dominating the preparations for it, the United States and Russia. Their relations make the conflict irrepressible. The conflict is imperialist on both sides, and that is what determines the predominant character of the war they will be (and in a sense are already) waging." (p. 195).

There follows what serves as analysis for Shachtman. We now find several pages demonstrating that the United States is an imperialist country. Apparently, some have to break through an open door in order to appear strong. As for Stalinism, here is what we find as a social analysis:

"The imperialism of the bureaucratic-collectivist states is different from that of the capitalist states. But the economic motive forces behind the one are no less powerful than in the case of the other. Only ignoramuses – people who know nothing about history and nothing about Lenin's theory of imperialism – can conceive of imperialism as a phenomenon unique to capitalist society." (p. 200).

We have learned to distinguish societies on the basis of the mode of production and of their property relations. We knew about a slave society, a feudal society, a capitalist society, and we did not think that one could usefully put ancient Rome, the Germanic Holy Roman Empire and Great Britain under the same label of "imperialism." We are very willing to concede our ignorance, but Shachtman should also in all fairness attribute it to Lenin, who wrote:

---

[41] We need not here dwell on Shachtman's studied effort to picture Lenin as a "democrat," in the most vulgar meaning of the term. As we shall see, Shachtman wishes to make use of the founder of the Bolshevik party for his own reformist purposes.

"Colonial policy and imperialism existed before this latest stage of capitalism, and even before capitalism. Rome, founded on slavery, pursued a colonial policy and achieved imperialism. But 'general' arguments about imperialism which ignore, or put into the background the fundamental difference of social-economic systems, inevitably degenerate into absolutely empty banalities, or into grandiloquent comparisons like 'Greater Rome' and 'Greater Britain.' Even the colonial policy of capitalism in its previous stages is essentially different from the colonial policy of finance capital." (*Imperialism*, Little Lenin Library, pp.81-82).

Although forewarned that he would degenerate inevitably into empty banalities or into grandiloquent comparisons, Shachtman set out on a road which, as we shall see, caused him to degenerate much more.

Still Another Definition

We cannot however hold it against Shachtman that he has remote and confused recollections about this work of Lenin, for his mind has a tendency to confuse everything. Several pages after having written that the third world war would be an imperialist war "on both sides," he gives a somewhat different definition:

"The Third World War will differ radically from the First and even the Second in that the two main belligerents find in one another not only imperialist rivals but class enemies representing antagonistic social systems" (p.201).

It will then be something other than an inter-imperialist war, at least in the minds of the belligerents; for the formulation of Shachtman is, to say the least, ambiguous. In any event, we will see two systems confronting each other which have different property forms. This being granted, Shachtman says that when the American ruling class speaks of a war against communism this is "not so stupid" from its own point of view, but it is "arch-stupid", from his point of view for "there is nothing in common between communism and Stalinism" (p.202). Shachtman is here referring to societies, the society of his dreams and Russian society. There is nothing in common between them except "the centralization of the means of production and planned production and distribution" (p.200). Only a Trotskyist could maintain the Marxist conception that only one social regime, and not two, corresponds to a given set of production and property relations. For Shachtman, production relations, property relations, are not very concrete; otherwise one would be compelled to accept the Trotskyist theory of the USSR as a workers state. But wanting a fundamental analysis, Shachtman decides his policies by means of statements of a psychological and subjective order:

In Place of Analysis - Stalinophobia

"Far overshadowing all other obstacles to the realization of the American imperialist objective – nothing less than domination of the world – stand the forces of Stalinism. Without hesitation or ambiguity, we can say that the only greater disaster that humanity could suffer than the war itself... would be the victory of Stalinism as the outcome of the war." (p.198). "We repeat: no greater disaster can be expected in connection with the Third World War than the victory of Stalinism... Until it has been utterly destroyed as a political force, the victory of the working class is impossible" (p.200).

Shachtman is so blinded by the possibility of a worldwide victory of Stalinism as to think that capitalism cannot be vanquished by the working class throughout the world unless Stalin is first overthrown. He has learned no lesson from the revolutionary struggles which have marked the world since 1943. He shuts his eyes to what took place in Yugoslavia, to the nature of the relations between the Kremlin and China. What is taking place in the countries of Eastern Europe is unimportant to him. He fails to see the revolutionary upsurge of the masses wearing away the foundations of Stalinism right within the Communist Parties themselves. So long as Stalin will be there, no victory is possible for the working class[42].

Shachtman "Transforms" Lenin's Strategy

At this point, whoever will have followed Shachtman in his intellectual tribulations will be led to conclude: we must first support

---

[42] We cannot follow Shachtman in all his "theoretical" promenades. It would be a pity, however, to let the following lines pass: "Stalinism is a powerful social force rooted and nurtured in the decay of capitalist society, which is incurable, and the decay of the labor movement, which, fortunately, is not at all incurable ... Stalinism remains an unshaken force in countries like France and Italy because the bourgeoisie is incapable of taking serious measures to overcome the social crisis on a capitalist basis and the non-Stalinist labor movement, the Socialist Party and the reformist trade unions in France, for example, remain appendages or allies of the bourgeoisie; whereas Stalinism is an insignificant force in a country like Britain because, even though the bourgeoisie could not solve the social crisis in its way, the official labor movement has taken serious, if hesitant and inadequate, measures to solve it in an anti-capitalist way. With all the necessary changes, the same explanation can be made for the difference between the situation in India and the situation in China, or even in comparing the situations in Indonesia and Indo-China" (pp.201-202).
The right-wing leadership of the Labor Party, the bourgeoisies of India and of Indonesia, they are the means of curing the decay of the working class! What is really incurable is Shachtman's decay.

the United States in order to vanquish Soviet imperialism; only then can we think of fighting for socialism. This follows so logically that it explains why the Shachtmanite organization has above all been a passageway for intellectuals between the workers' camp and the imperialist camp. Shachtman himself raises the question. He begins by conceding that a victory of American imperialism would not be quite so disastrous:

"If the United States were to win the war, in all likelihood it would not mean the automatic and immediate establishment of totalitarian rule that would result directly from a victory of Stalinism. It is far from certain but it is quite probable that an American victory would leave at least some degree of democracy under which the working class and socialist movements could continue to develop with greater or lesser freedom" (p.200).

Is it freedom of the type which the South Koreans are experiencing or of the type promised by that famous issue of *Collier's*? Shachtman does not tell us and he is not ready (not ready as yet) to go so far. He does not want, he protests, to march with American imperialism because the latter bases itself on the worst forces of reaction throughout the world. For want of more arguments, Shachtman proceeds to define his position in the last three pages of his article in the following way:

"The labor movement in this country is today a minority politically. The socialists are a much tinier minority. We have our responsibilities; the ruling class has its responsibilities" (p.204).

Shachtman's evaluation of the American working class is a bit summary and very static. But let us proceed further:

"The bourgeoisie is at the head of the nation. It is genuinely concerned with defense of the nation. But it conceives of it in the only way it can: as identical with the defense of capitalist property and imperialist power" (p.204). "The working class, too, is concerned with the defense of the nation. Unlike the bourgeoisie, it does not identify this primarily with the defense of capitalist property and imperialist power. Its patriotism is of a fundamentally different type, no matter how heavily overlaid it may be with bourgeois ideology. It identifies national defense essentially with its own class interests: with the preservation of its organizations, its relatively high standard of living, its hard-won democratic rights, as well as the right to rule as a free and independent nation. One of the outstanding differences between the coming war and the First World War is that all the things that the working class identifies with national defense are actually threatened by Stalinism. The triumph of Stalinist arms would completely change the social and political regime in the United States, a fact which we can state with as much firmness as Lenin insisted upon the opposite with respect to the main belligerents of the war of 1914. We socialists are as one with the working class in wishing to resist this threat and overcome it. We differ with the working class, as it is now, in that we cannot and will not support the American capitalist side in the war which aims at violating the rights and integrity of other people. Socialist policy in the corning war, then, does not put forward any such slogans as 'revolutionary defeatism' or 'transform the imperialist war into a civil war'." (p.205)

Thus the American labor organizations are not threatened by American imperialism (which aims merely at "the rights and integrity of other people"), but by Stalinism. At the same time the social and political regime of the United States – the capitalist regime – would fall with a defeat of the arms of American capitalism. Stated another way, the American working class organizations and American capitalism have a little something in common: they have the same enemy, Stalinism. If the latter wages war, an American worker cannot desire the defeat of his boss. Shachtman makes it even more explicit in these words:

"... To prosecute the class struggle in such a way that it would clearly 'imperil the military position of the government, even to the point where it may be defeated by the enemy and lose the war' – that, in the conditions of the Third World War, would be disastrous to the working class and to socialism. Instead, socialist policy must be based upon the idea of transforming the imperialist war into a democratic war, that is, adopting broadly the view put forward by Lenin in 1917, with all the changes required by the differences between the situation then and now, and working for its adoption by the labor movement as a whole." (p.205).

Bowdlerizing Lenin's Ideas

It now becomes clear why Shachtman began by seeking out that example from Lenin. He has given it a broad, a very broad interpretation. Under what conditions did Lenin modify his position? Let us see:

"We have been advocating the turning of the imperialist war into civil war, and now we have reversed ourselves. We must bear in mind, however, that the first civil war in Russia has come to an end; we are now advancing toward the second war – the war between imperialism and the armed people. In this transitional period, as long as the armed force is in the hands of the soldiers, as long as Miliukov and Guchkov have not resorted to violence, this civil war turns for us into peaceful, extensive, and patient class propaganda. To speak of civil war before people have come to realize the need of it, is undoubtedly to fall into Blanquism" (*The April Conference*, Little Lenin Library, p. 19).

The imperialist war having begun to change into a civil war, the masses being armed, to speak of civil war would no longer be a question of strategy; it would become a slogan, it would mean calling for an armed struggle against the government. The majority of the people must first become convinced that this is necessary before they will take such an action. Lenin temporarily abandoned speaking of civil war as a *slogan of action*, at a time when "it is the soldiers and not the capitalists who are in possession of the guns and cannons" (Lenin), and while the Bolsheviks were in a minority in the class. Shachtman abandons it as a *strategy* at a time when, according to him, "the labor movement is a minority, politically," while American imperialism is slaughtering the revolutionaries of Korea, of the Philippines, is helping to slaughter those of Vietnam, and is preparing to plunge the whole world into war. In order to take into account so vast a difference in situations, Shachtman changes Lenin a little bit more. Lenin wished to propose "a democratic peace to all the nations" in order to help the masses go through their experience with the provisional government. Shachtman wants to organize "a democratic war" against the USSR and the nations which may be allied with the USSR.

Not only is this one of the most impudent examples of bowdlerizing Lenin's thoughts; it also discloses in Shachtman the scarcely refurbished ideas of the social patriots and centrists which Lenin castigated during the First World War. When Shachtman speaks of the democratic rights and workers organizations he wants to defend against Stalinism, this is only a belated echo of the German social democrats of those days who carried out their betrayal under the pretext of protecting their organizations against czarism, and of the French Guesde socialists who did their betraying under pretext of defending their country's revolutionary traditions against the Kaiser.

The "Third Camp" to the Rescue

How is Shachtman going "to transform the imperialist war into a democratic war?" He calls upon the labor movement to champion a series of economic and political measures, such as control of production, of the distribution of commodities, of prices and profits, abolition of all measures of racial discrimination, economic aid to backward countries, etc. And, he adds, since only a workers' government would carry out this program, such a government

"... could mobilize such an international force – the force to which we refer as the Third Camp – as could be counted upon either to postpone the outbreak of the Third World War or, if it is precipitated by a desperate Stalinism, to bring it to a speedy, democratic and progressive termination" (p.206).

The "Third Camp" thus appears on the scene for the first time in the last twenty lines of Shachtman's article. There are the people who are not as yet ready to die for Wall Street today. Shachtman is presenting a political line for enlisting them under the stars and stripes.

But while one thing is clear in this political line, namely that Shachtman is set upon a war to the death against the USSR, he has omitted to tell us *how* and by what means he contemplates replacing the capitalist government of Washington by a workers' government. We know that he does not want to carry on the class struggle disturbing to the schemes of the Pentagon. What does he propose? In the history of the international working class movement we have heard of only two proposed roads: the (realistic) revolutionary road and the (Utopian) reformist road. Shachtman is abandoning the revolutionary road. Has he discovered a "Third Road," just as he invented a "Third Camp"? No, he has sunken into shame-faced reformism and does not want to admit this even to himself. His "Third Camp" has led him in practice to capitulation to American imperialism, for which he does not want to cause any serious difficulty in wartime and which he is trying to change gradually...

From the "Third Camp" to the Imperialist Camp

We have had occasion to point out in passing examples of incoherence in Shachtman's thinking, but his own evolution and that of his concept of the "Third Camp" are not at all incoherent. For a long time he was with us in the camp of the working class, with all its imperfections, despite its miserably inept and scoundrelly leaders, aware that that was the only road to the unfolding socialist showdown with capitalism. At that time he unconditionally defended the USSR, despite the criminal policies of the Kremlin. When great social pressures began to bear down, that is to say, at the beginning of the Second World War, when the petty bourgeoisie was shocked by the Hitler-Stalin pact, he took a stand for several weeks for "conditional defense" of the USSR, and called on the Polish masses to organize an insurrection simultaneously against Hitler and Stalin. Then he invented his "Third Camp," and abandoned the Trotskyist conception of the USSR in order to adopt the theory of "bureaucratic collectivism" which Burnham had whispered in his ear. Somewhat later, when Stalin and Roosevelt became allied against Hitler, his "Third Camp" had to find a reorientation. Incapable of distinguishing between the war which the USSR was fighting and that being conducted by imperialism he sought refuge in abstention. Now that a life and death struggle is developing between world capitalism girding for a decisive test and the organized masses which are under the command of the bureaucratic leaderships, his "Third Camp" is undergoing a new transformation: this "Third Camp" is also for a life and death struggle against the USSR, and while it must not jeopardize the decisions and the actions of the White House and the Pentagon, it must wait until the American camp has received a good coating of democratic paint. Again we find behind this position, just as in 1939, the same social force, but with greater intensity: that liberal petty bourgeoisie which chokes at the unsavory aspects which history assumes; which dreams, if not of an ideal development, then at least of a nice orderly camp, in which one could take one's place without the danger of getting dirty. This liberal section of the American petty bourgeoisie cannot determine the march of history, but it is sufficiently powerful to push Shachtman into the camp of imperialism.

The "Third Camp" of Shachtman has had its evolution – a rapid one in the case of its adherents (the erstwhile R.D.R.) in France where the situation hardly lends itself to equivocation, slower in the United States, just so long as the war did not take on definite form. But rapid or slow this evolution has led inexorably into the camp of imperialism. The Shachtman case illustrates, on a microscopic scale, the inevitable evolutions which the gigantic forces now prevailing and criss-crossing one another are provoking and will continue to provoke. For the petty bourgeoisie socialism has merit only as a moral idea and becomes odious when it takes on the form of an attack against the foundations of capitalist society. Under the pretext of not "capitulating to Stalinism," and yielding to the pressure of petty bourgeois public opinion these alleged revolutionaries, who cannot adjust themselves to a working class which is not dressed in a style they like, enter the "Third Camp" which brings about their capitulation to the imperialist camp.

The search for quotations from Lenin, the subtleties of thought or alleged subtleties of thought employed to prop up a theory of the "Third Camp" which abandons the fundamental Marxist concept of the class struggle carried on by the two main social camps – all these verbal acrobatics have led and inevitably lead those who are taken in by them right into the arms of the bourgeoisie. Stalinism, which is not a social system but an ultra-reactionary leadership of the working class, will be conquered only by those who remain rooted in the working class camp and fear neither Stalinism itself nor contamination in a united front struggle with Stalinists.

PIERRE FRANK

The Politics of French Stalinism

The situation in France has been marked by a whole series of events at the end of May and the beginning of June 1952 which were widely commented on in the world press but most often in a specious manner.[43] The real relationship of forces, the perspectives in view, were generally distorted; so too with the shifts of policy of the Communist Party of France. The object of the following remarks is to clarify several essential points.

France, Nerve Center of Western Europe

It is a commonplace that France is the most sensitive spot of the Atlantic coalition in western Europe. Not only is the majority of the working class under the leadership of the Stalinists (who have obtained 5 million votes in all elections since 1945 – and the CGT, Stalinist-controlled trade union federation, obtains some 60 to 70% of the votes in the elections of delegates in the industries). But a defeatist and anti-American feeling is harbored by the bourgeoisie and petty-bourgeoisie and finds daily expression in the newspaper, *Le Monde*. French capitalism – which takes a dim view of the rearmament of Germany – is dominated by American pressure and can do nothing but passively wait the advent of the war. It must attempt to disorganize the working class to the utmost and to weaken the hold of the CPF upon it. Hence the imperative need for French capitalism to engage in a series of attacks and provocations against the workers and against the CPF, short of civil war before the outbreak of the war itself. Antoine Pinay, the most reactionary premier since 1945, has attempted to push things furthest in this direction even to the point of running some risks. It should be noted that even some de Gaullists considered the arrest of Duclos an adventure.

However that may be, the government had prepared a conspiracy against the CPF on the eve of Ridgway's arrival in France and sought a pretext to carry it out.

---

[43] The Politics of French Stalinism (June 27, 1952) comes from *Fourth International*, Vol.13 No.4, July-August 1952, pp.108-113

To get an idea of the importance of France for imperialist strategy, it should not be forgotten that there are around a million workers voting communist in the Paris area where the headquarters of NATO and its military arm, SHAPE, are located.

Stalinist Policy

The fact that France is one of the weakest rinks of the imperialist chain must inevitably tempt the Kremlin to utilize the workers' movement and the strength of the CPF to try to break up the Atlantic coalition. The "radicalization"[44] of the CPF must be considered within this framework.

This "radicalization" began to take a particularly palpable form at the beginning of this year. The CPF countered the prohibition of the traditional annual demonstration on February 12 by an appeal for a general strike. The results of the action were inconclusive. Workers' preparation was not especially intense except at Renault (France's largest auto plants located in the Paris suburbs). The movement was spotty throughout the country. There was a clash at Renault between the workers and the police who, however, did not seek to push the fight too far.

The 12th of February action was to serve the purpose of an initial radicalization of the CPF membership as was very clearly indicated in the deliberations of the CPF Central Committee which took place around the middle of the month.

The radical note emerging from this session was further confirmed and sharpened by editorial articles in the *Cahiers du Communisme*, CP theoretical organ (March and May 1952) written by Etienne Fajon and Francois Billoux, members of the Political Bureau; Billoux had just returned from the USSR.

What was the nature of this "radicalization"?

It was pointed out that the political situation in France was marked on the government level by a series of more and more reactionary premiers since 1945, that discontent was general and, consequently that the situation was opportune to reverse the direction of events by means of widespread mass action regardless of the composition of the existing parliament. It was also pointed out that the principal enemy to be overcome for this purpose was the French bourgeoisie which was the main enemy although acting under American pressure; that the bourgeoisie *as a class* was betraying the

---

[44] Radicalization is the nearest we can come in conveying the meaning of the French gauchissement which literally means to become more left.

interests of the nation, and that even if some individual bourgeois were in favor of east-west trade, it was for individual motives and should not therefore lead to an attenuation of the struggle against them. The need for concrete actions of struggle against the war was emphasized (refusal to transport and handle arms). An impeccable position was taken against the French Union (the French Empire – Ed) and for the support of the colonial movements. They glossed over the policy of collecting peace petitions (Stockholm) and explained that the struggle for peace was part of the struggle for socialism. They explained that the reversal of political orientation in France should lead to socialism. The question of perspectives was emphasized as a means of insuring the cohesion of the party in action.

In effect, in extreme confusion and under the banner of national independence, the CPF ranks were raised to a higher political level and to greater combativity. On the other hand, the CPF leadership continued its policy of united front "from below," seeking to set the socialist workers against their leadership solely by denunciation. They retained their slogan of a government of democratic unity, sometimes using the expression of a peace government or a government of honest men, the dominant note being ambiguity. There was not the slightest hint of a united front of the Communist Party and the Socialist Party nor of a struggle for a united front socialist-communist government.

What was most interesting on the organizational plane was that while the CPF leadership formally recognized the right of Stalinist-front organizations (like the Peace Movement) to follow a different policy, in effect it renounced the previous orientation of adapting the party to these organizations and tended – bureaucratically, to be sure – to delineate the CPF in action and as an organization.

As a mass organization, the turn of the CPF and its leadership are not assimilated solely by the reading of resolutions of its Central Committee or of articles by members of the Political Bureau. Like any mass organization, the CPF is educated principally in action, and even if the leadership of the CPF was not bureaucratic in character, it would have been obliged to envisage the means of making its new policy understood through action. For so bureaucratic a leadership, there was no hesitation in precipitately involving the revolutionary vanguard in an action of which most of the participants were uninformed until the moment they were thrust into it. As has been pointed out above, the February 12th strike was broadly utilized by the CPF leadership to begin to radicalize the ranks of the party. (For example, the first clash with the police at Renault, the raising of barricades, etc.).

The Events of May 28th

The arrival of Ridgway, fresh from Korea, thus occurred in a situation where the government on its side was preparing a provocation and a conspiracy and a Stalinist leadership on the other side was seeking to raise the level of the struggles.

The government proscribed the demonstration called on the *place de la Republique*, but the call for the demonstration remained. Tension mounted as the day approached. The government arrested Andre Stil, editor-in-chief of *L'Humanité* (leading Stalinist newspaper). Local demonstrations were organized by communist branches. Then, as a consequence of the deportation of Messali Hadj (Algerian nationalist leader) from Algeria, North African workers demonstrated on May 23 on French territory; the police opened fire, killing four Algerian workers. On the morning of May 28, the police seized *L'Humanité*.

In the late afternoon, when the factories let out, only a vanguard was answering the call of the CPF. To outmaneuver the police who had concentrated their forces at *place de la Republique* and in a fairly large neighboring area, the demonstrators gathered at a dozen different points. The number of demonstrators, which is difficult to establish, may however be estimated at from ten to fifteen thousand, but more important was the extremely combative character of the demonstration. In most cases the demonstrators took the offensive, attacked the police cortèges, breaking them up, vigorously assailing the police and even a police station and police wagons in which demonstrators, were being taken off. A large number of police were wounded. There was one dead and many wounded among the demonstrators.

Although only a vanguard had taken part in the demonstration, it had transpired generally amidst the sympathy of the working masses.

This demonstration, and the extremely violent character of the clashes, cannot be considered as accidental, but as the prelude, the general rehearsal for the period in which civil war is ripening in France; it marks an important stage in the development of the class struggle to extremely high levels. It deserves a detailed study, because some of its features will appear in a more developed form in the struggles for power in the future.

Tactically, the communist militants had surprised the police and the demonstration had as its first result the raising of their combativity, their revolutionary potential, a series of questions becoming clearer to them (struggle against the state, arming of the workers...). But politically matters were to take another turn, for on the same evening the government put into operation its conspiracy by arresting Jacques Duclos, general secretary of the CPF since the departure of Thorez.

The Government Conspiracy and the Workers' Reaction

The day after the demonstration the government proceeded with the execution of its plans. *L'Humanité* was again seized. Some days later the police raided the headquarters of the Central Committee and a number of local CPF offices.

On May 29, communist workers attempted to arouse the workers to action in a number of factories. Despite general sympathy, they encountered considerable difficulties even in factories where their influence is very strong. The National Committee of the CGT met quickly to issue an appeal to action for the defense of democratic rights and for action on economic demands which were "to begin on June 4th." This action was to take broader forms as it proceeded. The CGT's appeal was extremely skillful and cautious. But the railroad workers federation called for an unlimited general strike.

On June 4th a strike was declared at Renault as well as in several Parisian metal factories, but generally speaking, despite all the sympathy the masses showed for the CPF and despite their hostility to the government repressions, the failure of the movement was almost complete, particularly among the railroad workers where there were not even partial movements as there had been on February 12th. On June 5, the movement also came to an end at Renault. At no times since 1945 had the ranks of the CPF found themselves so isolated in action from the working class.

The CPF and the Working Class

During recent years the members of the CPF had experienced the high and the low of their capacity to mobilize the workers, but never had they suffered as heavy a defeat, and this in face of the worst government provocation: the arrest of the principal leader of the party in violation of his parliamentary immunity. It was also evident that their leadership had been taken by surprise by this government aggression and by the absence of working class response to their appeals for action against the repression. Almost a week passed before they organized a mass meeting against the repression, which was attended by 30,000 people.

This situation (these relationships between the working class and the CPF) could not be explained to the satisfaction of the militants by the customary reasons used in defeats: inadequate preparation, faulty application of the policy of the party... A political explanation was necessary and the principal purpose of the Central Committee meeting of the CPF in the month of June was to give such a political explanation to the members of the party in order as much as possible to divert the members from seeking such an explanation on their own. But before examining the results of this meeting, let us recapitulate what arc the relations between the CPF and the masses and how they were manifested on May 28 as well as in the following days.

The failure of the CPF to mobilize the masses, its isolation in action, does not in any way signify that the broad masses are separating themselves from it or that the fighting potential of the French working class has been seriously impaired. At the very moment when these events were occurring elections for delegates were being held in many industries (Renault, railroad...). The losses of the CGT were at a minimum, from five to ten percent, while sixty to seventy percent of the workers continued to vote CGT. These votes were cast amidst extraordinary heavy employer pressure. Dismissals had mounted. Thus, at the Renault plant, where a few days after June 4, 63 percent of the workers had voted for the CGT, more than 400 militants had been dismissed since February 12. Under such conditions losses remained slight.

The *Force Ouvrière* trade unions (a trade union federation led by Social Democrats) did not progress either numerically or in influence. The Christian unions, who are to the left of *Force Ouvrière*, made very slight gains. The CPF maintained its positions in various municipal and legislative elections.

Generally speaking the working masses of France who, between 1936 and 1945. have in their majority gone over from the Socialist to Stalinist leadership, remained deeply tied to the Stalinists. There is not even the slightest movement back to the reformists despite the many defeats the working class has suffered since 1947. And the events of May-June 1952 have in no way modified the fundamental relations between the CPF and the working class.

This does not mean that the masses are blindly and uncritically following the CPF or that they are ready to reply to any appeal on its part. That had already been evident in the past but now it is necessary to understand why they did not react at the very moment when repression was at its height.

Beginning with 1947, the CPF has been thrust into opposition to the government; at times it had been sharply in conflict with the state, especially during the miners strike of 1948. However, from 1947 to the beginning of 1952, its general activity remained within the framework of propagandist opposition and consisted only from time to time of general mobilizations at an extremely low level (Stockholm petitions, mass meetings...). Its general policy was that these petitions and these rallies would stop the war makers... During recent years the masses have not heard any propaganda for struggle.

The stiffening of the CPF and its "radicalization" occurred bureaucratically and was not apparent to the masses. We have already pointed out that the large part of the membership of the CPF only became aware of the turn in the struggle itself. Because of this fact, the masses – whatever their sympathies toward those who were fighting the bourgeois state and the employers – were not politically prepared for action, above all because of the past policy of the CPF. But this was also due to its present policy.

Discontent is general among the working masses. Grievances are numerous. But more or less instinctively the masses feel that they cannot obtain satisfaction of their demands in limited struggles. They feel the question to be tied to the question of power and that any real change for them must result from some real change in the government. But this sentiment of the masses is not stimulated and not transformed into action because the CPF's position on the problem, to say the least, is equivocal.

The CPF does not carry on any campaign on the question of power. The Central Committee adopts resolutions which close in a ritualistic way by a call for a "government of democratic unity," which has no meaning for CPF members or for the masses in general. Three or four years ago when the formula of a "government of democratic unity" was first issued – about a year after the end of the Stalinist coalition with the petty bourgeois parties – the slogan could have given the appearance of seeking for a new period of collaboration. Under present conditions, such an eventuality being excluded by the very nature of things, the slogan loses all real meaning and in fact presents an obstacle to the only real slogan, that of a united front government of the workers, a communist-socialist government issuing from the joint struggle of the two big working class parties.

The broad masses do not rally today to the appeals to action, of the CPF. Although isolated in this sense, the militants of the party remain the leaders of the working class of the country. The masses will inevitably begin to act because of their absolutely intolerable conditions which will be worsened by preparations for the Third World War and by the war itself. This development can be aided or hindered by the CPF's policy but it cannot be eliminated by it. When the masses take their own road to radicalization they will inevitably turn to the communist militants for leadership. They will choose as leaders those who have had the courage to be in the vanguard of the struggle and they will not begin by a careful scrutiny of the policy of their party. Any other conception would be an anachronism.

Fajon's Report and the Central Committee Meeting

What is the significance of the June 19-20 Central Committee meeting?

The general opinion of the bourgeois press was that there was a turn of the CPF dictated by Moscow. Why the turn? It cannot be theoretically excluded that Moscow ordered a turn, but for. the present serious international objective reasons are lacking to substantiate such a hypothesis. The left emphasis, particularly given by Billoux' article, undoubtedly originated in directives from Moscow. It is to be explained objectively by the development of the situation. For the moment, the factors are lacking which would permit the conclusion that Moscow has reversed itself. On the contrary, a study of the minutes of the Central Committee meeting give rise to a much more plausible explanation. One cannot and should not explain all the actions of a Stalinist leadership solely by orders from Moscow. Especially when a mass party is involved such a leadership cannot but take into account the relationships of the party with the masses. Moreover it possesses a margin of maneuver within the general line established by Moscow.

What is even more striking in Fajon's report than its differences with Billoux' article, which are not to be discounted, is its self-criticism. And when we speak of self-criticism we can say regardless of its political content that for the first time this word can be used without quotation marks. In effect, Fajon says that *the Political Bureau is responsible* for the "insufficiently clear and incomplete" article by Billoux.

Jeannette Vermeersch (Maurice Thorez' wife) speaks of "errors of estimation" in one of her articles. The Political Bureau also declares itself party responsible for errors committed in important instances: an article in *L'Humanité*, a headline in *Liberté*, organ of the Communist Federation of the North, are called sectarian. The Railroad Workers Federation and the Union of Trade Unions of the Seine are also criticized.

All in all, the self-criticism is certainly still very guarded, but what is inescapable is that the leadership does not shift the blame, as is its custom, onto a scapegoat. This self-criticism needs explaining, for the leadership does not beat its breast without having serious reasons for so doing.

It did so for many reasons. First there is the idea, widespread in the party, that they were too far ahead of the masses. The leadership as well as the ranks understood that the first need was to re-establish contact with the masses. Moreover, this is unquestionably a real problem for any leadership and presupposes a whole series of measures to which we will return later. The greatest danger for the leadership would, be if the party members began to seek their own political solutions on the basis of their political development of recent months, the line set forth by Billoux, and the radicalization ensuing from recent struggles. On this basis, there was the risk that the militants would orient themselves outside of the roads mapped by the bureaucracy and would tend politically toward a more or less finished revolutionary conception. Under these conditions, the leadership shouldered part of the responsibility and outlined its political answer.

What are the principal differences between the Billoux article and Fajon's report?

None of the ideas expressed by Billoux is openly condemned or contradicted, except on the point of the socialist perspectives of the struggle, but the accent is placed on something else. Fajon's report insists on the contradictions existing within the French bourgeoisie. He no longer speaks of the need to defeat it as a class, but he also no longer says that it is necessary to support one faction of the class against another or something of the kind. The problem of a change of orientation in the policy of France is mentioned in passing instead of being the central theme. There is no change on the need of struggling side by side with the colonial peoples. He continues to emphasize the need of specific actions against the preparations of war. In order to continue to carry on the "struggle for national independence and peace," he emphasizes the need of linking a campaign for the freeing of Duclos, which would be a campaign in defense of democratic rights, to the struggle for the immediate demands of the workers and the middle classes. But the change occurs on the question of perspectives.

The struggle for peace, "which is the decisive question of the *present*, which overshadows all others," is dissociated from the "struggle for socialism which is our program for *the future*." How different from the editorial of the same Fajon in *Cahiers du Communisme* (March 1952) in which, explaining the February Central Committee decisions, he wrote that world socialism could be considered as a perspective for the near future. It follows from this change that "what is essential is *the broadest possible unity* to safeguard peace of all those opposed to war" which means a re-adaptation to the position of the fellow travelers. Finally, says the Fajon report, "it is to the degree that new strata of the population take part in the battle for peace and national independence, to the degree that this battle rises to a higher level... that a policy of peace... will triumph... under a broad government of democratic unity."

The change, as we see, while not unimportant in presentation or in emphasis, is hardly fundamental in nature. There is no repudiation, even in the Stalinist way, of the line defined in the Billoux article; no different line is presented. It is undeniable that the leadership in its own way is seeking to re-establish contact of the CPF with the masses so as to find a better opening for the application of the line defined in Billoux' article.

Obviously this is a Stalinist leadership, i.e., it is profoundly empirical and opportunistic. It could not subject its past policy from top to bottom to self-criticism; it is constrained to remain within certain limits, i.e., to a number of current decisions and articles.

What were the factors which were at play in the readjustment of the tactics of the CPF? Nothing clear on this score is to be found in Fajon's report and therefore one can only make certain presumptions. Did they take into consideration certain signs of wavering in the Atlantic coalition over the ratification of the general contract with Germany? It is possible, but this would prove that as a typical Stalinist leadership it still has illusions in the possibility that inter-imperialist contradictions can play the same role they did in the second world war. It certainly can count on the development in France of a broad expression of public opinion against the police regime being created by the government, which is already apparent in a whole series of verbal protests, resolutions, etc., arising from circles outside those controlled, animated, or influenced by the Stalinists.

Naturally a revival of contact with the masses requires a policy which takes the immediate demands of the masses and the defense of democratic rights as its point of departure. The Central Committee decision to carry on a campaign for the freeing of Duclos is not erroneous in itself. (This article was written prior to the quashing of the charges against Duclos – Ed.) And, as we have pointed out above, the climate is favorable for such a campaign finding a real echo.

But a campaign for such elementary objectives, must first of all be conducted through the medium of agitation for the united front. In this connection, in the trade union sphere, the CGT leadership has revived the proposals it has made since September 1951 on various occasions for unity of action to the other trade union federations. Nevertheless, the proposal is implemented in its usual way merely as a formal approach from the top without any systematic. campaign addressed to the ranks popularizing its objectives, as though it were merely a futile gesture.

On the other hand, the necessary scope can only be given by a struggle on a broader scale than the trade union field, i.e., by a *political struggle* involving all the working people of the country. But here the leadership of the CPF is much less at home. At the close of 1951, there were articles by Fajon in *L'Humanité* beginning a campaign for the socialist-communist united front. But this campaign never got beyond the local scale. And then it was suddenly stopped short. Then there was discernible a resumption of the practice of appealing to the ranks of the socialists against their leaders (particularly in Billoux' article)..

In recent days there have been signs that the question of this campaign, has been raised in the CPF again. In the campaign against the incarceration of Duclos, importance is given to the participation of socialists (notably of delegates from socialist organizations). Mention should be made of a proposal of the "Progressive Union" addressed to both parties and also to capitalist parties for a new "Peoples Front." An article by Lecoeur (a member of the Political Bureau) in *L'Humanité* warns against rejecting the united front on an organizations level. In a general way, what emerges from the conduct of the Stalinist leadership since the beginning of June is an empirical search to find a solution to the problems of establishing ties with the masses for action.

The weakest point is the question of government. According to Fajon's report, what is required is a struggle which by extending its scope eventually poses the problem of power. But the obverse is true. A systematic campaign in its many forms for a united front socialist-communist government is necessary because this conception, once accepted by the masses, becomes a means of launching partial struggles as an opener to broader battles. The withdrawal of perspectives by Fajon in his report that were contained in the Billoux article is precisely the important retreat that will hinder the communist militants the most in their search for a solution to the problem of their party leading the masses.

Although, in our opinion, Billoux' article was also "insufficiently clear and inadequate," but for different reasons than those of the Stalinist Political Bureau (the defeat of the bourgeoisie as a class, the changing of the political orientation of the country by a struggle which would unfold the perspective of socialism) this article could have had the effect of making the communist militants more susceptible to questions of united front and of the government of the united front as concrete means for winning the masses for a struggle for such a perspective. In conclusion, the obstacle to the progress of CPF militants in the Fajon report is not its attempt to find slogans to revive contact with the masses, but the elimination of what Billoux had presented as a perspective.

A General View of the Situation

But what is happening in the CPF should also be viewed on a more general plane.

France is facing growing tension, more frequent shocks and convulsions. Precisely because it is weak, very weak, the French bourgeoisie will seek through such devices as the Pinay conspiracy to create difficulties in the workers' camp. Duclos' arrest has not fundamentally changed the relationship between the classes in France any more than the arrests in Tunisia have fundamentally changed the relationship of forces between imperialism and the Tunisian people. But these arrests, by provoking premature actions of the vanguard, serve the purpose of gaining time for the bourgeoisie and of interfering with the normal progress of the masses.

The upsurge of the French proletariat under pressure of the conditions created by war preparations is proceeding slowly. A first start occurred in May-April 1951 but since then the bourgeoisie has succeeded in preventing a new outbreak.

Because of this situation and of a whole series of events, the radicalization of the CPF militants, which follows its own course of development appreciably different from the evolution of the broad masses, induces differentiations in the ranks of the CPF which cannot be normally expressed in a political form because of the bureaucratic regime. Nevertheless these stirrings do find forms of expression. It is noteworthy to recall the polemic last year of two Political Bureau members against a Central Committee member who had proposed the reestablishment of the Communist Youth. The events of May-June 1952 obliged the Political Bureau to indulge in self-criticism which for the moment serves the needs of the bureaucracy but in the long run undermines belief in the omniscience of the supreme leadership.

The reactions of the CPF to these events provide us with a close-up of the processes at work in mass Communist Parties as a result of the aggravation of the world situation. It was only after the event that we could grasp the overall consequences of what had happened to the Communist Parties of China and Yugoslavia. In France, we are now living at the onset of this process, which will still be a very complicated and tortuous one.

The radicalization today encompasses the vanguard elements and not yet the masses. Other events will shake up Stalinist monolithism even more. But these processes will develop within the ranks of the CPF. The militants will not seek a solution to their problems on the outside. Basing themselves on this or that phase of the searchings and groping of their top leaders their political thought will take shape and mature. The development of the situation will provide the Trotskyist vanguard, on condition it takes the work of the Third World Congress seriously, with numerous opportunities to influence the poltical evolution of the best cadres of the French working class who are outstanding Bolshevik elements despite the Stalinist hoop that now binds them.

A Review: *Diary in Exile*

As a revolutionary militant, Trotsky did not usually resort to the literary device of a diary; but at certain periods of his life, when he found himself in a sort of captivity, he set down notes on paper.[45] This was the case in 1935 at a moment when -- the French government having just notified him of a new expulsion order, and there being no country that would grant an entry visa -- Trotsky was forced to live in a village in the Dauphinois, under a police surveillance that deprived him of normal conditions for work, without a secretary, and receiving his mail only at rare intervals, He noted down, more or less daily, remarks and observations, both on political events and on his reading, on the incidents of his life and that of his companion Natalia, the fate of his family in the USSR, etc. Soon after his arrival in Norway, he again found normal conditions for work, and... forgot this "diary," which was rediscovered in the archives deposited at Harvard University.[46]

Before going on to this unpublished document of Trotsky, one cannot refrain from smiling at the preface by the university dons who edited it. Imbued with bookish knowledge, there gentry express an unusual incomprehension of men, events, and ideas. For them, the turn from the reform of the Third International to the struggle for the Fourth International is "the abstract political level of Trotsky's crisis in exile"; the general character of the man is that of the "revolutionary intellectual in politics, the 'outsider' with his ideologies." These Harvard gentlemen see politics only at the level of US bourgeois parties. Astonished to find in Trotsky a man of deep sensitivity, they cannot understand that in this diary there are to be found "no ideological doubts that in this diary there are to be found "no ideological doubts or even soul-searching." We can imagine into what a laugh Trotsky would have exploded on reading such lines about himself.

But let us leave these distinguished university scholars, and come to Trotsky's diary itself.

On all the purely political part there is no need to insist. The notes here relate above all to the events that were then occurring in France, between the reactionary coup de force of 6 February 1934 and

---

[45] This review appeared in the Winter 1959 Amsterdam-published *Fourth International*.
[46] Trotsky's Diary in Exile - 1935. Translated from the Russian by Elena Zarudnaya. 218 pages, Cambridge (Harvard University Press), 1958.

the rise of the Popular Front: they have been worked up, in a much more finished form, in articles which the Fourth International reprinted a few months ago in French.

The interest of this diary lies in the fact that it gives an insight into the Trotsky of the last exile, of the Trotsky who, after having created and led the Red Army in the first years of the revolution, had been exiled and harried by Stalinism. In the literature about Trotsky, there are many remarkable pages written during the extraordinary years of the Russian revolution, describing either the pre-1917 militant, or "the sword of the Revolution" (Radek); but up till now it is at best only episodically that anything has been written on the last period of his life, from 1928 to 1940, on years such as none of the great revolutionaries ever experienced. After he had twice in his life been at the head of a revolutionary movement, after he had held second place in the leadership that removed one-sixth of the globe from capitalist domination, the state thus created had turned its forces against him, had driven him out, and had forced him to live a life alien to his temperament: he was everywhere under observation, he could not mix freely with people, his activity was inevitably limited to a small number of persons. He was cut off from his companions-in-arms, who were to be broken by Stalinist terror. Still more, in the workers' movement outside the USSR, he no longer had any comrade of his own generation; those who joined him were young people -- of whom many turned out to be migratory birds incapable of resisting the rigors of the climate caused by the parallel rises of fascism and Stalinism -- young people with whom, in spite of everything, he could not have as close relationships as with men of his own age. And lastly, though no great revolutionary has escaped the infamies and calumnies of those whose existence and petty interests he disturbed; nobody -- not even Blanqui -- experienced such an avalanche, such a downpour of muck and lies, backed by the authority of the first workers' state. And they are still far from having been wholly swept away.

Trotsky, whose personal life and revolutionary activity were one and the same, gave many details about him in his autobiography; but that ended practically at the beginning of the third exile. In addition, there were depths in his being that could be glimpsed by living close to him or by reading his works, but which he did not reveal: he was not "soul-searching," to use the expression of the Harvard University scholars, but his deep inner life can perhaps be appreciated, more than in any other of his writings, in the "diary" that has just been published.

There are in this diary, as one might expect, abundant reflections about literature and art. Though in many other fields there have not been lacking Marxists of uneven value in the field of aesthetics on the contrary, those who contributed something, can be counted singly. Marx, Engels, and Lenin, in this field, did not go beyond a few remarks, though these were worthy of their genius. Mehring and Plekhanov were the first to work in this field. Trotsky has, without any doubt, made a most considerable and eminent contribution. But at the very moment when "destalinization" has affected Communist intellectual circles, they not only do not dare look Trotsky's way in the matter of the analysis of Stalinism and the economic and political problems of transitional regimes (that would run the risk of leading them to revolutionary conclusions), but they are also unaware of Trotsky's work as a Marxist literary critic. Among the causes of this state of things, there is evidently the difficulty, the impossibility, of disassociating the two fields in an absolute way but there is also the fact that Trotsky, showing himself be an incomparable master, stimulating the thought of his readers in whatever field he treats, never resorts to the fashion of the professors, never pontificates, and his thought always concerns itself with the immediate present, yet without losing historical perspective. What has not been said of late about Soviet literature? In any case, nothing as concise and profound as this note made in the diary under the date 9 March 1935:

Aleksey Tolstoy's novel is a work remarkable for the immediacy of its feeling for the remote Russian past. Of course this is not "proletarian literature": as a writer A. Tolstoy has his roots in old Russian literature -- and world literature as well, naturally. But undoubtedly it was the Revolution -- by the law of contrast -- that gave him (and not him alone) an especially keen feeling for the peculiar nature of Russian antiquity--immobile, wild and unwashed. It taught him something more: to look beneath the ideological conceptions; fantasies and superstitions for the simple vital interests of the various social groups and of the individuals belonging to them. With great artistic penetration A. Tolstoy k, lays bare the hidden material underpinnings of the ideological conflicts in peter's Russia. In this way individual psychological realism is elevated to social realism. This is undoubtedly an achievement of the Revolution as an immediate experience and of Marxism as a general doctrine.

Mauriac, a French novelist whom I do not know, an Academician (which is a poor recommendation), wrote or said recently: we shall recognize the USSR when it produces a new novel of the calibre of Tolstoy or Dostoievsky. Mauriac was apparently making a distinction between this artistic, idealistic criterion and a Marxist, materialist one, based on relations of production. Actually, there is no contradiction here. In the preface to my book Literature and Revolution I wrote about twelve years ago:

"But even a successful solution of the elementary problems of food, clothing, would in no way signify a shelter, and even of literacy, complete victory of the new historic principle, that is, of Socialism. Only a movement of scientific thought on a national scale and the development of a new art would signify that the historic seed has not only grown into a plant, but has even flowered. In this sense, the development of Art is the highest test of the vitality and significance of each epoch."

However, it is impossible in any sense to represent the novel of A. Tolstoy as a "flower" of the new epoch. It has already been stated why this is true. And the novels which are officially regarded as "proletarian art" (in a period of complete liquidation of classes!) are as yet totally lacking in artistic significance. Of course, there is nothing "alarming" in this. It takes some time for a complete overturn of serial foundations, customs and assumptions to product an artistic crystalization alone new axes. How much time? One cannot say offhand, but a long time. Art is always carried in the baggage train of a new epoch, and great art -- the novel -- is an especially heavy load. That there has been no great new art so far is quite natural and, as I have said, should not and cannot alarm anyone. What can be alarming, though, are the revolting imitations of a new art written on the order of the bureaucracy. The incongruities, falsity and ignorance of the present "Soviet" Bonapartism attempting to establish unlimited control over art -- these things make impossible any artistic creativity whatsoever, the first rendition for which is sincerity. An old engineer can perhaps build a turbine reluctantly; it would not be first-rate, because it had been built reluctantly, but it would serve its purpose. But one cannot, however, write a poem reluctantly.

It is not by accident that Aleksey Tolstoy retreated to the end of the seventeenth century and the beginning of the eighteenth in order to gain the freedom essential to the artist.

In addition to general observations like the foregoing, how many remarks about a book or an author! In 1935, Jules Remains, the first volumes of whose Hommes de bonne volonlé had appeared, was setting out in politics. In a few lines Trotsky judges him as both politician and writer:

As a writer (and even more as a politician) he is evidently lacking in character. He is a spectator, not a participant. But only a participant can be a profound spectator. [...] A spectator like Romains can be a remarkable writer, but he cannot be a great writer.

One day chance caused Trotsky to read Frapie's La Marlernelle, a winner of the Goncourt Prize in a period when this distinction made less fuss. About the work of this of whom he knew nothing, Trotsky wrote :

[...] He shows very courageously the back yard -- and the darkest corner of the back yard -- of French civilisation, of Paris. The cruelty and meanness of life strike hardest at the children, at the smallest ones. Frapié, then, set himself a problem of looking at present-day civilisation through the frightened eyes of the hungry maltreated children with hereditary vices in their blood. The narrative is not sustained artistically; there are breakdowns and failures; the heroine's arguments are at times naive and even mannered; but the author succeeds in creating the necessary impression. He knows of no way out and does not even seem to be looking for one. The book is charged with hopelessness. But this hopelessness is immeasurably higher than the smug and cheap recipes of Victor Margueritte.

The same acuteness of observation, joined with the same superior ability to deduce general ideas and social conclusions, is to be found again when, leaving the field of literature, he notes the contacts he was having with people, inevitably forced contacts with various "authorities" and official figures, or inevitably brief and scarcely developed contacts with people who, more often than not, did not know who he was. Prosecuting attorneys, policemen, clerks of court, prefects, hotel or pension proprietors, barbers, etc. Little touches, graphic and full of irony, toward officials anxious not to get on his account into any trouble that might impede their careers. And these words that cannot be read without their evoking so many miserable memories:

There is no creature more disgusting than a petty-bourgeois engaged in primary accumulation. I have never had the opportunity to observe this type as closely as I do now.

Always extremely sensitive to the contrasts between human progress and knowledge and superstition and prejudices, and the combinations that result therefrom : the radio on the one hand, and, on the other, the manifestations at Lourdes or a royal ceremony in England. On the plane of intelligence, Trotsky does not fail to conclude:

There is a much greater distance between Baldwin and Lenin, as intellectual types, than between the Celtic druids and Baldwin.

He is on the level of Marx, Engels, and Lenin ; with them he breathes the fresh air of the mountains, which clears out lungs full of pettiness and insolence, obsequiousness and ignorance. From the pages of this diary, let us excerpt a few all-too-brief lines on Engels, "one of the finest, best integrated, and noblest personalities in the gallery of great men" :

PIERRE FRANK

Alongside the Olympian Marx, Engels is more "human,," more approachable. How well they complement one another! Or rather, how consciously Engels endeavors to complement Marx; all his life he uses himself up in this task. He regards it as his mission and finds in it his gratification. And this is without a shadow of self-sacrifice -- always himself, always full of life, always superior to his environment and his age, with immense intellectual interests, with a true fire of genius always blazing in the forge of thought. Against the background of their everyday lives, Engels gains tremendously in stature by comparison with Marx -- though of course Marx's stature is not in the least diminished by this. I remember that after reading the Marx-Engels correspondence on my military train, I spoke to Lenin of my admiration for the figure of Engels. My point was just this, that when viewed in his relationship with the titan Marx, faithful Fred gains -- rather than diminishes -- in stature. Lenin expressed his approval of this idea with alacrity, even with delight. He love Engels very deeply, and particularly for his wholeness of character and all-round humanity. I remember how we examined a portrait of Engels as a young man, discovering in it the traits which became so prominent in his later life.

At the moment that Trotsky was writing his diary, the Stalinist repression, which had already hit heavily at the oppositionals, was about to pass on to a new stage by striking at their families and friends: only a year later the first big "Moscow Trial" began. Trotsky, who had already been hit by Stalin through several members of his family, saw several others threatened. Trotsky and his companion Natalia were going to be painfully affected already in 1935 by the arrest of their youngest son, Sergei, who, having in his childhood turned away from politics, had become a teacher in an institute of technology and was devoting himself entirely to his technical work.

Anyone who was close to Trotsky and Natalia in these years of exile when they were to learn of the suicide of Zina, the disappearance of Sergei, and the death of Liova, cannot read many pages of this diary without reliving painful hours and without making the striking rediscovery of the incomparable example of these two beings, suffering deeply but showing to the entire world, to the few friends, and to powerful and shameless enemies, a firmness of character of the highest inspiration for young revolutionaries.

In this diary one learns of Trotsky's and Natalia's worry about the way that their son Sergei, lacking in political interest, would stand up to his executioners, inspired by an insatiable hatred. Some months ago an unimpeachable witness came to us to bring an account of a chance encounter in 1937, between a communist militant and Sergei, in a prison of the GPU; Sergei, he informed us, behaved in a way full of the dignity and courage whose example he had had before him in his parents.

Among the very moving lines in this diary, perhaps the most touching of all are those that Trotsky devotes to Natalia: they must be read; any commentary would be too poor.

In this diary, Trotsky appears also to be concerned with the idea of death -- purely as a revolutionary conscious of the tasks he is accomplishing -- and seems to have felt certain premonitory signs in himself:

My high (and still rising) blood pressure is deceiving those near me about my actual condition. I am active and able to work but the outcome is evidently near.

What he feared was not sudden death but prolonged invalidism, and, in that case, he declared flatly that he intended a "suicide" like that of the Lafargues. But at the same time he could not fail to think that, under the conditions of the fierce slanders of the Stalinists against him, this would run the risk of giving rise to erroneous and malevolent interpretations; and so he considered it indispensable to reaffirm in a few lines his unshakable conviction in communism and in the future of humanity, in case he should have been led to take such a decision.

Many other passages give food for thought, whether it be his regret at not having had more time to devote to philosophy, or that dream in which he was talking with Lenin. But of this diary, which was not written for publication and which was forgotten by Trotsky among his papers, it is not possible to fail to reproduce this passage, where a Marxist treats of the role of personality in history, this personality being himself, with impressive objectivity:

Rakovsky was virtually my last contact with the old revolutionary generation. After his capitulation there is nobody left. Even though my correspondence with Rakovsky stopped, for reasons of censorship, at the time of my deportation, nevertheless the image of Rakovsky has remained a symbolic link with my old comrades-in-arms. Now nobody remains. For a long time now I have not been able to satisfy my need to exchange ideas and discuss problems with someone else. I am reduced to carrying on a dialogue with the newspapers, or rather through the newspapers with facts and opinions.

And still I think that the work in which I am engaged now, despite its extremely insufficient and fragmentary nature, is the most important work of my life -- more important than 1917, more important than the period of the Civil War or any other.

For the sake of clarity I would put it this way. Had I not been present in 1917 in Petersburg, the October Revolution would still have taken place -- on the condition that Lenin was present and in command. If neither Lenin nor I had been present in Petersburg, there would have been no October Revolution : the leadership of the Bolshevik Party would have prevented it from occurring -- of this I have not the slightest doubt! If Lenin had not been in Petersburg, I doubt whether I could have managed to overcome the resistance of the Bolshevik leaders. The struggle with "Trotskyism" (i.e. with the proletarian revolution) would have commenced in May 1917, and the outcome would have been in question. But I repeat, granted the presence of Lenin the October Revolution would have been victorious anyway. The same could by and large be said of the Civil War, although in its first period, especially at the time of the fall of Simbirsk and Kazan, Lenin wavered and was beset by doubts. But this was undoubtedly a passing mood which he probably never even admitted to anyone but me.

Thus I cannot speak of the "indispensability" of my work, even about the period from 1917 to 1921. But now my work is "indispensable" in the full sense of the word. There is no arrogance in this claim at all. The collapse of the two Internationals has posed a problem which none of the leaders of these Internationals is at all equipped to solve. The vicissitudes of my personal fate have confronted me with this problem and armed me with important experience in dealing with it. Then is no one except me to carry out the mission of arming a new generation with the revolutionary method over the heads of the leaders of the Second and Third International. And I am in complete agreement with Lenin (or rather Turgenev) that the worst vice is to be more than 55 years old! I need at least about five more years of uninterrupted work to ensure the succession.

To conclude these few reflections on this brief diary which evokes so many things in us, we cannot do better than to apply to Trotsky the diary's words on Engels, that fit Trotsky himself so well:

Engels' prognoses are always optimistic. Not infrequently they run ahead of the actual course of events. But is it possible in general to make historical prediction which -- to use a French expression -- would not burn some of the intermediate stages?

In the last analysis E. is always right. What he say in his letter to Mme Wischnewetsky about the development of England and the United States was fully confirmed only in the postwar epoch, forty or fifty years later. But it certainly was confirmed! Who among the great bourgeois statesmen had even an inkling of the present situation of the Anglo-Saxon powers? The Lloyd Georges, the Baldwins, the Roosevelts, not to mention the MacDonalds, seem even today (in fact, today ever more than yesterday) like blind puppies alongside the farsighted old Engels.

REVOLUTION AND COUNTER-REVOLUTION IN EUROPE

Eighty Years Ago

Next November 7th will complete eighty years since Leon Trotsky was born. By his theoretical contribution and his militant life, he takes his place in the class of the most eminent proletarian revolutionaries, that of Marx, Engels, Lenin, and Rosa Luxemburg.[47]

But if these others are accepted as such in the workers' movement (which does not mean that their teachings are not trodden underfoot), the place of Trotsky, even at the present beginnings of "destalinization," has not yet been recognized. True, the crudest Stalinist lies are no longer repeated, for they would no longer find any listeners; but a number of lies and false ideas continue to drag on, including among those who think that they have been delivered from Stalinism. How many try to get out of it by saying: The struggle between Trotsky and Stalin is ancient history, outlived, a personal rivalry about more or less abstract theories, and Trotskyism -- apart from a few faithful followers -- no longer exists. This was not at all the opinion of Stalin who, after claiming that Trotskyism was dead, went on setting up -- in vain -- the most monstrous judicial machinations to kill it. Nor is it the opinion of Stalin's present successors, either. If they have not rehabilitated Trotsky and the Left Opposition, it is because they realize that it is not outlived ancient history, but one of the burning problems of the present day.

The figure and the teachings of Trotsky will inevitably find the place they deserve in the course of the anti-bureaucratic movement of the masses, and not in the bureaucracy's measures of self-defense to protect its political power and privileges.

Among some who perhaps do not lack sympathy but do lack a sense of history, what contributes to their failure to appreciate Leon Trotsky is the contrast between the last part of his life (from 1928 on) and his period of glory and power in the first years of the Russian Revolution. Max Eastman wrote in a recent article that Trotsky was a man of indecision who did not know how to fight against Stalin -- all this based on "psychoanalysis" for the American petty bourgeois. Without expressing themselves so stupidly, there are not lacking people who think that if after all Trotsky was defeated by Stalin, it was because he pierced himself with his own sword at a given moment by his vision of the glorious period of the Russian Revolution, without

---

[47] *Eighty years ago,* appeared in issue 7 of the Amsterdam-published *Fourth International,* Autumn 1959.

understanding the new situation that was then opening up. It is, however, easy to verify the fact that it was Trotsky who really understood the new situation, whereas Stalin did not have the faintest idea of where he would be led by the struggle he started after Lenin's death. Power not only contributes to corrupt those who wield it; it also sets them on a pedestal which deforms their real stature. If someone like Trotsky lost the power, that must be his fault, and he was not so great a man as all that -- such is the reasoning of petty-bourgeois thinkers. We are convinced that the future will say that the whole greatness of Trotsky was shown most clearly in that last and so dramatic period of his existence -- such a period as none of the other great revolutionaries had to go through. Marx and Engels at the end of their days saw the workers' movement accept the doctrines that they -- for a long time almost alone -- had developed and advocated. Rosa was assassinated in a revolutionary period. Lenin died respected, just It the turning in the Russian Revolution, before he could join battle against the rising bureaucracy. It was to Trotsky, who, together with Lenin, had had the glory of leading the proletariat to power, that it fell to carry on that struggle. In it, the state that emerged from the first victorious proletarian revolution became the instrument of a narrow-minded and reactionary social layer of the new society, who systematically resorted to methods of violence within the workers' movement against the revolutionaries, cite a degree that even the reformists had not reached. In the Soviet Union alone, the number of members of the Bolshevik Party liquidated by Stalin -- according to the statement of Khrushchev at the session of the Central Committee in which he defeated Malenkov, Molotov, and Kaganovich -- reached 1,600,000. This figure alone indicates what was then the power of the bureaucratic reaction. Its hatred was aimed with its full force against Trotsky.

Trotsky's third exile never had an equal not so much because of the agents of Stalin who never ceased to exist around Trotsky and Leon Sedov; but this exile was in practice doubled by a cloistering imposed by various capitalist governments and by the interventions of the Soviet government. True, Trotsky could leave his home, engage in physical exercise (walking, fishing, hunting, etc), but it was in fact forbidden to him to take a direct part himself in the workers' movement. It is necessary to recall the rage poured out by the Soviet press when it was learned that Trotsky had left Istanbul to give a lecture in Copenhagen. The lion had escaped from his cage; few interventions were necessary to make the Social-Democratic Danish government understand what attitude it must take. Trotsky, a man of the masses to the highest degree, a militant the essential part of whose life had been passed in workers' organizations, in fact during this last exile found himself in a sort of prison with invisible bars, for he could communicate with the world and especially with the workers' movement only through visitors under the more or less discreet control of the police of the country he was in.

What is more, he had no exchange of thoughts, no relations, with the workers' leaders of his generation: the Social-Democracy and Stalinism had divided up between them the old leaders of the workers' movement. The more recent strata -- those of the First World War and its postwar period -- provided the elements for the bureaucratic apparatuses. Those who gathered around him were quite young militants, without a past, without training. It is easy to understand that this great difference in age and experience added to his isolation from the big labor formations kept up by apparatuses.

On the occasion of the publication this year of his *Diary* for the years 1934-35, some persons have discovered a "human" side to Trotsky. That is because they never knew how to read Trotsky. It is not at all hard to see in all his works how much he understands -- because he shares -- the feelings of the masses risen up against all oppression. And with him, as with Marxism's other great ones, these feelings take on all the more force in that they find their source in the understanding of causes and in the conviction that mankind now possesses the means to put an end to those inhuman conditions in which the great majority of them live. Nobody was more sorely tried than he and Natalia by the most hideous manifestations of Stalinism; those who were at their side saw how they suffered each time that their children were struck down by Stalinism. But they also saw the firmness with which they faced it, and how Trotsky in his grief redoubled his strength to carry on the struggle to which he had devoted his existence.

It is not simple to summarize Trotsky's theoretical contribution to Marxism, so considerable is it.

Above all, there is the theory of the permanent revolution, formulated when he was 26, in connection with Czarist Russia, but which, because of the trend taken by the world revolution from the U S S R toward the East, in colonial and semi-colonial countries -- contains its strategic basis for nearly two thirds of humanity in our times. While the Stalinist conceptions about "socialism in a single country" and "revolution by stages" have been swept away by such gigantic facts as the Chinese Revolution, the theory of the permanent revolution is still officially ignored by some, reviled by others, who remain in tow to native bourgeoisies without strength and without future.

PIERRE FRANK

The fundamental strategy for the struggle for power in the advanced capitalist countries (united front and transitional programme) had been formulated by the Communist International at its IIIrd and IVth Congresses, in fact by Lenin and Trotsky. It was defended and systematically elaborated by Trotsky against Stalinist revisions (sometimes sectarian, sometimes opportunist, conceptions of the united front -- renunciation of the struggle for power and a transitional programme, and a policy of alliances with wings of the bourgeoisie, such as the Popular Front etc). Trotsky further proceeded to study in a practically exhaustive way declining capitalism's forms of defense (fascism, Bonapartism).

The creation of a first workers' state in an economically backward country and its isolation in the world raised the most complex problems on every plane. The victory of the bureaucracy and its absolute power under the tyrannical leadership of Stalin helped to aggravate all these problems. It is to Trotsky that we are indebted for the greatest clarity about these questions. On the problems of industrialization, planning, the proportions of the various branches of the economy, relations with the peasantry, relations of economic questions with soviet democracy, on political problems in the workers' state (separation of state and party, plurality of parties, etc), on cultural problems, on all problems posed today with a force rendered doubly explosive, both because of the level attained by the Soviet Union and because of the Stalinist methods of repressing independent initiative in any field whatever -- on all these problems Trotsky provided the correct method of approach, and often indeed solutions that are still valid today. That the bureaucracy, forced to take action along lines indicated by him so many years ago, should continue to manifest hostility toward Trotsky, without however resorting to the worst calumnies of the Stalin era, is easy to understand: at the basis of all Trotsky's answers there is to be found as the essential element the intervention of the masses by the reestablishment of soviet democracy.

We are leaving aside very many manifestations of Trotsky's thought in the most varied fields, in which most often he no more than sketched out the way of treating them, but which will unquestionably constitute for future Marxists -- as is the case for very many passages in the work of Marx -- a guide for tackling new problems.

There is in Trotsky's work one point on which many an admirer of today is skeptical: that is his creation of the Fourth International and his conviction that it was, as early as before the Second World War, indispensable for ensuring the future of revolutionary Marxism and of the workers' movement. We shall not take up this whole question again here, where the militants of the Fourth International have so often had occasion to deal with it. We wish only to insist on the continuity of the international and internationalist activity of Trotsky. He had been one of the representatives of the Russian Social-Democratic Workers' Party to the Second International, and had seen its weaknesses; he had been at the foundation of the Third International, had there, together with Lenin, played the leading role, and had tried to make' it into a genuine international leadership of the revolutionary workers' movement; and had seen that one of the essential factors in its disintegration had consisted of abandoning an internationalist conception in favor of "socialism in a single country." To that it must be added that Trotsky had taken not at all lightly the error he had committed, compared to Lenin, on the question of the *party*. It was necessary to keep revolutionary Marxist principles intact, including that of the party -- and, after 1914, there could be no question of anything except an international party. It is there that is to be found the explanation of the immense efforts expended by Trotsky in his last years on the turbulent problems of an organization so numerically weak as the Fourth International, efforts which remain incomprehensible to those who do not understand that in so doing Trotsky was showing that he had adopted the Leninist conception of the party. On this question too, we are sure that the future will show that Trotsky was right. No one can yet foresee the forms of organization by which we shall pass from today's Fourth International of cadres to tomorrow's Fourth International of mass parties, but for us there is no doubt that the mass revolutionary Marxist movement of tomorrow will connect up with the Third International of the time of Lenin and Trotsky through the Fourth International founded in 1938 under Trotsky's leadership.

The error that Trotsky most often committed in more than one circumstance was to be ahead, and even very much ahead, of events. In that also, it may be said in passing, Trotsky found himself in the company of Marx and Engels. Although the brakes of reformism and the Soviet bureaucracy continue to have a strong effect on the mass movement throughout the world, they have lost much of their power. There is very little left of the Stalin cult five years after his death. And so we can, on this eightieth anniversary of Trotsky's birth, affirm with the greatest confidence that on his ninetieth anniversary his memory and his work will be honored by the great masses of the entire world.

PIERRE FRANK

The workers' parties and De Gaulle

In its history France has experienced several Bonapartist operations prior to that of de Gaulle, and comparisons between them still offer some interest. From both the bourgeois and the proletarian point of view, the de Gaulle operation presents an extraordinary picture.[48]

It was the war of Algeria following on that of Vietnam which led the French army to bring off its *coup de force*. This was carried out in an atmosphere unconnected with this political operation. There was no economic crisis as in 1851, no military collapse and exodus as in 1940. The war of Algeria had lasted three and a half years, and throughout that whole time in the metropolis the bourgeoisie had gone on showing indifference, a really surprising unconcern, about the war. Everyone was occupied with his own business, which was prosperous. Everyone was thinking about his coming vacation. The parliamentary regime had become the least of the worries of the bourgeois.

But if there was really one thing that differentiated the de Gaulle operation from its predecessors, it was the situation of the working class. It was not suffering from a bloodletting, as after June 1848. It was not, as in 1940, mobilized and with the CP in illegality. It had not been pushed into the background of the political scene. It had its parties, its trade unions, its press.

But, just like the bourgeoisie, it was but little concerned with the war in Algeria in the immediately previous years. These years of prosperity had assured it of a limited but unquestionable improvement in its living conditions; it had obtained three weeks of paid vacations. It also looked with contempt on the parliamentary game and the interminable ministerial crises. For this state of mind in the working class, it was the traditional leaderships — of the Socialist and Communist Parties that bear the responsibility. If, for the first time in French history, a Bonapartist operation could succeed without the prior defeat of the working class and the popular masses, it was

---

[48] Dated 21 June 1958. From the Summer 1958 issue of the Amsterdam-published *Fourth International*.

owing to those leaderships, and it is not unuseful to point out how they prepared such a defeat.

I: *The Socialist Party*

The overall line of the Guy Mollet leadership is well known, but his perfidy appears still more in the de tailed examination of his various proceedings. Guy Mollet reached the leadership of the SP in 1946- 1947 at the head of a *left* tendency that blamed the Daniel Mayer leadership for too timorous a policy.

But Guy Mollet quickly turned right, anticommunism becoming the fixed quantity in his political variations. He also constructed, for the first time in the history of the SP, an apparatus that guaranteed him control of the party. As French policy, beginning with the Liberation, evolved toward the right, the SP ended up by finding itself in the opposition between 1952 and 1955. It returned to power at the beginning of 1956 after the election victory of the "Republican Front" composed essentially of a combination of the SP and the Radical Party then led by Mendès-France.

Although the latter was the recognized leader of the "Republican Front" during the election campaign, Guy Mollet became the head of the new government, in view of the preponderant place held in the Nation al Assembly by the SP — with the exception of the French CP, to which, at that moment, no attention was paid in the parliamentary world. In the legislature elected in 1956, everything depended on the Socialist group: this was seen in May 1958.

During the election campaign Guy Mollet had vigorously criticized the war of Algeria: an idiotic and hopeless war, he called it. The victory of the Republican Front, paralleled by the strengthening of the Communist parliamentary group, meant that the country was expecting from the new parliament a policy of peace in Algeria. Willingly or not, Guy Mol let fell into the traps of the ultras and settlers of Algeria. His first choice for Minister of Algeria had been General Catroux, a "republican" who was saying that he would stop at nothing. But when Guy Mollet was received at Algiers with tomatoes, he persuaded Catroux to resign and in his place named Lacoste, who was to give a full demonstration of his socialism. In proceeding to make this designation, Guy Mollet, who had retreated before the fascist riot of 6 February 1956 at Algiers, considered it some thing "healthy."

Beginning with that moment, it was a steady retreat before the settlers and the army. In Algeria itself Lacoste was not directing anything; but he was covering up everything and had become the principal traveling salesman to make France accept the war of Algeria and all the infamies that it brought in its train.

As for the Guy Mollet ministry, it was "special powers," it was "pacification" by the sending of about half a million draftees, it was the Ben Bella affair. It was also the Suez campaign. It was the whitewashing given the torturers.

This policy which was nowise countered by that of the FCP) aided the progress of the reaction in France. In the SP itself, there could be observed the development of a fascisizing wing (speeches of Lacoste and Lejeune at the SP Toulouse Congress). But, unlike what happened in 1933-1934, when the Blum leadership was forced to expel the "néos" (Déat...), the Guy Mollet leadership made a bloc with this current against those who were calling for another Algerian policy, however moderate it might be. The leadership took sanctions against its opponents, going as far as expulsion (Philip) and above all depriving in practice almost the whole minority of its right of expression in the party congresses and conferences.

Overthrown as premier, Guy Mollet became the power behind the throne in the two following cabinets Bourgès-Manoury and Gaillard) who kept Lacoste on as Minister of Algeria. Guy Mollet also forced his party to swallow the formation of these governments and to support them, although resistance to this policy began to develop in the party. When the Gaillard government was overthrown, Guy Mollet pretended to be angry with the right "the most stupid in the world," he claimed and had the National Council on May 2nd and 3rd vote that the SP would no longer take part in any government, being satisfied to assure it of its support. He thus succeeded in strengthening his authority over the SP, an authority that had been somewhat damaged. At the time the Pflimlin government was formed, the SP was outside the government, and, by this fact, Lacoste was no longer Minister of Algeria.

It was then that the Algiers plot took an open form. Lacoste, who was informed about it, let it go on, hoping that he would be the beneficiary from it. He refused to return to Algeria at a time when constitutionally he still had to assure "current affairs," i.e. public order against the fascists, and in speeches spurred the ultras on to action.

Guy Mollet and the Socialist Parliamentary Group

As soon as the Algiers coup occurred, there could be noted dissonances between the attitude of Guy Mollet and that of the Socialist parliamentary group. The very day of the Algiers coup, May 13th, Guy Mollet was trying to discourage Pflimlin from going through with his appeal to be invested by the National Assembly. The Socialist parliamentary group, on the contrary, which was not aware of this intervention by Guy Mollet, was pushing Pflimlin to ask for this vote by the National Assembly, which granted it to him.

The next day, May 14th, the Socialist group and the Directing Committee decided on participation in the Pflimlin government. "When the Republic appears menaced, the Socialist Party is always present," declared Guy Mollet, who was becoming vice-premier accompanied by other Socialist ministers, among them Jules Moch at the Interior, where ten years before he had distinguished himself by a ferocious repression of the miners' strike.

On May 15th, a joint appeal by the Directing Committee and the parliamentary group:

"The Republic is threatened. Civil and military insurrection in Algeria and the manifesto of General de Gaulle are evidence that the assault against the republican regime has been launched [...] To face this peril, the Socialist Party has decided to participate in the government [...] But the Republic is defended not only in parliament and the government [...]"

But in face of a declaration by de Gaulle, there were to be noted two different attitudes, that of Guy Mol let and that of the spokesman of the Socialist parliamentary group at the National Assembly in its 16 May session. Guy Mollet asked de Gaulle to make an effort:

"It is true that General de Gaulle has given the Republic back to the fatherland [...] We see that Algeria's belonging to our national community is brought into question, and we greatly regret that we do not read the slightest phrase of condemnation of this in General de Gaulle's message. We should need to have the general complete his declaration, clearly insufficient."

Naegelen, in the name of the Socialist group, uttered a condemnation:

"We were expecting something quite different from General de Gaulle. His statement is only an accusation harking back to all candidates for dictatorship in all countries, against the regime of parties [...J Over the head of the parliament elected by the nation, over the head of the legally invested government, over the head of the chief of state, General de Gaulle has addressed the country to say that he is ready to assume the powers of the Republic: this plural is indeed an indication that he is demanding dictatorship. To this overweening pretention, we rise in opposition."

On May 18th, Jules Moch made a thunderous declaration on the radio, alluding to his role as a strike breaker:

"The fate of the Republic is at stake [...] Strengthened by former experience, I can give the assurance that the government will not disappoint or fail in its duty."

Following a new declaration by de Gaulle, which was in part an answer to the solicitation of Guy Mollet, on May 19th, the Socialist parliamentary group and the Directing Committee stated:

"The SP notes that General de Gaulle has demanded powers that would be conferred on him as a result of an exceptional procedure whose modalities he would himself determine, and has thus denied the Constitution of the Republic. The SP has confidence that the government will maintain order and legality, resist all pressures, and maintain national unity within the framework of the Republic."

But on this same day, Pinay announced that he had advised Guy Mollet to make contact — either alone, or, better, together with Pflimlin — with General de Gaulle in order to find out his intentions. But, he added, the vice-premier refused to undertake such an initiative... Indeed!

On May 23rd, on emerging from a meeting of the Socialist group, its president, Deixonne, stated:

"The Socialist group would not lend itself to a compromise from which our freedoms would suffer [...] We will not pay for the return of Algeria to legality by the loss of the Republic [...]"

At this moment still the Socialist group was unanimous. It is true that Lacoste was not present. But on the 24th an article by him appeared in *The new Republic of Bordeaux* (Gaullist), in which he wrote: "I am overwhelmed and filled with admiration" (by what was going on in Algeria).

On May 25th, following on the Ajaccio coup, the SP associated itself with a declaration of the "National Committee for Republican Defense" (Radicals, MRP, SFIO, etc. in which can be read:

"[...] calls on the members of the organizations signing this message to be ready for any eventuality and to consider themselves mobilized for safeguarding our endangered national unity and freedoms."

Late on the 26th, the Socialist parliamentary group voted a resolution supporting the strike decided on by the CGT:

"The group has expressed the wish that the success of the strike launched by the CGT will be aided to the maximum extent. It furthermore hopes that there will be organized tomorrow in Paris a big mass demonstration. The Directing Committee of the party will meet in order to take an official decision and to plan the modalities."

But that did not suit Guy Mollet, and later, on the 27th, the Directing Committee issued the following communiqué:

"The Directing Committee of the SP formally denies the information appearing this morning in certain newspapers according to which it might be taking a decision in favor of demonstrations in agreement with the CP or the CG T. The party's members are asked to con form strictly to the instructions that have been communicated to the federal secretaries."

But for the first time there occurred a division in the Directing Committee, composed of 43 majority Molletists out of 45 members. This text was adopted by 17 votes against 9

During the night of the 26th-27th there occurred an interview between Pflimlin and de Gaulle, and on the 27th de Gaulle made a statement according to which he had begun the process of constituting his government. The same day the Socialist parliamentary group adopted, by 112 votes against 3, and 1 abstention, a manifesto in which it was said:

"General de Gaulle has just made it known that he is undertaking what he calls the "regular process" in view of forming his government."

The Socialist parliamentarians declare:

"[...] 2° that they will in no case rally to the candidacy of General de Gaulle, which, by the very form in which it is posed and by the considerations that accompany it, is and remains under any hypothesis a challenge to republican legality."

Thus, parliamentarily, de Gaulle seemed not to have a chance. On the 28th the great demonstration from the Nation to the Republic took place.

But the same day it was learned that Guy Mollet had got in touch with de Gaulle through the intermediary of a Socialist deputy, Piette, more familiar with certain services than with the class struggle, and that as a result of these relations Guy Mollet (vice-premier, let us not forget) had written de Gaulle a letter, without the knowledge of the premier and naturally with out the knowledge of the Directing Committee of the SP. The text of this letter has never been published. The 29th of May was to be the day of the final maneuvers. Coty was to send a message to parliament. Within the SP Guy Mollet — the bureaucrat — was running the risk of no longer carrying weight with either the Directing Committee or the parliamentary group. So we saw the intervention of the former President of the Republic, Vincent Auriol — the "democrat" — who, in the last previous months, had given his support to the minority against the Guy Mollet leadership. The exchange of letters between Auriol and de Gaulle has been published. It was a maneuver in the grand style to pacify the "consciences" of a few Socialists and republicans.

On May 30th *Le Populaire* was still trying to save appearances:

"In spite of everything, and having weighed all the risks and dangers, the SP will take a position in conformity with its traditions and its past: it will not disavow itself."

The same day Guy Mollet went to de Gaulle's home at Colombey, accompanied by the president of the Socialist parliamentary group, who is not usually mistaken for a master-mind, and who returned convinced. Guy Mollet finally obtained the capitulation of part of the Socialist deputies (among them that swaggerer Jules Moch), enough to give a pseudo-appearance of legality to de Gaulle's accession to power. The powerful demonstration of May 28t pressure on the Directing Committee and on the parliamentary group in the opposite direction to the pressures and maneuvers of the Guy Mollets, Auriols, Lejeunes, *et al.*, who were carrying on a campaign for de Gaulle. It finally ended up in the following votes: Directing Committee and parliamentary group, meeting jointly: 77 for de Gaulle, 74 against. But the figures, broken down, give the following: Directing Committee: 18 for, 23 against; deputies: 40 for, 50 against. It was the Socialist senators who brought about the Gaullist majority.

At the time of de Gaulle's investiture by the National Assembly, the parliamentary group divided up: 42 for de Gaulle, 49 against, 3 absent. True, the deputies who had voted against de Gaulle were not going out side the framework of parliamentary democracy, but such a vote constituted a very hard blow to the Guy Mollet leadership. Mollet himself, furthermore, at one moment turned in his resignation, but withdrew it again soon afterward. Since then, the Directing Committee has decided to postpone the party congress first set for the end of June and to replace it by a national conference.

The minority — who hope to become the majority — are organizing to demand this congress. They are counting on the support of the Socialist International. It is, however, possible that things will not be pushed to a split before the presentation of the draft constitution worked up by the de Gaulle government, about which any ambiguity will be all the less possible in that it can be answered only by a Yes or a No.

Thus the de Gaulle operation was able to be carried out with the complete support of Guy Mollet, accompanied by all his artful dodges as an old maneuver in parliament and at congresses. The SP's general secretary has a seat in the de Gaulle government, and tries thereby to give it a surety of republicanism and liberalism.

The Meaning of the Division in the Socialist Party

Guy Mollet has not only betrayed the working class (that was done long ago; he has betrayed even his own party, whose natural milieu is bourgeois parliamentarianism. Without such a betrayal, de Gaulle could not have had the slightest appearance of legality, he would not have had a parliamentary majority and would have had to push the *coup d'etat* to the point where it fully took on the aspect of a military intervention against the National Assembly.

The resultant situation within the SP, the state of split that has aroused savage rightists against Guy Mollet, has something very surprising about it. But this situation is quite explicable.

The SP, at the Liberation, found itself with a diminished working-class base, especially among the most decisive layers of the working class that went over to the FCP. But the place occupied by the SP on the chess-board of the Fourth Republic guaranteed it (save for a short period) a key position in governments, and caused various currents to converge on this party. In the south of France, it replaced in some areas the Radical Party, with a petty-bourgeois peasant electoral base. In addition, while at the time of the Third Republic it already had a clientele of petty functionaries schoolteachers, postal employees...), after 1945 it saw its ranks swelled by high and middle functionaries (prefects, governors of colonies, ministerial administrative assistants...) who came to it especially to aid their careers.

In this situation it was automatic that the SP tops, already far from the working-class ranks, were going to become even more strongly bourgeoisified. In appearance, the SP had succeeded in winning important positions in the state. The reality was that the state had topped the SP, and the apparatus created by Guy Mollet was often very close to the state apparatus.

The recent crisis tends to break up what was, socially speaking, artificially united. In spite of where it has been led by ministerial participations, the SP, by its origins and by the place it occupies in the political structure of France, had remained the traditional reformist workers' party, whose existence is fundament ally bound up with that of parliamentary democracy. It would be wrong to claim that the lines of the present division are already unchangeable and that they are of impeccable class purity. But the resistance to de Gaulle has shown itself there where the SP has a serious working-class base or clientele, whereas the careerists were turning toward de Gaulle. A remarkable example was afforded during the crisis by the Nord Federation. It is, together with that of the Pas-de-Calais, the most numerous in the SP, one of the most rightist and anti-communist. For years Guy Mollet was guaranteed a majority in his party just by the addition of a few votes to those of these two federations. The Nord Federation was at all times one of the most hostile to any united front with the CP, even in the short periods of collaboration at the time of the 1935-1936 Popular Front and the 1944-1946 Liberation. But on May 27th the Socialist Nord Federation supported the strike order given by the CGT miners' union.

We shall certainly see some comings-and-goings among the Socialist deputies and leaders in the next months; but on the organizational level, the tendency that will stand out is that of the SP appearing as the reformist workers' party, struggling to defend or restore the parliamentary frame that is its natural working milieu.

Thanks to such a change, essential questions like that of the Communist-Socialist united front will appear in a new aspect.

II: The Communist Party

The policy of the French CP, majority party of the working class since the Liberation, has since that period had a steady line which, in the same way as that of the SP, caused the recent defeat.

Thorez claims priority in the conception of the parliamentary "new paths" toward socialism. We shall leave verification of the matter to those whom the question might interest, but there is no doubt that the whole policy that he has followed since the Liberation was — even during a few leftist jolts basically parliamentary, and nowise aimed at going on to a society building socialism. In fact, during the whole period elapsed since the Liberation, the FCP leadership has never stopped saying that the alternative for France was not capitalism or socialism, but democracy or fascism. It would be easy to give several pages of quotations from reports to the Political Bureau. As we shall see further on, the FCP leadership persists in the same conception even after de Gaulle's arrival at power.

This policy is explained above all by a lining up with Moscow, which constantly seeks maintenance of the status quo. That implies a bourgeois France in which the FCP tries to aid a bourgeois wing less dependent on Washington, anti-American if possible. Because of this, it can be said without exaggeration that, though the FCP leadership criticized the authoritarian conceptions of de Gaulle, it has long handled him person ally with kid gloves because of certain hopes the Kremlin had in him. Let us not forget that Thorez was a minister of de Gaulle, and that at that period — on his return from Moscow — he made the "patriotic workers' militias" dissolve and give up their arms, in order that there might be "a single army, a single police, a single state" (Thorez, Ivry Speech, 1945).

When de Gaulle, after giving up power, made a first political incursion in 1947 against the "system," the then editor-in-chief of l'Humanite was censured be cause he had allowed himself to engage in a mere irreverent pleasantry against de Gaulle. Even during the last period of the crisis, de Gaulle was never treated on the same level as the Soustelles and Massus. The slogans for the May 28th and June 1st demonstrations were to spare de Gaulle any harsh epithets. And anyone could note the deferential and respectful attitude of the Communist deputies in the National Assembly when de Gaulle presented himself there for his investiture and later for the vote of the project granting the power to prepare a new constitution.

The search for bourgeois allies had led the FCP leadership to the worst of betrayals, that of the Algerian revolution. The FCP's variations in this matter have been numerous, but it has never made recognition, frank and consistent in application of policy, of independence for Algeria. We refer our readers to the document written on this question by the FLN itself, which we published in our last issue. It is the most crushing indictment, showing that the FCP's policy was never in conformity with the principles professed by this party in the name of Marxism-Leninism on the colonial question. Since then we have seen even during the crisis — the FCP deputies again vote "full powers" to Pflimlin, who was flaunting his intention of carrying out a more intense military action in Algeria and who turned these "full powers" over to General Salan the orders of the "Public Safety Committee" of Algiers and not those of the Pflimlin government.

"L'Humanite" Day By Day

Let us see how the FCP evaluated the events then taking place and what policy it followed. The main accent was laid on parliamentary action. On May 13th, the coup de force at Algiers. The same day, investiture of Pilimlin. The Communist group abstained, making the following declaration:

"The proposed premier having affirmed the desire of his government to continue the war in Algeria, the source of all the evils from which the country is suffering, the Communist group decides not to grant him its votes. But at the hour when, faced by the riots in Algiers and by generals entered into rebellion against the Republic, the proposed premier declares that he will not yield to the factious coup de force, the Communist deputies unanimously decide on voluntary abstention from voting, thus giving the government a possibility of being formed."

Thus it was above all on the "firmness" of the government and the parliament that the FCP leadership was laying its stake.

The mass meeting at the Cirque d'Hiver planned for the 14th was prohibited by this "firm" republican government. The FCP leadership simply accepted this prohibition and sent its functionaries to disperse those who had come in spite of the prohibition: The slogan was:

"Go back to your neighbor hoods, disperse, go find other republicans to pre pare the answer to the fascist coup de force." (L'Humanite, 15 May)

May 15th: first declaration by de Gaulle exploiting and encouraging the coup de force at Algiers. *L'Humanite* promptly published an extra, in which were recommended, among other things, appeals to Coty:

"Multiply, by thousands and thousands, protests to the President of the Republic, for safeguarding the Republic."

May 16th: the government obtained the vote of the state of emergency (including the Communist votes), which was never to be used against Algiers or de Gaulle, but only to prevent any interventions by the workers.

In *L'Humanite* of May 17th, an article by Fajon, member of the Political Bureau, the director of the newspaper, presented this vote as a victory for democracy:

"In the great combat undertaken to bar the road to de Gaulle and military dictatorship, yesterday was a good day [...] By launching theft attack against the Republic four days ago, de Gaulle and his accomplices thought they would win without striking a blow. Their coup did not come off. It is democracy that has won a first great victory."

May 19th: press conference by de Gaulle, who was taking one step forward toward power. In answer to this conference, a Political Bureau statement of the same day affirmed: "Victories have been won. For five days fascism has been held in check."

May 20th: the National Assembly voted special powers for Algeria, powers entrusted by Pfllinlin to Salan. The Communist deputies voted in favor.

In *L'Humanite* of May 21st, an editorial by Pierre Courtade thus commented on this vote:

"It was a good day [...] The Republic is asserting itself. It is winning not only time which was only twenty-four hours ago a dramatic necessity —it is growing stronger [...] We are stronger today than yesterday. And the whole left is with us. So is the Republic which will emerge improved from this test."

In *L'Humanite* of May 22nd, an editorial by Waldeck-Rochet, a Political Bureau member, who repeated the argumentation of Courtade:

"The National Assembly condemned the men of the plot by according immense majorities to the nation's legitimate government which, despite its weaknesses, has stated that it wants to fight for the respect of republican legality [...] Last Tuesday's vote on the special powers enabled the government to consolidate its position."

An editorial by Fajon in L'Humanite of May 23rd:

"On the parliamentary level, [our party] has given the Pflimlin government the possibility of getting formed, next of obtaining the means it demanded in order to defend republican legality, and finally of consolidating itself as a result of massive votes. **Thus the danger has retreated.** [Our emphasis]"

On May 25th, far from retreating, the danger was expressed by the coup de force at Ajaccio. Beginning with this moment, the FCP's leadership was to raise timid protests toward the Pfllmlin government: it is not energetic enough, it does not turn to the country...

L'Humanite of May 26th: "The government limits itself to yesterday's timid decisions."

L'Humanite of May 27th, in a report on the previous day's speech in parliament by Duclos: "The government has fallen behind the state of mind of the republican country..."

But on this same day de Gaulle made a new declaration that openly announced that he had made official contacts with members of the government, that he had set going the process that would bring him to power.

At the National Assembly, Duclos spoke up to say to Pflimlin: you want to leave and make place for de Gaulle. But the conclusion to such a quite correct affirmation was just simply: we shall vote in favor of your project of reactionary revision of the constitution.

On May 28th, when Coty turned officially to de Gaulle, the Political Bureau, in a statement, was still counting parliamentary noses: "Yesterday there were only 165 supporters of de Gaulle at the Assembly, whereas 408 votes were cast for the defense of the Republic."

Thus the emphasis was put on the firmness to be given to the official authorities of the Republic to defeat the plot of the rebels. And, what is more, it was announced day after day that this parliamentary policy was winning successes.

Beginning with May 13th — if we are to believe *L'Humanite* directly inspired by the FCP's Political Bureau we were going from success to success against fascism, the Pflimlin government and the parliament were growing stronger in their determination to defend the republic, and then suddenly, at the very moment when several hundreds of thousands of workers were demonstrating in the streets of Paris, an accident happened: the government collapsed, the parliament capitulated, and Gaullism carried the day While the deputies were carrying on the battle "for the Republic" by supporting a government which, in the shadows, was conspiring de Gaulle's coming to power, what was asked of the workers?

The most current term, "vigilance," in practice meant most of the time immobilization in headquarters. Street demonstrations were cut down, and, when the authorities forbade them, called off.

There were work stoppages, strikes, but these were carried out in a sporadic way, without coordination, and never with the perspective of an active general strike that would bring about a conflict with the state forces that were raising de Gaulle to power.

On the whole, the workers' actions were subordinated either to the parliamentary and legalistic tactic to ward the Pflimlin government, or to the intentions and decisions of the other "republican" groups.

Toward the Bourgeois Tops

This whole policy, in the opposite direction to the real evolution of the class, found its expression in the mammoth demonstration of May 28th.

The coup of Algiers occurred on May 13th. Demonstrations had taken place in various provincial cities, but working-class Paris had not demonstrated in any force. What was going on? The FCP leadership did not dare issue in its own name alone a call for a big street demonstration: it knew that a call from itself alone — would not have produced much of an echo. Formally there was no joint appeal, there was no united front, for the leaders of the left bourgeois organizations and the Socialist Party, of Force Ouvriere and the CFTC, rejected any agreement with the Stalinist leaders. Granted, there were tacit agreements, and the Radical and Socialist leaders were well aware, when they launched the call for the demonstration of 28 May, that the FCP and the CGT would join in it.

The masses answered on May 28th because for them it was in fact a question of a joint Communist-Socialist demonstration. While all the leaders, from the bourgeois to the Stalinists, were still in agreement that there should be no shout or banner other than "Long live the Republic," the Paris workers were spontaneously shouting: Popular Front, Unity of action, The left to power, Peace in Algeria. For the workers, Popular Front has another meaning than what it has for the leaders. For the workers, the Popular Front is in fact Communist-Socialist unity in action, for down in the ranks they see only a few Radical shopkeepers to whom they attach no importance, and they do not grasp the role of the bourgeois leaders at the Popular Front's summit.

The FCP leadership, therefore, lined up with some uncertain parliamentary top people, and was way behind the aspirations of the masses.

It did not try to correct itself either the next day or in the following days. But, when de Gaulle's coming to power became sure for June 1st, it decided to cover up its whole opportunistic policy by an operation of a pseudo-leftist appearance, street demonstrations in which only members of the party were in practice to participate, in order to be able to say that only the party had fought to the end and that the defeat was owing to the others.

Like the Bourbons

Soon after the end of the crisis, on June 9th and 10th, there was held a session of the Central Committee of the FCP, in which the leadership showed that, like the Bourbons, it had learned nothing and forgotten nothing. The champions of self-criticism found that everything had been very good, that the leadership had been clear-sighted, that the party had showed itself to be a "fine party," and that it should just go on as in the past.

When Thorez said that he had a "fine party," he specified immediately what he meant thereby: the apparatus has not experienced break-ups like those in 1939-1940. Thorez perhaps spoke too soon.

There are *two* explanations by the FCP leaders about what has just happened. In his closing speech at this CC meeting, Thorez said:

"A crisis of the regime opened and has wound up in the formation of a government of personal dictatorship which opens the way to fascism.

"The army, in its present composition, has taken on more and more the aspect of praetorian troops, it has been led more and more to set itself above the nation.

"The Gaullist plot is the sign, not of the strength of the bourgeoisie, but of its weakness. By having recourse to personal power, to dictatorship, it recognizes that it is unable to guarantee its domination any longer by traditional means. It makes the confession of its impotence to solve the problems of its own decline, by which it is assailed."

In an article in the June 21st Humanite, devoted to Algeria, he repeats the same explanation:

"The malfunctioning of institutions was not the deep cause of the crisis that France is passing through. It was, rather, the expression an sign thereof. The dominant reality was and re mains [...] the incapacity of the ruling classes to solve the problems posed by our epoch. First of all must be emphasized their impotence of the questions raised by the general crisis of colonialism."

Thus the profound cause is capitalism, unable to solve the problems of the period, whose weakness force to throw itself into the desperate measures of dictator ship. Quite right.

But here is another explanation in the resolution adopted by the same CC:

"The cause of the evils from which France is suffering is neither democracy nor the parliamentary regime, but on the contrary the permanent violation, by anti-communism, of the wishes of universal suffrage and the principles of the representative regime."

It is no longer the incapacity of the bourgeoisie, but the bad way in which parliamentarism is applied. But by whom, if not by the representatives of the bourgeoisie, and precisely because parliament is no longer a good instrument for capitalist domination?

And so, instead of calling on the proletariat to solve the problems by the seizure of power and the building of socialism, Thorez declared to the CC: "What is necessary is to correct that bad application that has been made of institutions and to guarantee at last their normal functioning."

And the C resolution specifies:

"The remedy for governmental disorder and impotence does not consist in throwing democracy overboard, but on the contrary in guaranteeing its normal functioning by reestablishing the country's independence and by giving the working class and its party, side-by-side with the others, the place belonging to it in parliament and in the government. Nothing but its place, but its full place [...] The choice is not between fascism and communism. It is between a personal dictatorship backed by reaction and militarism leading to fascism, and a regime of democracy so as to carry out the policy desired by the majority of Frenchmen."

What impeccable reasoning! The bourgeoisie is incapable of solving problems by the parliamentary regime. It is therefore necessary to go back to this regime, while asking the bourgeoisie only to give the working class — read, the FCP leadership — the place belonging to it in the bourgeois parliament also a few seats in the government.

At the CC session held some weeks before the crisis the reporter Servin was explaining that it could be a question of fighting for socialism because the relationship of forces was not in favor of the working class, which was weak. Now the FCP leadership explains the reactionary *coup de force* by the weakness of the bourgeoisie. But in any case, whether the relationship of forces between the proletariat and the bourgeoisie is in one direction or the other, for the FCP leadership it is never the moment to put the struggle for power on the order of the day. In fact the situation in France has shown that the parliamentary regime is at its last gasp, and that as the Communist International declared in its early years either the working class would go over to the attack on the regime, or else capitalism, savagely defending its domination over society, would not hesitate to go beyond parliamentary forms to install regimes of open dictatorship.

The evolution of the Stalinists on the question of workers' power is truly significant. At the beginning of the struggle against the Left Opposition in the years 1923-1929, the proletarian revolution was, according to them, on the order of the day in economically advanced countries, but not in underdeveloped countries like China. Thirty years later, when capital ism has been broken as a social system over a third of the globe, including China, socialism is no longer on the order of the day even in the advanced capitalist countries of Western Europe!

Now let us see how the FCP leadership proposes to carry on the struggle against the rising dictatorship:

"All toilers, all democrats, all adversaries of personal power, owe it to themselves, from now on, to prepare a massive NO by our people at the time of the October consultation. The organization of this great campaign from now on dominates all our activity." (Thorez)

"They will fight with all their energy both for peace in Algeria and so that, at the time of the referendum, universal suffrage will say no to the personal and military dictatorship that would open the road to fascism." (Thorez)

Against the violence of the parachutists, against the armed might of the bourgeois state, the FCP leadership opposes... universal suffrage, in this case by answering *no* in a plebiscite, i.e. a mockery of universal suffrage itself.

The FCP leadership had praised to high heaven the conception of the "new paths," i.e. the use of parliament to build socialism. But in fact there is no more parliament. How, even if one accepts the perspective of a reestablishment of bourgeois parliamentarism, an illusory perspective, how can it be arrived at without recourse to violence? The leadership is a prisoner of its parliamentary and legalistic conception just at the moment when its preferred instrument has ceased to function. The FCP leadership has not brought the slightest criticism to bear on its conception of the "new paths" it has not even retained a certain reservation which it had introduced into its conception, namely, that violence must be resorted to if the bourgeoisie resorts to it. By omitting, after the Algiers coup, this part of its conception of the "new paths," the FCP leadership shows that for it what was in question there was just a stylistic clause, without any real value, that it had just plain settled down into bourgeois parliamentarism, and that it was no more concerned about the fight for socialism than the SP leadership was.

The FCP leadership believed that it could profit by this period of crisis and the days immediately following, in order to strike blows at oppositionals, engaging particularly in expulsions in the intellectual circles where for so long now it has wanted to strike. This bureaucratic offensive, however, happened to be topped by the bureaucratic offensive of the Kremlin, signalized by the assassination of Imre Nagy and his companions. Soviet intervention in Hungary had much cut off the FCP from other labor and socialist formations of all tendencies. Events in France — the war of Algeria, the reactionary danger, and finally de Gaulle's coming to power had not permitted it to surmount this situation, but at least openings had been created. This time its cutting-off threatens to be irremediable, for the feeling of broad layers of workers is: With you? why, that would be worse than de Gaulle. Truly Khrushchev has worked for de Gaulle better than anybody could have done.

A New Stage

A stage in the history of the French workers' movement, opened at the Liberation, is now closed. After having had the possibility at that moment to set up, almost without striking a blow, a Socialist-Communist government that would have opened the road to the European socialist revolution, that movement was led by these two leaderships of ill omen to see de Gaulle come "coldly" to dictatorship.

The slope to climb back up will be hard to scale. French capitalism has occupied controlling positions from which it can be dislodged only by the action of the working class raised to the highest level. All the old political formations set up in the Third and Fourth Republics will undergo shakings-up, overturns, and disappearances. There must be added to them the old workers' leaderships which — originating at different periods out of the class struggle — have, under different forms, settled down into the parliamentary political world of French society. We are entering in to an era of struggles, of splits, and of regroupments in these old formations. The present background of defeat will generate difficulties during a whole period for the revolutionary Marxist current and for those who will try to find a line of revolutionary behavior again. But at a later stage, that cannot be far off, the exigencies of the objective situation will on the contrary operate in the direction of a pitiless elimination of half-measures, of unfinished ideas, of timorous thinking, and will stimulate the creation of a new leadership capable of leading the revolutionary struggle for the seizure of power.

PIERRE FRANK

The Algiers putsch of April 22

The recent putsch in Algiers attempted by a few Generals and Colonels followed a number of attempted armed coups which, since 1956, have aimed to modify the policy and regime in France. From February 6th 1956 to May 13th 1958 these armed coups have succeeded in imposing the policy of so-called "French-Algeria", and the elimination of Parliamentary democracy.[49]

Since May 13th 1958 these armed coups have neither reversed the regime of the Fifth Republic, nor reversed the march of Algeria towards self determination -- towards independence.

Until May 13th 1959 these coups succeeded, thanks to the union of the European-Algerians and the army, combined with the wearing down of the democratic regime and the needs of Big Capital for a power "independent" of French society. Once de Gaulle was installed in power this combination was not maintained. We will come later to the attitude of the bourgeoisie in France. For, whatever they did in Algiers, the army (the professionals of course) wanted to maintain an Algeria indissolubly tied to France and did not want to serve the *particular* reactionary interests of the European-Algerians. It is this which explains both their attitude of wait and see in January 1960, when Lagaillard and Ortiz attempted the "coup des barricades" in Algiers and their recent attempted putsch, prepared entirely in the back room, truly as a "Kriegspiel", outside any ties with the political formations of the "ultras" of France and Algeria, and of all preparations of a political order — unless one calls a few plastic bombs preparation of a political order...

We see once again, as in the whole post-war period, that fascism has been revealed to be extremely feeble. In France itself it reached its height as a movement with Poujadism, which grouped the generally old and small merchants ousted by the capitalist concentration in certain underdeveloped regions, but who never dared attack the workers' organisations. In Algeria it was more important; it was founded on the desperate resistance of the Europeans to the rising colonial revolution.

---

[49] This article appeared in the Amsterdam-published *Fourth International*.

But there also without the support of the army it would not have been very important. Fascism has not known a serious development in the post-war period except in the very particular form of the transformation of an important part of the professional army into a political faction, seeing in the "subversive war" and the "psychological war" the means of bringing an end to communism and the colonial war.

Bonaparte and his sword

De Gaulle was brought to power following the coup of May 13th 1958, but as we said at the time he was not at all a political representative of the forces which made the operation.[50] He came to power pushed by a small but dynamic wing of Big Capital which has modernised the basic industries in France but which, in order to carry out its work, must accelerate the process of concentration in light industry, in distribution and in the countryside, and which finds the parliamentary regime a big obstacle on this road. De Gaulle was installed following an old political tradition — that of Bonapartism — as an arbiter above society. The Bonapartism of de Gaulle uses well the philosophy of the "Grandeur" of France but he does not hold the sword that is to say the army — firmly in his hand. On the one side there is no lack of officers of the old school still imbued with Petainism and who have not forgotten that in June 1940 de Gaulle gave a dangerous example of disobedience. On the ether side, there is the young neo-fascist school of "expeditious and limited savoir faire" who reproach de Gaulle with selling out the Empire in the manner of Mendes-France.

From May 13th de Gaulle sought by all sorts of manoeuvres, tricks and corruption (promotions, dismissals. . .) to take the army in hand and make it an instrument of his "strong State".

He did not fail as well to give a new reason for its existence. If, with the march of events, France must let go the ballast of the Colonies, he, de Gaulle, will keep it in the ranks of a Great Power, creating that which at present is the mark of a Great Power, that is, atomic weapons and not colonies. Amongst other things the "striking force" serves to regroup around de Gaulle the most technical part of the army far removed from the memories of Diên Biên Phu[51] But, this

---

50 See various articles in the *Fourth International* and also Frank's 1958 introduction to the French edition of "Whither France" by L. Trotsky (Reprinted in the February 1969 number of *Quatrieme Internationale*).
51   Diên Biên Phu was the climactic battle of the First Indochina War between the French army and Viet Minh communist revolutionaries. The battle occurred between

attempt to take over control of the army by these means will prove in vain. If it is true that the adventure of Challe, Salan, et al, failed quickly and miserably, it is no less true that the plot was widespread in the army and that only the course of circumstances prevented the participation of a larger number of officers implicated in the plot.

Also, this time, under the cover of a few arrests and of a certain number of sanctions, de Gaulle proceeds with a much more serious plan. He is obliged to dissolve the units which constitutes the spearhead of the French army -- the four day putsch itself contributed to the breaking up of the army. De Gaulle clearly felt the danger of the putsch and he did not hesitate to appeal to the troops to refuse to obey all rebel officers, *even when they were involved in operations against the FLN*, to crush the military plot if necessary with arms. Never have the "democrats" and the workers' parties dared go so far, not even on May 13th 1958.

The greatest obstacle the "putschists" encountered in Algeria were the conscripts. They did not act as a malleable mass, who would be sympathetic to the sentiments of the European. Algerians, and would not oppose the plot. From the beginning the conscripts were hostile to the armed coup. The resistance first of all manifested itself as inertia, passivity, in front of the orders of the rebels and here and there an active resistance. The appeal of de Gaulle gave to all soldiers who wanted to act against their officers a point of support.

The remaining rebels rapidly retreated with the regiment's professional soldiers whom they used to commence the operation. One sees now in the army a number of signs of distrust, of refusal o serve under the orders of those officers who have been dilatory in the course of the putsch. In short to the growing distrust between the officers and de Gaulle, is now added distrust between the troops and the officers.

The "strong state"

The same dubious attitude of the military cadres is rife in the other armed forces of the State (police...) and this explains why on the evening of Sunday 23rd April panic reigned in the high apparatus of the State, and why, after de Gaulle's "aidez-moi" appeal to the French people, Debré appealed to the people to oppose the Parachutists whom, he thought, threatened to land within a few hours. This is why the ministers such as Malraux and Frey were forced to form a militia of odds and ends, and why the "government" closed it' eyes, more or less, to the possibility of the formation of workers' militias. The

---

March and May 1954 and culminated in a comprehensive French defeat that influenced negotiations over the future of Indochina at Geneva.

attitude of the manager of Renault in his relations with the trade union organisations, more particularly with the CGT, was at least ambiguous on this point for some hours. It is hardly necessary to say that, once the danger became remote, the government recovered itself and even swaggered, attributing to itself all the merits of success. In fact, within a few hours, all the mystique of the "Strong State", spread abundantly for nearly three years, had collapsed.

The Bourgeoisie and De Gaulle

In the course of this operation, amongst other things was shown the isolation of the regime even with regard to large layers of the bourgeoisie, both middle and big. Incontestably these layers were not favourable to a coup d'Etat. Business goes well — why upset the market? But at the same time these layers did not show any solidarity towards de Gaulle. The Conseil National du Patronat Français (National Council of French Employers) only made a declaration against all disturbances of order three days after the collapse of the putsch. The Confédération des Petites et Moyennes Entre prises (Confederation of Small and Medium Enterprises) made no declaration. The Confederation Général des Cadres (General Confederation of Managerial Staff) was not associated with the strike of April 24th, refusing, they said, to participate in a political movement. The organisation par excellence of people of influence, the Independants et Paysans, made no declaration, and its General Secretary, Duchet, refused as Mayor of his commune to send a pro-de Gaulle declaration. He has since left his post as General Secretary but this does not cancel out the fact that he expressed the sentiments of large layers of the well-established bourgeoisie, who accept de Gaulle as a last resort. The political editor of "Le Monde", Jacques Fauvet, who conveys with a slight Leftish touch the positions of the intelligently conservative bourgeois strata, in a conversation with some journalists, replied as follows to the question: "If de Gaulle was to disappear what would remain of this regime?"

"Nothing! For the time being, nothing!... I believe that de Gaulle has been necessary to set the affairs of Algeria in order. The suspension of certain democratic forms was also a necessity... But we shall not he committed much longer to this road and wait first for Algerian affairs to be solved, and second for de Gaulle to go. Afterwards we shall see!"

How much is expressed in these few words! The cynicism of a bourgeoisie rich in political experience lends support to the impression that de Gaulle will go once the affair of Algeria is settled.

PIERRE FRANK

The attitude of the working class and its organisations to the putsch

Faced with the rising of the army the "Strong Government" turned towards the working class. Their reply was rapid and firm. Not only was the strike of April 24th general, the demonstrations large, but the slogans launched by the CGT and the FCP for arms and militias were accepted without difficulty, even though the same organisations in the past and again on May 13th 1958, denounced as "provocateurs" those who advanced such a policy.[52]

It is not sufficient to say that the working class reacted immediately against the fascist putsch, it is necessary to analyse their feelings and reactions more fully. Generally, though there is much resolution among the workers and though one does not doubt they would have faced this show of force without weakening, nevertheless, at the same time, they have been deprived of any of the enthusiasm which is normally associated with combat, and they have been very preoccupied with making clear that their action cannot be considered as political support for dc Gaulle. It is true that the FCP and CGT and, in the same way, the PSU have denounced the Gaullist regime which has placed the leaders oi the putsch in the highest positions, whereas the leaders of the SFIO, FO, CFTC have lined themselves up behind de Gaulle. But this anti-dc Gaulle feeling has developed over the years just gone and this explains largely the lack of enthusiasm which marked the workers' intervention.

At the same time as denouncing the responsibilities of de Gaulle, these organisations did not develop the least perspective for the workers. To them it is obviously necessary to bar the way to a military dictatorship. But, this done, one comes up again against de Gaulle. And afterwards? In actual fact the FCP, CGT, and PSU have all brought forward the "Defense of the Republic", the watchword of the

---

[52] The recourse to the slogans of arms and of militias does not signify any change in the conceptions of the FCP on the "parliamentary and pacifist road" to Socialism, as one could to verify a few days later at the 16th Congress of FCP. These slogans were launched under pressure of these very same events which led the government, faced with the possible landing of the Parachutists, to add to its appeal to resist, the necessity not to do this with empty hands. Moreover the leaders of the FCP and the CGT launched these slogans in a very legalistic manner, demanding arms from the Government, and leaving it at that. At no time was this step intended as a maneuver to make better understood these slogans in the way Lenin so powerfully expressed it: "Arm the workers with the desire to arm themselves." All this being stated, it is nevertheless clear that the use of these slogans even in the way it has been done can lead much further than is the wish of leaders who, in their past career have gone no further than to call the masses to insurrection to replace Marshall Petain with General de Gaulle. More than one militant thinks that an opportunity was lost once in 1945, and that that was already too much.

socialists, the Gaullists, the MRP and all the other opponents of the putsch. The FCP have forgotten to propagate their "renewed democracy" and the PSU the "socialist front." These organisations forgot, at this crucial time, the pivot of their policies; this alone suffices to show their feebleness. Let us add that the right wing of the PSU has gone further, it joined the "left Gaullists" in their effort towards the Minister of the Interior to get arms.

Finally these organisations in Paris bowed to the decisions of a government whose powerlessness was evident, they did not ignore a government ban on street demonstrations at a time when millions of workers left their work and would have responded in very great numbers to an appeal for street demonstrations. Only the students ignored the government ban and once again in this period showed themselves acting as the advance guard, leaving behind the traditional leaders.

The suspicion of the workers towards the government was expressed as early as the day after the collapse of the putsch by a stepping up of the wages drive. There had been, a short time before the putsch, many demonstrations over wage demands. Halted during the four days which it lasted, they were taken up immediately it came to an end. But, at this moment, the reformist top TU leadership of the FO and of the CFTC in order to be forgiven for making a certain rapprochement with the CGT and the communists, wished give a breathing space to the government and the bosses. The workers would not listen to this. This was very clear in the Paris transport undertakings. Though the workers in this industry are very divided from a trade union point-of-view (twenty-odd unions) which meant that in the past these movements did not happen except when a limited unity of action was realised by the principal unions, this time the appeal of a single union, the CGT, produced twice the number of strikers. The same day the railway workers, encouraged by the CGT and the CFTC, largely brought the traffic in the whole country to a halt. In the factories numerous demonstrations sprang up, initially for better wages.

However important this surge of wage claims might be, however promising it could be for the cohesion of the working classes and for their future struggles, one must not mistake its limits, it must be placed in the framework of the regime. It is from de Gaulle they are demanding an in crease. It is not, but must become, a battle against the regime.

PIERRE FRANK

Once more in search of the "strong state"

The general effect of this situation: the feebleness of fascism, the indifference of the bourgeoisie, the working class affected politically by the disillusionment of the post-war period, the defeat of the 13th May, and the flabbiness of the traditional leaderships, gives to French political life a rarefied atmosphere in which the personality of de Gaulle takes on a particular importance, and which also gives him, in spite of the narrowness of his support in the country, a significant amount of room to manoeuvre in internal policies. The putsch has much enfeebled French imperialism by dislocating its army, but present day political conditions in France mean that in the immediate future in internal affairs it will be de Gaulle who will hold the political initiative and -derive an advantage from the operation. Realising at the same time his strengths and his weaknesses de Gaulle has brought into play article 16 of the Constitution, which consists precisely of suppressing all legal or judicial rule and of giving all power to de Gaulle, of installing in French society completely arbitrary government.

The pretext is that it is very convenient for the suppression of the instigators of the putsch. But nobody doubts that it will translate itself into some measures, probably quite stringent, but extremely limited, against the fascist Right, and into play article 16 of the Constitution, which of the political revolutionary vanguard of the working class and the intelligentsia.

Has de Gaulle succeeded in building his "Strong State"? If he has only the traditional leaderships he will he able to achieve this. But there are, throughout the world, problems much less easy to deal with than these leaders. In the first place, there is Algeria. It was seen in what an unpredictable way the Evian encounter was prepared. The downfall of the would-be fascists of 1960 and 1961 has not advanced things more than in a very limited fashion. On the one hand de Gaulle has not renounced the at tempt to conserve the serious holdings of French capitalism in Algeria; he still has remote 'hopes of what the men of the GPRA will sign and accept, even if, under the pressures exerted on them from all sides, they show themselves unwilling to make extended concessions. For there are the Algerian people whose aspirations are growing more and more radical. In spite of the chatter of a sycophant press de Gaulle appreciates the negotiations in an aura of enfeebled power, for he has had to strike at the unity of the army which throughout the past years has to de Gaulle and the fact that French Imperial ism has accepted its defeat in Algeria. We must therefore expect long negotiations before agreement can be reached. During this period one could think that the political re awakening witnessed on the Left in France would grow, nourishing itself precisely on the resistance to de Gaulle and the fact that French Imperialism has accepted its defeat in Algeria.

More long-term perspectives

Political re-awakening, let us say, but without having illusions with regard to its extension and rhythm in the most immediate period, all the more that the good economic conjuncture con tributes to maintaining a settled situation.

Nevertheless many elements are preparing for a more active political future, as much on the Right as on the Left.

On the Right we have seen a series of defeats of a particular form of fascism. It is possible that the putsch of the 22nd April is the last important political action -- exclusive of some "plastic" bombs. But fascism will find itself new forms later on when the independence of Algeria is recognised. Ex-officers returned to civil life, European-Algerians who have left Algeria, petty-bourgeois nursing the humiliation of the "selling out" of the Empire, others displaced by the growing concentration of capitalism, will furnish a clientele for the fascist politicians. The danger of a conquest of power by the fascists in the longer run seems to us very limited, but one must expect intense fascist political activity, so much the more acceptable to capitalism because they would wish to counterbalance a resumption of political activity of the working class.

On this side, from now on, the re-awakening of which we have spoken, although it seems feeble, manifests itself above all on the level of a critical approach, in two groups of great importance for the future: the militant workers and the youth, student youth more particularly.

Although Mollet and Thorez continue to boast, each in his own party, the crisis of the lack of confidence grows and deepens. As far as the FCP is concerned the unanimity of the Congress no longer succeeds in disguising the misgivings of the great majority, the irreducible disagreements of a minority.

Although cut short, the Casanova - Servin affair reflected this state of things in the party apparatus. The perspective of "renewed democracy", the question of the "roads to socialism" are problems which pose themselves to a growing number of militant communists.

It is among the youth that one feels a growing political interest which is not at all conformist either towards the government or to wards the old leaderships. Instinctively it is towards revolutionary solutions that a vanguard turns, disgusted with the policies pursued by these leaders. One remembers the affair of the 121 intellectuals recognising the right of "insoumission" (i.e., refusal to he conscripted into the army). The role played by the conscripts in the debacle of the recent putsch allowed those who, inside the workers' movement had denounced this demonstration, namely the leaders of the FCP. to say: "We advised you, you should not have deserted, you should have done work inside the army!". This "argument" does not take into account a certain number of facts: First, the position of the 121 could not be a call for a mass action, it was a demonstration of op position towards war in Algeria aimed at an awakening of the public opinion which no political leadership with a mass influence called upon for action; second, the "insoumis" and deserters were the result of this inefficient leadership and treason after six years of war! Third, as for the work of these organisations inside the army, it never existed; the conscripts reacted spontaneously, under the pressure of weariness towards war in Algeria, which is felt by most French people, and of the desire not to help people whom they know pretty well ('paras", "legionnaires" and also the European-Algerians) and whom they hate.

But if the organised workers' movement has no direct responsibility in the attitude of the conscripts during the putsch, one 'may say, with out fear to contradiction, that the young men who have made such an experiment in Algeria, however short this experiment may have been, will certainly stay profoundly influenced there by and that later there will be repercussions inside the workers' movement. The attack against Order in its most oppressive form, the military hierarchy, cannot but lead to a capacity to stand against disfigured forms of the bourgeois order as are the apparatus of the organizations established in this society.

New generations are arising to political life, in a climate of oppression and stifling of political thought both by the regime and the old leaderships. They reach political life with much con fusion resulting from the whole policy and teaching of the old leaderships. But at the same time they are rebelling against these policies, these teachings.

The putsch which recently failed, struck a big blow against French imperialism, obliging it to chop off a part of its armed forces. It will have contributed also in allowing thousands and tens of thousands of young people to have an unforgettable experience which will stimulate in them the spirit of criticism and rebellion. It was not bad that Reaction should have made a faux pas. Unfortunately benefits will not be immediate, except for de Gaulle, but they will nevertheless exist in the future.

Mr. X Versus de Gaulle

The French Left Unveils Their Candidate Mr. X

PARIS, Jan. 15 – Since the arrival of de Gaulle to power, political life in France has been almost nonexistent. The few referendums and elections have left the masses largely indifferent, preoccupied as they are with the daily struggle (The figure for strike days during 1963 was the highest in ten years.) The workers' parties receive big votes in the elections but mobilize nobody.[53]

However, the so-called opposition of the left; that is, under the circumstances, the clubs of the politicians, top functionaries, etc., feels that a means has been found to revive political life. This is around the election of the President of the Republic.

It is more than 110 years since a President of the Republic was elected by universal suffrage. The experience of the Second Republic with the election of the man who was to become the second Bonaparte (see Karl Marx, *The 18th Brumaire of Louis Bonaparte*), following a *coup d'etat*, created among republicans a tradition hostile to the election of the head of the state by means of universal suffrage. The fear was that a man backed by a plebiscite would go beyond the parliament. The republican tradition was even opposed to political leadership by the President. On de Gaulle's gaining power through the *coup d'etat* of May 13, 1958, the Bonapartist tradition replaced the republican tradition, and the President of the Republic is to be elected through universal suffrage.

Legally, the election must take place by 1965, but de Gaulle can precipitate matters at any time. During a recent tour in the provinces, he let it be understood in his usual equivocal way, that he might seek a new mandate. It is likewise not impossible that he will seek reelection not through an electoral campaign but through a referendum.

Democratic Pond Stirred Up
For all these reasons, the democratic frogs have been stirring for some time in their little clubs, seeking to settle on a candidate for the presidency from here on out in opposition to the candidacy of de Gaulle.

It should be noted that among these frogs are to be found quite a number of neocapitalists who seek a "modern state"; that is, a "strong"

---

[53] Mr. X Versus de Gaulle (1964), a series of articles, comes from *International Socialist Review*, Vol.25 No.2, Spring 1964, pp.45-48

bourgeois state, with a vigorous President of the Republic, in which parliament in the final analysis would play a permissive role. In brief, these gentlemen are not too displeased with the present regime. What they want in place of the arbitrary de Gaulle, who is hostile to the elected intermediary bodies, is a personage who acts in a more regular way with the traditional political circles.

Under present conditions, a candidate running in opposition to de Gaulle does not appear to have any chance of coming out ahead. But our frogs are busy with intricate calculations. There will likely be a candidate of the right who could take about five per cent of the votes. If the candidate of the left obtained a little more than forty per cent of the votes, then taking into account the abstentions, de Gaulle would risk being elected by only a minority instead of an absolute majority, and he would be quite capable of rejecting these results. Even if he doesn't pull out in a huff, our augurs add, de Gaulle is close to 75; he is not immortal; and it is good to run a candidate to get him known and prepare his triumph over a candidate of the right who will not have much weight once de Gaulle is no longer here.

To all these considerations, there must be added the fact that two big workers' parties exist, the French Communist party (PCF) and the Socialist party (PS), without whose support a candidate cannot hope to win a massive vote.

The astuteness of these strategists is limitless. It is necessary to find in the Socialist party an adequate personality, one who adheres unquestionably to "socialism," but who, at the same time, is able to maintain his "independence" in relation to the party. To have him nominated as a candidate by his own party would, under present conditions, tend to force the hand of the leadership of the Communist party. This party, not wanting to bear responsibility for splitting the votes of the left, must likewise hesitate at presenting a Communist candidate who would not be able, given the character of the electoral rules, to register under his name all the votes won by the Communist candidates in the legislative elections.

What We Want Is Mr. X

We have not yet come to the end. To have a candidate meeting such qualifications is not sufficient. It is still necessary to find the means of making him acceptable without too much trouble. Looking across the Atlantic, something might be learned, it seems, concerning presidential elections. It is necessary to operate the way advertising campaigns are launched: create the demand, publicize the features of the product in demand, and do this in such a way that the consumers will conclude: the only product I want is the Such and Such brand.

The first part of the operation was launched without a hitch. An opening press campaign raised the disturbing thought: the left runs the greatest risk if it doesn't have a candidate right now for the presidency of the Republic. Came the second round: we're not concerned about the name of the candidate; let's call him "Mr. X" for the time being; but let's reach agreement on the features he needs!

With the appearance of the very first article, there were plenty of explanations as to what was going on behind the scenes, but that didn't stop things from proceeding in their course. Those in on the game began to say during the speechmaking windup at some of the truly republican banquets: "For me, 'X' can't be anyone but Deferre."

On being interviewed, Gaston Deferre, the Mayor of Marseilles, candidly replied, "I don't know if I was made for that. I'll have to think it over."

The timing required a major move, otherwise the campaign could lose momentum and end in something the very opposite of what was wanted. The leadership of the Socialist party was summoned to take a stand. The movement was strong enough among the party chieftains to bring this about and they decided to call a special congress of the Socialist party on February 1 with only one point on the agenda, the candidacy of Deferre.

Mr. X Unfurls His Banner

Some fifteen days before the congress, the Marseilles Mayor, during a congress of his federation, announced his views. The press, radio, television, gave him top billing. All his speech was concerned about was to make clear that he stood on a neocapitalist platform. Socialism is not involved, neither now nor later. Deferre stands for the firm application of the Gaullist constitution, against the poor record of de Gaulle in this respect.

In other words, he stands with both feet planted in the present Bonapartist regime. For him, his candidacy is thus not a challenge against the regime but a proposal for trimmings. He does not intend to talk about any "program" which he promises to carry out in one way or another; he will attempt to solve problems as they arise.

Finally, while affirming his loyalty to the Socialist party, he wants to be the candidate of the whole "left." There is no question of drawing any line to the right. On the other hand, he took a categorical position against any negotiations over his candidacy with the Communist party. The Communist party, he said, must vote for me or assure the election of de Gaulle.

This is the way things stand on the eve of the special congress of the Socialist party. Guy Mollet and the official Socialist party newspaper *Le Populaire* are silent. It is known that Deferre's candidacy does not exactly enjoy Mollet's blessing, but it seems that he will not be able to block it at the congress. The congress may see some shrewd maneuvering to deny Deferre the free field he demands; but how this will turn out cannot be predicted.

An Indignant Cry from the CP

The Communist party reacted strongly to Deferre's speech, particularly his haughty attitude in their direction and insisted on the necessity of agreement on a program – bourgeois democratic, it should be noted in passing – letting it be known that a Communist candidacy is always possible for the first round of balloting in the absence of an agreement.

We have summarized the circumstances surrounding the preparations of the left, a very respectable left, for the presidential election to be held in the still undetermined future. As of now the maneuvers of narrow circles, of smalltime Machiavellian hopefuls, seem to be succeeding. But the real problem is not touched by these combinations.

The only force that can bring an end to the Gaullist regime is the working class; and, at the present time, its activity – including its interest in a candidate for President of the Republic – hinges first of all in the relations between the Communist and Socialist parties. Minimum agreement between these two parties would give different meaning to a candidacy. The relations between the Communist and Socialist parties are no longer war to the knife as they were for the past fifteen years; they are undergoing a change, although it cannot yet be discerned where the discussion now underway between these two formations will end.

Can French Socialists and Communists Get Together?

PARIS, JAN. 22 – France has passed through a series of political and social shocks since 1934 and will not find stability until the working class, led by a revolutionary party, takes power. One of the essential tasks of such a party will be to achieve revolutionary unity in action of the French working class which has been divided on the political level since 1920. One of the greatest failures of the French Communist party in the period when it sought to be a revolutionary party as well as later when it was dominated by Stalinism, was that it could not orient itself correctly on the question of unity of action, of the united front of the working class. In general, it could be said that it has oscillated between a sectarian policy towards the Socialist party and an opportunist policy in the wake of the same rival.

The question of the relations between the PCF and the PS is again on the agenda. The setting for this was de Gaulle's coming to power and the installation of a Bonapartist regime that does not bother about playing parliamentary games. But it is likewise placed in a historic development that weighs on these parties and on the workers. To understand current developments and what is projected, it is necessary to bear in mind, at least in broad outline, the history of these relations.

After the split at Tours in 1920 which gave birth to the Communist party, nothing outstanding occurred until 1934, due to the lack of big struggles in the country. Each of the two parties acted without paying much attention to the other. The Communist party at certain times made proposals for a united front with the Socialist party; at other times it sought to undermine it with a policy of "united front from below"; i.e., with the ranks of the PS to the exclusion of their leaders – a bizarre concept of Stalinism not noted for its success.

In 1934, after Hitler's victory in Germany, reaction and fascism rose dangerously in France. On February 6, 1934, a reactionary coup d'etat was attempted. Immediately following this, an almost spontaneous mass movement surged up in France, giving birth everywhere to anti-fascist vigilance committees. The two leaderships were impelled under this pressure to sign a pact for joint anti-fascist action. The leaderships hastily transformed this agreement, widening it to include the bourgeois radical party, thus creating the Popular Front.

This alliance between the workers' parties and a wing of French capitalism coincided with a rapprochement between France and the USSR on the plane of international relations. In 1936 the Popular Front won a parliamentary majority; then it limited and halted the gigantic movement of occupation of the plants and left capitalist property and the capitalist state intact. Once this was achieved, the capitalists seized the initiative, and in 1937-38 the Popular Front was ruptured, relations between the Communist party and the Socialist party becoming envenomed.

The Ups and Downs

From the signing of the Hitler-Stalin pact in August 1939 up to the day of Hitler's attack against the Soviet Union, the PC and the PS were virtually at sword's points; the Socialist ministers, during the first months of the war, underwriting the repression of Communist militants forced into the underground.

During the Resistance and Liberation period, Communists and Socialists cooperated again, first of all in the struggle against the German occupation, then... in the reestablishment of the capitalist state and economy; the principal differences between the experience of 1944-47 and that of 1936-38 being that this time the MRP (Christian Democrats organized in the *Mouvement Republicain Populaire*) replaced the Radical party as the bourgeois ally, and the Communists had representatives in the government, beginning with Thorez, Vice-President of the government presided over by de Gaulle.

In April-May 1947, partly under the pressure of the workers at Renault who went on strike against the advice of all the trade-union leaders (Stalinists and reformists), and more directly because of the "cold war" that erupted, the break between the PCF and the PS widened again.

Parallel with these developments on the political level, the trade-union movement, split in 1921 by the reformists, was reunified from 1935 to 1939, then again from 1943 to 1948.

It is to be noted that the relations within the workers' movement have hinged considerably on relations between the leading factions of French capitalism and the Soviet power. At bottom, the interests of the French bourgeoisie have counted much more to the Socialists than the specific interests of the French working class. With the leadership of the PCF the primary interests have been those of the Soviet bureaucracy.

Since the end of the Second World War and, above all, since the "cold war," two factors have not ceased to weigh on the Socialist cadres in their relations with the PCF. Unlike the period before 1939, the PCF has largely held the majority in the working class[54]. There is this and the "Prague coup"; that is, the events that assured the transformation of Czechoslovakia into a workers' state in 1948[55].

* * *

From 1947 until de Gaulle's coming to power in 1958, the "cold war" raged continually between the PS and the PCF. Even in 1956, during the administration of the PS leader, Guy Mollet, although the Communist deputies voted for this government, and particularly for its infamous "special powers" which were aimed at bolstering the war in Algeria and installing a fascist power there, the Socialists refused to take the Communist votes into consideration.

---

[54] Whereas in 1936, the relation of votes was around 65 to 35 in favor of the Socialist party, since 1945 the same relationship shifted in favor of the PCF. It is understandable that in view of this important change, many Communist militants, not grasping the conditions as a whole that led to this result, have not been able to see tha policy of the Popular Front as injurious since it led to the strengthening of their party. Contrariwise, the Socialists, without condemning the experience of the Popular Front, have felt some bitterness over the results it appeared to bring their party.

[55] It is pointless to cite the details of the Prague affair, which the Khrushchevists refer to as an example of the peaceful and parliamentary road to socialism, whereas the Socialists point to the way the Communists utilized their posts in the government. Both of them appear to forget the presence of the Soviet Army at the time in Czechoslovakia.

Even more, in distinction from what had always been the practice in the past, this attitude was widely supported by Socialist voters. In the second round of balloting, a Socialist candidate would continue to oppose a Communist candidate who had made out better in the first round, or would withdraw in favor of a bourgeois candidate. Unlike former times, the Communist candidates did not receive even a small part of the Socialist votes.

It is absolutely true that the important, even decisive, factor of the prewar period had definitively disappeared – there was no perspective whatever for an important wing of French capitalism to seek an alliance with the USSR against American imperialism. The factor of "foreign policy" went directly against a rapprochement between the PCF and the PS.

Affected by the Workers

But both of them are workers' parties, both of them distant from the revolutionary struggle for socialism, but both with deep roots in the working class, unable not to take into account the interests and the democratic rights of the workers in capitalist society. If this was evident for the PCF, it was likewise true for the PS, no matter how it had been affected by the bourgeoisie and petty bourgeoisie during the years of the Fourth Republic (1945-58) when the Socialist party was in power or never far from it. This was rapidly shown upon the installation of the Gaullist regime.

If the rebellion in Algiers on May 13 permitted de Gaulle to make his bid as a candidate for power, it was Guy Mollet above all who succeeded in having him accepted by the political circles of the Fourth Republic and who, despite strong resistance from the Socialist parliamentary caucus, blocked any united action by the workers against the turn.

Up to this day, Guy Mollet defends his attitude toward de Gaulle at that time, even declaring that in identical circumstances he would do it again.

But the installation of the Gaullist regime resulted from the beginning in bringing about a profound change in relations in the working class. This did not take any of the spectacular forms of the years 1934-35. On the contrary, the new tendency was not easily perceptible. In the municipal elections of 1959, for the first time an appreciable percentage of Socialist voters were noted to have voted on the second round for Communist candidates despite the slogans of the Socialist party.

But it was on the occasion of the legislative elections of November 1962 that the turn was taken by the Socialist leadership.

In the elections, the Socialist party appeared in a combination called the "cartel of the no's," an assemblage of parliamentary formations extending from the right to the left of the Fourth Republic (PS, Radical party, MRP, independents) who came out against the election of the president of the republic by universal suffrage. This cartel had no common program, the candidates being united solely on a commitment to withdraw on the second round for those who made out best on the first.

Four days before the election, Guy Mollet made a public declaration the gist of which was that he saw no reason for not withdrawing on the second round for a Communist candidate. Such a declaration was equivalent to breaking the electoral cartel of the no's, and the other partners interpreted it as a break. On the second round, the Socialists withdrew in many areas in favor of Communist candidates, and their appeals were met with enthusiasm by more than seventy-five per cent of the voters. A chapter had ended. What would the future hold?

Miners Judge the Turn

Guy Mollet declared that only an electoral operation against the personal Gaullist power was involved, that there was no political agreement between the two parties, no common program, no reciprocal engagement. This was formally true, but it was no less true that this could not be the end of the matter. The mass of workers, who had something to do with this Socialist decision because of what was developing silently within their ranks, felt stimulated; for them it heralded a new situation. A few weeks later a great strike was staged by the miners, a fraternity where these relations have always been decisive for their struggle.

In 1963 the Socialist party congress decided to hold a public discussion with the PCF on their reciprocal relations, and a delegation of the PS that included Mollet and Deferre went to Moscow where they talked at length with Khrushchev.

The discussion between the PS and the PCF was launched at the beginning of 1964 with a rather odd opening: the two participants began talking about different questions without entering into a dialogue. The leadership of the PCF raised the question of the *program* for joint action, including the presidential campaign. The leadership of the PS raised in its way the *problems* of *the split* of *1920*, the "21 conditions" for adherence to the Communist International, etc. The leadership of the PS has remained silent on the question of the program for current action; the leadership of the PCF has said nothing about the doctrinal questions underscored by the Socialists.

It is evident that the leadership of the PCF is seeking above all to mobilize their party for an action in the direction of the Socialists and towards the outside, whereas the leadership of the PS does not want to become engaged in a possible action without having previously prepared their ranks. For them, joint action is equivalent to supping with the devil, and, as is known, to do that it is necessary to have a long spoon.

Soon the special congress of the Socialist party will be held. Perhaps new factors will enter into its deliberations. We shall see...

Special Congress of French Socialist Party

PARIS – The special congress of the Socialist party, which met at Clichy February 1-2, ended in a unanimous decision to run Gaston Deferre as candidate for the presidency of the republic. But the congress was greatly divided throughout its sessions. "They asked us for an amicable agreement on nominations [to a resolutions committee], Deferre said at one time, "in the name of a friendliness and spirit of conciliation which, I must say, has been rather scarce for several weeks." It took five hours of argument behind closed doors to reach agreement.

However, on the big political problems there were actually no differences. In substance, the quarrel involved mainly the relations between the candidate and his party. (Not the party and its candidate.)

Guy Mollet is incontestably the man who best understands the importance of the Socialist party in French politics as the hinge between the bourgeoisie and the working class. He understood the role it could play in 1958 in bringing de Gaulle to power; and he seeks to maintain its capacity for the inverse operation, in case of need. Deferre, in contrast, is one of those Socialist politicians, common in France, who utilize the Socialist party to gain election but who have their own electoral following and who feel no need to abide by the decisions of a congress if they find it inconvenient. One of the strongest objections to his candidacy – from Mollet to activists in the most distant provinces – was that he was imposed upon the party by a series of maneuvers. From the way he treated his party in becoming its candidate, it can be guessed how he would act toward it if he were elected president of the republic. If he were elected...

Count Chicks Before Hatched

A comic aspect of the debates at the congress was the care which both Mollet and Deferre displayed through hours of oratorical dueling in refraining from calling things by their right name. Deferre saw himself already elected; Mollet similarly visualized himself – the head of a victorious Socialist party – as prime minister. A lot of wind went into haggling over the relationship between the president of the republic and his prime minister.

But can they be thinking, in case they win, of maintaining the Gaullist constitution of 1958? Certainly. "Elected in accordance with the constitution of 1958, he will carry out the duties pertaining to his office and will uphold the constitution in spirit and letter," declares the unanimously adopted resolution of the Socialist congress.

What they accuse de Gaulle of is not having respected his own constitution, of having made "improper and erroneous interpretations" of it.

Finally, don't think that it's only a short-time business. The resolution also mentions "reefs to be avoided," among them "an upset, innovations so great that there would be a risk that the public would not understand clearly what we want."

Moreover, in undertaking an electoral campaign, "the party maintains its complete freedom for the day, *without doubt very distant*, when the problem will be posed of over-all structural reform." (My emphasis.)

There is not much to be said on the "program." The truth is that the candidate Deferre does not want a program but only "options" (?); the partisans of Mollet don't want a program either, the pretext being that it is up to the head of the government and not the president of the republic to handle this. The net result was a document of less significance than the platforms produced by the major party conventions in the United States. It commits no one.

Avoid "Force de Frappe" Issue

However, one point should be noted. Not a word is said stopping the "*force de frappe*" (de Gaulle's nuclear striking forces.)

Deferre's eel-like capacity to wriggle was well demonstrated when he was asked what his stand was on this at a press conference February 5.

"We are for general, controlled disarmament," he said, "thus we are for the suppression of national striking forces. To ask French political figures today, 'Are you ready to stop everything?' is a false problem. The real problem will be posed in two years. If many are taking a stand against the national striking force, a part of the public is in favor of a European striking force. At the moment, it is not possible to undertake a formal engagement. My intention is not to say what I would do if elected. Thus I will refrain from any demagogic promise. What is certain is that it is necessary to provide France with a modern, and if possible European, force."

Still another very significant aspect of the Socialist congress should be noted. At a time when the Socialist party leadership is attempting to "discuss" with the Communists (in a bizarre way, as I noted above), the rare times when the question of the French

Communist party came up clearly the intention was revealed to ignore it in this business of the presidential election. No one asked that the Communist party be consulted in regard to the campaign.

The explanation is very simple. So far as the election is concerned, the Socialist delegates (there was not a worker among them) had their eyes turned to the right, toward the Radicals, the Christian Democrats in the *Mouvement Republicain Populaire*, and others who would be repelled by dealings with the Communist party.

To this passing consideration should be added something more profound, related to the fact that sooner or later contact must be established. "At a time when a thaw is beginning in the Communist world," one of the delegates said, "we must keep the CP dangling on our ideological conceptions."

The "left" thus has a candidate now who does not wish to frighten anyone. It would be incorrect to believe that this nomination will not exercise a certain influence on political life in France. This will come much less from the "style" that Deferre is trying to give his candidacy, and the vague themes he is now elaborating on, than from the fact that regardless of what is said about the spirit and letter of the Gaullist constitution, the candidacy, in the eyes of the masses, will appear as an alternative – for or against de Gaulle.

In short, whether Deferre likes it or not, the struggle can force him to take positions on the problems of genuine interest to the masses, and the struggle can have a certain logic which is not necessarily that of a candidate who fears innovation.

PIERRE FRANK

The Transitional Program

The first Marxist transitional program appeared in the ***Manifesto of the Communist Party*** of 1848, at the end of the chapter Proletarians and Communists. Formulated in ten points, it presents both a program for mobilizing the workers in the struggle for the conquest of power, and a program to be instituted in the period following the seizure of power by the workers.[56]

The programs of the big working-class parties that arose during the second half of the nineteenth century, the most famous of which was the Erfurt program of 1891, consisted of two parts having no dialectical relationship to each other whatever: There was a maximum program calling for a socialist society in the indefinite future, and a minimum program which the working-class party defended in the immediate period within the framework of capitalist society; for this was the era of the development and worldwide expansion of capitalism and the problem of the seizure of power by the proletariat could not be posed as an immediate objective.

With the advent of the imperialist phase of capitalism at the beginning of the twentieth century, the struggle for power was again on the agenda; the Russian Revolution of 1905 was its first and most striking manifestation. In 1917, the Bolshevik Party advanced what was a transitional program in fact even though it did not use the name (it is to be found in the April Theses as well as in Lenin's pamphlet *The Threatening Catastrophe and How to Fight It*). In 1918, Rosa Luxemburg, who was first in sensing the danger of dividing the program into two parts (see footnote two below), called attention in her programmatic speech at the founding congress of the German Communist Party to precisely those passages in the *Communist Manifesto* which we mentioned above, as well as to the Erfurt program. Declaring that it was necessary to return to the ideas of the *Manifesto*, she went on to assert:

"[Our program] is in conscious opposition to the point of view on which the Erfurt program was based, in conscious opposition to the separation of immediate demands, called minimum, in the economic and political struggle from the final socialist goal as the maximum program. In our conscious opposition to this, we draw a balance on the results of the past seventy years of development and especially

---
[56] The Transitional Program (1967) comes from *International Socialist Review*, Vol.28 No.3, May-June 1967, pp.1-12.

their direct consequence, the world war, by stating: For us there is no such thing as a minimum program and a maximum program; socialism is one; socialism is the minimum which we must achieve today."

Having established itself organizationally and taken measures to shut its doors to reformist and centrist currents at its first two world congresses, the Communist International, at its third and fourth world congresses (1921 and 1922) advanced the idea of a transitional program in these terms:

"In place of the minimum program of the reformists and centrists, the Communist International mounts a struggle for the concrete needs of the proletariat, for a system of demands which taken together will disintegrate the power of the bourgeoisie, organize the proletariat and constitute stages in the struggle for the proletarian dictatorship, and in which each particular demand will express a need of the great masses, even if these masses are not yet consciously in favor of a dictatorship of the proletariat." (Third Congress, 1921, *Thesis on Tactics*).

"3. The programs of the national sections must clearly and decisively establish the necessity of the struggle for transitional demands, making the necessary reservations about the dependence of these demands on the concrete circumstances of time and place.

"4. The theoretical basis for all transitional and partial demands must be clearly stated in the general program, and the fourth congress likewise decisively condemns the attempt to depict the inclusion of transitional demands in the program as opportunism, as well as all attempts to gloss over or replace the fundamental revolutionary tasks by partial demands.

"5. The general program must clearly explain the basic historical types of the transitional demands of the national section, in accordance with the basic differences in the economic and political structure of the different countries, for example Britain on the one hand, and India on the other." (Fourth Congress, 1922, *Resolution on the Program of the Communist International*)

As the gangrene of Stalinism set in, the Communist International abandoned the idea of a transitional program. After some ultraleft convulsions, its main orientation became opportunist (Popular Front, National Fronts, etc.), and collaboration followed with various wings of the bourgeoisie or was sought after within the framework of the capitalist system. The Communist parties returned de facto to the concept of a minimum program. For them the question no longer existed of a system of demands so interrelated as to develop and raise the class struggle from the level of a struggle for partial and transitional goals to that of the struggle for a workers' government.

PIERRE FRANK

Trotskyist Contribution

It was the Fourth International which, in the transitional program as well as all other fields, continued and enriched the work of the first four congresses of the Communist International. After a number of initial efforts by national sections (*Action Program* of 1934 of the Communist League of France, *Action Program* of the Belgian section, etc.), the Founding Congress of the Fourth International adopted, in 1938, the document which has entered the history of the Trotskyist movement under the name of the *Transitional Program*. It is this document which we are reprinting here, along with the preface to the French edition of 1946.

The work should not be thought of as the fundamental program of the Fourth International, for the latter consists of the totality of lessons drawn from the struggle for socialism since the beginning of the working-class movement. A program of that kind cannot be drafted in the form of a single document. It is based on the teachings of the Marxist classics, the first four congresses of the Communist International, the fundamental documents of the Russian and International Left Opposition and the documents of the congresses of the Fourth International. Within this historical context, the *Transitional Program* of 1938 constitutes a part of the fundamental program of the Fourth International. It is its most important part politically in the sense that on the basis of the totality of teachings contained in the fundamental program, it formulates a political program aimed at mobilizing the masses into actions which correspond to their level of consciousness at a given moment, in order to lead them, through the education they receive in the course of these actions, to the highest level of consciousness, which will carry them to the conquest of power.

Key Elements of Program

The *Transitional Program* is therefore based upon two essential elements:

the condition of a capitalist society that has lost its stability on the historical scale (not necessarily at every moment and in any and all countries) and where the struggle for the conquest of power has become the major task for this historical period;

a series of slogans linked to national and international conjunctural conditions which in combination have the objective of raising the masses to the highest political level during the process of their struggles.

With the validity of each slogan being determined by its correspondence with the internal logic of the mass movement, the key piece in the program is precisely the culminating slogan of the whole chain – the slogan for a workers' and farmers' government or for a workers' government. Here again the Fourth International has both revived and enriched the teachings of the third and fourth congresses of the Communist International by using the slogan as a transitional governmental formula corresponding to the organizational conditions and consciousness of the masses at a given moment, and not as a synonym for the dictatorship of the proletariat. A program without the perspective of a government of the working masses to carry out anti-capitalist measures, is not a transitional program.

Another enrichment contained in the 1938 program, in comparison with the teachings of the Communist International: Stalinist degeneration in the Soviet Union posed the question of a political revolution against the bureaucratic power, and the *Transitional Program* of 1938 contains a section dealing with this struggle, with slogans having a conjunctural character which Trotsky explained in this way in *The Revolution Betrayed*:

"The program of the new revolution depends to a great extent upon the moment when it breaks out, upon the level which the country has then attained, and to a great degree upon the international situation."

Written on the eve of the second world war, the *Transitional Program* received its most striking verification a few years later, right after the war. All the great struggles in Europe in the immediate postwar period developed along lines corresponding with the internal logic and slogans of the *Transitional Program*, but the struggles were most frequently under Stalinist leadership, operating under directives from the Kremlin, which in turn was committed to the imperialists under its Yalta, Teheran and Potsdam agreements. Since these leaders had no desire to overthrow the capitalist regime, they never conducted the struggles toward the objective of installing a government of the laboring masses, and the struggles ended up in failure. The colonial revolution subsequently verified that part of the Program relating to colonial uprisings against their imperialist mother countries. The uprisings of the Polish and Hungarian masses in 1956 brought their verification of the document's guidelines for the Soviet state, which was the only workers' state in existence at the time the *Transitional Program* was written[57].

---

[57] See in particular the resolution adopted on November 12, 1956, by the Workers Councils in the eleventh district of Budapest, reproduced in our introduction to *The Revolution Betrayed*, (1961 edition), and the program advanced by K. Modzelewsky and

This threefold verification should be enough to emphasize the importance and value of this document. It remains just as valid today, provided, of course, we make certain necessary changes corresponding to developments which have taken place during the years since it was drafted.

But before we turn to that, it is necessary to deal with another question which does not have a purely conjunctural character. There are people who have brought the fundamental meaning of a transitional program into question by their very use of the term. In fact, the expression "transitional program" has now been used for several years in a completely opposite sense from that which it had in the Communist International originally and then in the Fourth International. The leadership of the Italian Communist Party has been its most eminent exponent. It advances the following point of view: The Italian constitution contains articles which make it possible to shift over from capitalist society to a society that could presumably construct socialism; the world is now in the period of the transition from capitalism to socialism; all that is necessary, therefore, according to Togliatti and his disciples, is to advance a program, utilizing the provisions in the present Italian constitution, the realization of which would signify a transition from one mode of production to the other.

A Peaceful Transition?

This point of view, as is immediately apparent, raises a fundamental question with regard to the Marxist conception of the state, which Lenin reaffirms so strongly in *The State and Revolution* (the leaders of the Italian Communist Party do not deny this moreover). In the transition from capitalist to socialist society, this viewpoint disregards – one could say conjures away – what Marx, Engels, Luxemburg, Lenin and Trotsky considered to be the essential turning point, the moment when the working class conquers power and destroys the bourgeois state. The "transitional program" advanced by the leaders of the Italian Communist Party does nothing more than bring back the type of program envisaged by Eduard Bernstein at the beginning of the century, predicated on a gradual evolution of society through a series of reforms, with the question of power being posed only on the parliamentary road, and, as an inescapable extension, socialist participation in bourgeois governments. This sort of "transitional program" is therefore no novelty; it takes us right back to

---

J. Kuron in their *Open Letter to the Polish Workers Party*, in which the lessons of the Polish October in 1956 are drawn.

the debates on revisionism which took place in the Second International in the early years of the twentieth century[58].

The ultraconservative leadership of the French Communist Party has long opposed this "Italian" notion of a "transitional program," but not from the revolutionary direction. Its opposition is more in the Kautsky style, "theory" being preserved as a dogma having no relevance to daily practice, which is just as parliamentary and opportunist in France as it is in Italy with the Italian Communist party. In France, it is inside the Parti Socialiste Unifié that partisans of the Italian-style "transitional program" are to be found. They hold the following point of view: Present-day capitalism, or "neo-capitalism," to use that rather vague expression for it[59], is a phase in the transition from capitalism to socialism; this transition is not taking place along the lines of the old schemes of political struggle; the question of governmental power has become of secondary importance; social power is now lodged in the great economic organizations, and socialism can advance precisely by means of men, animated by socialist convictions, attaining leadership in these economic organizations, in these "centers of decision" (in the plural).

As in the case of the Italian Communist Party, the question of power has been eliminated from their concerns and struggles. That decisive center of decision represented by governmental power within the state is conjured away and replaced with multiple centers of decision. Instead of making mass struggles converge toward the question of power, their tendency is to disperse these struggles in

---

[58] In *Reform or Revolution* Rosa Luxemburg insistently emphasizes the dialectic of the two terms, minimum program and maximum program, in her arguments against the opportunists who were abandoning revolution. "The daily struggle for reforms, for the amelioration of the condition of the workers within the framework of the existing social order, and for democratic institutions, offers ... the only means of engaging in the proletarian class war and working in the direction of the final goal," she writes on the first page of this book. She cogently points out where separation of these two terms must lead: "As soon as 'immediate results' become the principal aim of our activity, the clear-cut, irreconcilable point of view, which has meaning only in so far as it proposes to win power, will be found more and more inconvenient. The direct consequence of this will be the adoption by the party of a 'policy of compensation,' a policy of political trading, and an attitude of diffident, diplomatic conciliation."

[59] The term "neo-capitalism" was introduced by various bourgeois and petty-bourgeois reformists, without any real attempt at a definition, in order to spread the notion of a capitalism which had presumably found the way to overcome its objective laws, its crises, its contradictions. What they were really doing was idealizing the unexpected period of capitalist prosperity which followed the Second World War. Since the term has spread widely and found acceptance, provisionally at any rate, we must understand its real meaning, which is not one of a miraculously transformed capitalism, but only a period in the imperialist stage of capitalism characterized by a prolonged boom, the causes of which can be grasped without having to question the Marxist analysis of capitalism.

space and in time over multiple objectives. Ideas like these become associated with others which are already widely diffused, reaching even into certain bourgeois circles, ideas which are derived from a superficial evaluation of the Liberman reforms in the workers states on the one hand and of planning in the capitalist states on the other. On the basis of this, it is concluded that the question of the differences between capitalism and socialism has become outmoded and the problem of the conquest of power is now passe. Of course the capitalists themselves do not share these ideas when it comes to their daily practice. The most authoritative voice in the City of London, where the wealth of yesteryear has been lost but not the solid notion of capitalist interests, puts the matter in a way which, while not being put in Marxist terms, reveals a most lively capitalist class consciousness on these questions:

Capitalism Speaks

"Indeed the more one looks at the effort of the eastern and western economies to move closer to each other – the communists by turning towards 'market relations,' the capitalists by experimenting with planning – the more they seem to resemble two tethered goats trying to get together but checked by the length of the leash that ties them to its own particular stake. The stake is where the basic power of economic decision rests, with the state or with private men." (*The Economist*, November 28, 1964, p. 955; our emphasis.)

In capitalist society, despite all the changes which may have occurred, the state remains the center of decision serving the capitalists. Only by attacking it, by attacking governmental power, is it possible to go over to the building of socialism. Ignoring it and working surreptitiously for the accession of well-intentioned men to the leadership of multiple centers of decision will not achieve this. The theory of "centers of decision" no doubt offers some advantages... particularly to those who get the jobs. Here, too, the matter is not altogether new. When Jouhaux became a regent of the Bank of France (one of these centers of decision, and hardly the least important), his reply to revolutionary critics was that he was doing it for the cause of workers' emancipation, and he made out that he was making more sacrifices for the cause than anyone else.

For our part we absolutely reject such a conception of the "transitional program"; we unreservedly support the conception that governed the elaboration of the program of 1938, not out of any simple attachment to the past and feelings of respect for it, but because this conception continues to be more valid than ever for every portion of the globe.

In the countries which previously had a colonial or semi-colonial status, the conquest of formal political independence has yielded no solution whatever to the major problems of underdevelopment. On all the continents which experienced colonialization, the necessity imposes itself with ever increasing force for the colonial revolution to pass over into the socialist revolution. Parallel with this the need for a transitional program becomes more imperative.

In the workers states, "de-Stalinization" did not challenge the political power of the bureaucracy, and because of the continuation of this bureaucratic power, none of the demands formulated in the 1938 program or in *The Revolution Betrayed* has been completely satisfied. The events in Poland and Hungary in 1956, among others, have demonstrated the need for a political revolution, in the sense which Trotsky gave to this term, and consequently, the need for a transitional program for that part of the world as well.

In the economically developed capitalist countries, years of economic prosperity which no one expected, not even the most optimistic capitalists, have engendered a reformist euphoria and a setback for revolutionary currents. The opportunists and reformists find no need to be vindicated by theory: For them, sufficient unto the day is the evil thereof, and besides, aren't the conditions pre-eminently favorable for a minimum program?[60]

Imperialist Decline

But economic prosperity has not eliminated the essential characteristics of capitalism in its imperialist phase; it has not brought capitalism back to its period of full bloom, such as existed in the last third of the nineteenth century, which was likewise the period of the minimum program. Behind the facade of extraordinary economic prosperity, we find a capitalism which has lost control over a third of the land surface and a third of the population of the globe, a capitalism which is under continuous attack from the majority of mankind, a capitalism which sees that the material might of the United States is unable to break the will of the Vietnamese people, a capitalism whose economic system is visibly inferior to that of the workers states despite the fact that the latter is not yet beyond the preliminary stage, started from an extremely low level and is operating under a bureaucratic leadership characterized by its wastefulness.

---

[60] The bad luck of the socialist leaders lies in the fact that the bourgeois parties are the only ones to profit from good times whereas the socialist leaders are only called on to enter governments (Wilson in Great Britain, Brandt in Germany) when things get bad. The job given to them is to plead poverty in order to impose restraints on the working class and in that way restore capitalism to health.

PIERRE FRANK

The boasts about capitalism's capacity for adaptation, about its superiority over socialism, certainly do not deceive the capitalists themselves or their most responsible and clear-sighted servants in maintaining the system. Despite all the accumulated economic wealth and an unquestionable improvement in the living conditions of the working class within the economically developed countries, we are not witnessing any parallel flowering of bourgeois democracy as was the case during the expansion of capitalism in the last century. On the contrary, the tendency in all these countries is toward installation of a "strong state" at the expense of democratic forms, a strengthening of the "executive" at the expense of national parliaments and local institutions, and this is happening even in that model country of bourgeois democracy, Great Britain, and even under a Labour government. This tendency is not the result of some mental aberration but of capitalist necessity. It requires only some relatively limited event, whether it be the Belgian general strike of 1960-1961, the Greek crisis of the summer of 1965, or some similar episode, to demonstrate the social fragility of the European countries. Even in the United States, society has been shaken to its depths by the aspirations of the Negroes. In the most economically developed countries, the need for a transitional program has no more vanished than in the other parts of the world.

The present dialectics of the world revolution[61] will only sharpen the need for a transitional program to mobilize the greatest masses around slogans engaging them in struggle with the existing order and with the aim of establishing a government that will begin to implement the demands of the program, and by so doing begin the process of putting society on the road toward construction of socialism.

A few words remain to be said to complete our earlier remarks regarding the necessity for working out the slogans of the transitional program and linking them up on the basis of conditions existing in a given place at a given time. Compared with 1938, certain slogans have become, if not outdated, at least of secondary importance relative to others. Their justification, in particular, becomes quite different in the context of a different reality. The need for changes is greatest in the case of the economically developed countries, since the 1938 program was formulated in a period when they were in the throes of a prolonged chronic crisis, with massive unemployment which was altogether different from the limited kind now appearing after a long period of full employment. The transitional slogans such as workers'

---

[61] See the document *Dynamics of World Revolution Today* adopted by the Reunification Congress of the Fourth International in June 1963.

control, opening the books, reducing the work week, etc., no longer coincide with the conditions of a chronic crisis and massive unemployment but are now juxtaposed even to conditions of temporary prosperity and the need for maintaining or defending full employment. Defense of the organized working-class movement is not being posed in the face of a direct threat from fascism, but against the far more complicated and insidious threat or establishment of the strong state. The struggle against the danger of nuclear war poses problems and consequently slogans (unilateral nuclear disarmament, for instance) which would make no sense whatever for so-called conventional weapons, in view of the fact that it is generally easy to set up a conventional armament industry starting with normal industrial tooling, whereas the same cannot be done for nuclear weapons. The increase in leisure time poses new problems which must find a place in a program of action, etc., etc. But on all these points and in all these cases, it is merely a matter of adjustment to present conditions and in no case one of repudiating the principles which lie at the foundation of the *Transitional Program*.

This new edition of the *Transitional Program* of 1938 will become, we are sure, a multi-purpose tool for youth who are now turning toward Trotskyism. In it they will find a document showing how the Fourth International after years of struggle by the Trotskyist movement in defense of the theoretical and political teachings of revolutionary Marxism, established itself and translated its will to fight for the leadership of the working class movement into a programmatic application of these lessons to the conditions of our era; a document whose spirit can only continue to inspire the activities of revolutionary Marxists inside the mass movement; a document whose content still remains very largely valid almost thirty years after it was written, despite the substantial upheavals which have taken place in that span of time.

PIERRE FRANK

"We Will Emerge Stronger Than Ever!"

I learned from a press agency that the Parti Communiste Internationaliste [PCI] has been placed on the list of organizations whose dissolution has been decreed by the Council of Ministers.[62] I have had no official notification of this measure but it does not surprise me[63].

The PCI, it should be remembered, was built in the underground during World War II through the fusion of various Trotskyist groups of that time. It has been active in public life since the liberation. Among other things, since 1946 it has run candidates in legislative elections many times.

Our members were persecuted and arrested during France's war with Vietnam and again in the war with Algeria. The government measure, which has struck at various revolutionary youth organizations along with us for allegedly organizing commando groups, is a completely arbitrary administrative directive. The government does not dare to present its case in the courts, where it would have to formulate exact charges and present evidence.

The government move coincided with the frenzied campaign which the leaderships of the PCF [Parti Communiste Français – French Communist Party] and the CGT [Confederation Generale du Travail – General Federation of Labor – the CP-led union] are conducting against the "leftists." These leaderships have not protested at all against the repression which can turn in their direction in the future.

We are studying the legal aspects of the measure and are reserving our right to challenge it. We are confident that many labor and civil liberties organizations will speak up against the dissolution measures taken by the government against a series of vanguard organizations, and will struggle against these decrees until they are abrogated.

In any case, the Trotskyists, who have undergone many repressions before, will emerge from this attack stronger than ever.

---

[62] From *International Socialist Review*, Vol.29 No.4, July-August 1968, pp.3-4.
[63] The following statement by Pierre Frank, secretary of the Internationalist Communist Party, the French section of the Fourth International, was issued June 13. Pierre Frank was one of the first revolutionists arrested after the Council of Ministers decree.

May 1968: First Phase of the French Socialist Revolution

I. Introduction

May 1968 will go down in history as the month the French socialist revolution began.[64] Opening with the struggle of the students against police intrusions into the Latin Quarter and the university, this month saw the entire working class entering into struggle, and with it all strata of the working population (the new middle class, the intellectuals, the peasants, etc.). This happened with a unanimity never before known in the past.

All of the country's youth were to be seen in this struggle: the high-school students, university students, the young workers – both employed and unemployed – including the "young hoods" that the bourgeois press, the government ministers, and so many others have slandered, though they are nothing more than the victims of "consumer society." The youth took the lead of a struggle which unfolded in the streets including extremely violent clashes with the repressive forces of the bourgeois state. Strikes, factory occupations, occupations of all sorts of buildings, street demonstrations took place not only in Paris but throughout the entire country. No region was untouched by the gigantic hurricane which swept the country. The capitalist state foundered for several weeks. It recovered its bearings *in extremis* much less thanks to its own strength than to the default, worse, the betrayal of the leaderships which controlled the great majority of the country's vital forces.

The French economy, which had already passed through great struggles like June 1936, had never been paralyzed as it was in May 1968. According to the statistics about 10 million workers were on strike but this does not give a complete picture of such a situation. Tens of thousands of workers (in gas, electricity, the waterworks, and newspaper printing, etc.) continued to work only to provide for the

---

[64] From *International Socialist Review*, Vol.29 No.5, September 1968, pp.1-48. On June 14, 1968, the day following the French government ban of revolutionary organizations, Pierre Frank was seized by French police and held incommunicado for ten days. Frank completed this article on June 10 – four days before his arrest.

most elementary needs of the civil population. And they did so by decision of their unions.

The bosses and the government found themselves bereft of all authority over the industrial, commercial, and banking enterprises, the means of communication, and the great modern mass media. The armed forces were obviously insufficient to suppress the movement. The police department employees were on strike. The police themselves threatened to go on strike. It was hard to envisage use of the army, in view of the consequences it would have provoked. The repressive troops (CRS, the *Gardes Mobiles*, etc.) were tired out after several nights of fighting in the streets of Paris and incessant mobilizations throughout France.

In a situation where the government was disabled for a period of several weeks and the workers traditional political and trade-union leaderships were bypassed by events, the revolutionary center of the Sorbonne arose with extraordinary improvisation. The most diverse revolutionary currents, previously subjected to implacable repression by the bureaucratic apparatuses of the reformists, came together in close proximity. Day after day, for several weeks, out of the ferment of this socialist democracy, an orientation emerged from this center which made it possible to carry the movement beyond all possible expectations.

In the opinion of all observers, this movement went far beyond June 1936. The historic parallels cited went back to Petrograd 1917, to the revolutionary movements of 1918 and 1919, and the first weeks of the Spanish revolution of July-August 1936. No doubt was possible: We were experiencing the first great revolutionary thrust which would reach a peak in a few days and put the question of power on the order of the day. This took place in an economically developed capitalist country (the fifth-ranking in the world). All the problems of the society (economic, political, social, cultural, etc.) were posed on a knife's edge. These problems are those of all highly industrialized capitalist countries. But they are also, in part, the problems of colonial countries (concerning relations of the working class with other social classes), and even of countries where capitalism has been abolished (concerning relations of the working class with the bureaucracy). With good reason, the entire world turned its eyes to France in May 1968.

The battle was still not over in the early days of June. The strike was still being vigorously pursued in the biggest plants, in vital sectors of the economy, in education, etc. But its peak had passed. The conquest of power was no longer on the order of the day. In the wake of this first phase of the socialist revolution a series of great economic struggles are continuing whose results will be very important for future revolutionary waves, determining their initial slogans and their objectives. There also remain a whole series of bases, large or small bastions, where the state, capitalist property and numerous institutions of capitalist society have been more or less completely put in question.

It is essential to draw a balance sheet of this month of May 1968 as soon as possible, to define what has been achieved, to clarify the perspectives which have opened up, to lay out the main lines of the tasks to come. This is the objective of this pamphlet. In the conditions under which I am writing it I make no claim that it is complete, or that it is exempt from certain inadequacies and perhaps even errors in detail. Nonetheless, I am sure that it will answer the main questions raised in the course of the events and will provide a sufficiently clear basis for the discussion which will inevitably begin in the workers movement and more particularly in the vanguard of the workers movement on the problems posed in May 1968 by the socialist revolution which has begun.

II. The Fundamental Crisis of French Capitalism

For an understanding of the historic meaning of May 1968, the major features of the crisis of French capitalism must be outlined. The great crisis of French capitalism began after the First World War. During part of the 19th century, France was still the second-ranking economic power in the world. After 1918, despite the advantages it drew from the Versailles Treaty, it was no longer anything more than a second-rate country, which moreover had suffered crippling losses. French capitalism had to adjust to its new position at the expense of the workers, by lowering wages or creating unemployment, or else the workers had to eliminate French capitalism. This crisis took spectacular forms starting in the 1930s. There was a succession of great convulsions in which the political regime changed a number of times: February 6, 1934, a right-wing coup, for the first time succeeding in damaging the parliamentary system and the Third Republic; June 1936, a thrust from the left, the first factory occupations; 1939-40, an abrupt shift to the right, the overthrow of the Third Republic and the establishment of the Vichy regime; 1945-47, a new thrust to the left following the war and the establishment of the Fourth Republic; and in 1958, the coup in Algiers, de Gaulle's coming to power and the establishment of the Fifth Republic. May 1968 fits into this succession as the beginning of a new drive to the left moving toward the overthrow of the Gaul-list regime and opening up the perspective of a socialist republic. While each of these convulsions had its immediate cause in conjunctural phenomena of greater or lesser political importance, each of them developed in such a way as to pose all the social problems. I will not go into all the details which would be brought out by a thorough history of France since 1918, but a fundamental fact must be noted. In none of these thrusts to the right has French capitalism, owing to a lack of sufficient inner forces, been able to carry its offensive to the point of imposing a fascist solution, a solution which would involve crushing the working class, completely eliminating its organizations, and a merciless decimation of the cadres of these organizations. It was incapable of doing so even at the time which was most favorable to it, the occupation of France by Hitlerite German troops. It has been able only to institute solutions of a Bonapartist type.

The most stable of these has been the Gaullist regime. This regime succeeded for some time in deceiving a part of the masses about its real nature because it ended the Algerian war, because it pursued a demagogic international policy, and because it received support from the governments of many recently decolonized countries, and also some workers states, for example the Soviet Union. The Soviet Union saw the Gaullist regime as a disruptive element in the Atlantic alliance and a possible ally for "peaceful coexistence."

In contrast, in each of the left thrusts, the workers first of all and the working masses in general have never lacked militancy and combativity. In every case, they stopped short of overthrowing capitalism only because the leadership of the mass organizations failed to give the order. "You must know how to end a strike," Thorez declared in 1936 [Maurice Thorez, longtime head of the Communist Party of France]. This same Thorez succeeded in getting the resistance (FTP) to disarm voluntarily by invoking the need for "one state, one army, and one police force." The state, the army, and the police force were then under the command of de Gaulle. In May 1968, Seguy [Georges Seguy, head of the CP-led General Federation of Labor (CGT)] could not continue his speech to the point of saying "you must know how to end a strike"; he had to change his line right in the middle of his speech.

But once again – as we will see in another chapter – this movement, which had gone further than ever, which was on the point of bringing the Gaullist government down by its own momentum, did not accomplish this, did not arrive at an anti-capitalist conclusion, because of the policy of the working-class leaderships, essentially the CGT and the PCF, because the other leaderships did not have a decisive weight in the working class (the FGDS, the CFDT, and the PSU).

While it can be argued in retrospect how far the movement could have gone in 1936, and while only a minority thought that the *"boat had been missed"* in 1945-47, a great many understood the betrayal in 1968. These diverse mass thrusts have this simple common denominator: The leaderships have repeatedly betrayed, when all that would have been necessary to overthrow capitalism was for them to have wanted to do it. These leaderships will certainly never change. But there have been important differences in the objective and subjective conditions of these great working-class mobilizations in France.

In 1936 and 1945-47, the leaderships enjoyed very great prestige and authority among the masses (the Socialist Party and the PCF in 1936, and mainly the PCF in 1945-47). But in May 1968, even before the mobilization began, the Mollet and Mitterrand leaderships in the FGDS and the Waldeck Rochet leadership in the PCF, while still enjoying extensive control over their members and their constituencies, were beginning to encounter critical feelings, doubts, and even a malaise. Before this movement was unleashed it was hard to discern much more than that, and it was impossible to know the real situation that was first manifested in the course of the mobilization itself.

In 1936, the movement in France did indeed carry over into several countries. In Spain also the mass movement attained revolutionary breadth in the face of the Franco coup. But the international context was then dominated by the rise of Nazism in Europe and moreover by the rise of Stalinism in the USSR (the Moscow trials, etc.). In 1945-47, Hitlerism was defeated by the alliance of the imperialist democracies and the Soviet Union. However, the Soviet Union under Stalin's leadership pledged itself not to challenge the capitalist order. And in the Soviet Union, the government was again preparing to begin its bloody purges (the "Doctors' Plot," Zhdanovism, etc.).

In 1968, the international situation was marked first of all by the victorious Tet offensive, as well as by numerous uprisings in the colonial countries. It was marked also by the resistance of the Afro-Americans in the United States, by a "de-Stalinization" which, however shallow, had eliminated the most oppressive aspects of Stalinism in the movement which swept away Novotny in Czechoslovakia. And finally, it was marked by growing student movements everywhere in the imperialist countries.

In all the great mobilizations of the French workers, one element has played the role of detonator. In 1936, it was the electoral victory of the Popular Front, that is, an event of an essentially parliamentary character. In 1945-47, it was the liberation brought about by the joint military victory of the imperialist democracies and the Soviet Union over Nazism. This victory was thus stamped with an equivocal character, an ambiguity from the class standpoint – an equivocality and ambiguity which was one of the characteristics of the Resistance. This resulted in an inner weakness in the movement of the period which made it possible for it to be liquidated relatively quickly.

The detonator in May 1968 was the student struggle. Nothing could be more misleading than to characterize this struggle as "petty-bourgeois" simply because the great majority of students are the children of the bourgeoisie or petty bourgeoisie. The ideology inspiring the students of opposition to the neo-capitalist consumer society, the methods they used in their struggle, the place they occupy and will occupy in society (which will make the majority of them white-collar employees of the state or the capitalists) gave this struggle an eminently socialist, revolutionary, and internationalist character. Thus, while the detonator in the preceding mass movements was either "to the right" of the movement, or eclectic from the class point of view, this time it was to the left of the movement, with a very high political level in a revolutionary Marxist sense.

There were revolutionary minorities in the 1936 and 1945-47 movements which were in the vanguard of the movement as a whole and opposed the mass reformist leaderships. But these minorities were, all told, extremely few in numbers. They were really "grouplets." For example, in the big parade that took place at the end of May 1936 at the Mur des Federes on the eve of the factory occupations, the group rallied around the Trotskyists – the only minority really existing at the time – was on the order of a thousand persons, who were ejected after a few brawls. In 1945-47, the revolutionary minorities were stronger, but in the climate created by the military victory, left oppositionists were unpopular. A few slanders were enough to keep the revolutionaries from gaining a broad hearing among the masses.

However, the May 1968 experience showed – at the Champ de Mars, at the Gare de Lyon, at the demonstration in Charlety stadium, at the demonstration in Montparnasse, at the Gare d'Austerlitz – that while the notorious "wildmen," "grouplets," "provocateurs," etc., depending on whether you choose the terminology of the government, *l'Humanité* [official organ of the PCF], or some others, were of course still a minority, they were by no means an insignificant minority. This minority was capable of bringing together tens of thousands of people in demonstrations, who effectively stood up against the repressive forces of bourgeois order.

To sum up, May 1968 occurred under political conditions far superior to those governing the previous mobilizations of the French workers. The new mass upsurge began at a much higher level with initial conditions much more favorable than in the past to a socialist outcome. It would certainly be wrong to draw only optimistic conclusions from this. The fight, although not a simple or easy one, comes in circumstances which objectively and subjectively offer much better perspectives than in the past.

III. The bourgeois leadership

A revolutionary situation is also distinguished, according to Lenin, by the bourgeoisie's inability to govern the country. What was the condition of the bourgeois leadership in France during the month of May 1968.

The bourgeois leadership was itself notoriously deficient. Let us leave aside Pompidou's and de Gaulle's trips abroad, which testified to their failure to face up to the situation. The almost total silence of these two men was not the result of calculation. The student movement and then the workers movement had exceeded anything the bourgeoisie had experienced in its history. There was talk in a number of quarters, for example in a newspaper like *Le Monde*, noted for the seriousness of its analyses, about the government's "errors." This, however, was disregarding the lessons of history which show that a worn-out system commits such "errors" from the simple fact that every one of its acts rebounds against it. It cannot be said that de Gaulle decided to launch a referendum with the idea of giving it up a few days later. Just like the working-class leaderships, the leadership of French capitalism found itself left behind and outflanked. De Gaulle really considered resigning. His radio interview can be believed on this score. The statements of Mitterrand, Mendes-France, Giscard d'Estaing, and several others on May 28 were also in line with such an assumption. In those days the bourgeois political world was searching for an alternative.

It was only when he found himself in an extremely difficult, almost desperate situation that de Gaulle, who is a political tactician in the grand style, decided to move with the utmost audacity. The movement was close to breaking through all restraints. De Gaulle understood that in these circumstances, the final impetus could only be given by the opposing leadership. On spontaneity alone, by its own undirected strength, the movement had advanced much further than anyone could have imagined. To continue to advance it now needed a leadership which would dare to give the signal. De Gaulle knows the Communist Party's men well; he was able to use them in his 1946 government[65]. He knew that they were incapable of such audacity. Having nothing but contempt, moreover, for "politicians on the shelf" of the Mollet or Mitterrand type, he decided to throw a scare into the lot of them. He accused the PCF of a policy which it had not the least intention of pursuing. He threatened a repression which made these spineless leaders tremble. And he offered them elections in exchange for their torpedoing the movement. Elections! These men found themselves back on their favorite ground! And thus de Gaulle saved his regime *in extremis*.

There was no long premeditated operation on his part. He resorted to a last-minute improvisation, a very slick improvisation which produced a guaranteed effect. However, it would be wrong to view this as a real solution for the situation. The strikes are continuing with great firmness. The elections are not entirely safe for de Gaulle. And even if he succeeds in surmounting this hurdle, difficulties will very soon reappear. If, for a period, a certain degree of repression could produce some results, other mass thrusts will show up profoundly marked by the experience of May 1968.

In conclusion, the French bourgeoisie, which is probably the world's most experienced in the matter of mass movements, showed in the May mobilizations that it was not its intelligence and slickness that saved it this time. It was the reformist policy of the PCF leadership and its still very strong control over decisive masses of workers which saved the de Gaulle regime and the capitalist system. The bourgeois economist, P. Uri, a member of Mitterrand's "shadow government," talked in the London *Times*, June 5, about an "objective conspiracy" between the Gaullist government and the PCF leadership. As two British bourgeois journalists described it:

"But the paradox which underlies this controlled chaos is that the Communist unions and the Gaullist government they appear to be

---

[65] Here is what de Gaulle wrote in his memoirs on the presence of PCF leaders in his government in 1945: "Taking into account previous circumstances, events since then, the necessities of today, I hold that the return of Maurice Thorez as head of the Communist Party can yield more advantages at present than difficulties ... Inasmuch as in place of revolution, the Communists seek preponderance in a parliamentary regime, society runs less risk ... As for Thorez, while trying to advance the affairs of Communism, on many occasions he was to serve the public interest. On his return to France, he helped put an end to the last vestiges of the 'patriotic militia' whom some of his people obstinately sought to maintain in a new underground. Insofar as the gloomy, hard rigidity of his party permitted him, he opposed the attempts at encroachment of the liberation committees and the acts of violence to which the overexcited groups turned. Among the workers – they were numerous – particularly the miners, who listened to his harangues, he did not stop advocating the slogan of working to the utmost and of producing, cost what it might. Was this simply a political tactic? It's not my business to figure it out. It was enough for me that France benefited." (*Le Salut*, pp.100-101.)

challenging are really on the same side of the barricades. They are defending French society as we know it... The Communist Party thus stood revealed as the ultimate bastion of the consumer society which the student Bolsheviks are pledged to destroy. It is as if Washington and Moscow had got together to put down North Vietnam." (P. Seale and M. McConville, *The Observer*, May 19.)

IV. The stages of May 1968

Following the movement day by day, one can distinguish stages which succeeded each other with a thoroughly remarkable internal logic.

The first stage began on May 3 with the entry of the police into the Sorbonne courtyard and the immediate resistance of the students on the Boulevard Saint-Michel. It reached its peak on May 10, when the high-school strike was followed by the demonstration which started out from the Place Denfert-Rochereau and returned on the Boulevard Saint-Michel, to end in the night of the barricades on the Rue Gay-Lussac and the neighboring streets.

This opened the way for the second stage, which began with the 24-hour general strike and the demonstrations of May 13. Under the impetus of this gigantic demonstration, the workers began to strike about 48 hours later, beginning a general strike with factory occupations. The movement reached a very high point (about 10 million strikers, to say nothing of numerous and many-sided demonstrations of all orders) toward the end of the week of May 20 to 25. During this week the dreary CGT demonstrations were politically juxtaposed to the demonstration at the Gare de Lyon, which culminated in a new night of the barricades and revolts in many parts of Paris. At this point, the government, the bosses, and the trade-union leaders hurriedly plunged into marathon negotiations lasting about 30 hours.

On Monday May 27 the trade-union leaders were barely given time to present the provisions of the Grenelle agreements to the workers in the principal factories (Renault, Citroën, etc.). These agreements were indignantly rejected by a unanimous hand vote. Then the movement entered into a third, politically decisive stage in which the question of power was posed. The government was impotent. There were demonstrations in the street in favor of different formulas for a government to succeed the de Gaulle regime. At Charlety stadium, the ranks were for "power to the workers." However, the silhouette of Mendes-France stood out on the speakers' platform, offering himself both to the bourgeoisie and the working masses as a 'left de Gaulle" to replace the right-wing de Gaulle. On

May 29, from the Bastille to the Gare Saint-Lazare, the workers of Paris and its red suburbs responded to the appeals of the CGT and the PCF for a "people's government of democratic union" "with Communist participation."

But these were only whims of the leaders since no slogan was given for any action aimed at overthrowing the Gaullist government. Strengthened by this indecision, this inertia, and by the electoral and parliamentary cretinism which deeply marks all the left leaders, de Gaulle decided to turn and fight. He stirred up every poltroonish, craven, and conservative element in the country. He denounced a purported danger from the PCF, which was completely nonplussed. He threatened to resort to military means. And, in place of a referendum which nobody even wanted to consider, he offered the left a goody – legislative elections in the coming weeks, following the dissolution of a National Assembly which had made itself an object of ridicule by the servility of the Fifth Republic mini-majority and the impotence of the minority to gather the few votes necessary to get a motion of censure adopted.

With de Gaulle's May 30 speech a new stage opened up. The mass leaderships accepted the elections, creating an extreme fragmentation of the movement. The all-out general strike which objectively posed the question of power gave way to powerful strikes for essentially economic objectives, which were negotiated separately with the bosses or the leaderships of the overseeing ministries. This, as I write, is the phase we are in now. As a revolutionary thrust, a revolutionary crisis making possible the overthrow of the Gaullist regime and even the capitalist system, May 1968 is now ended.

The strike movement will not dissipate itself overnight. These strikes will continue for a more or less prolonged period in many sectors. Analyzing these strikes in detail is outside the scope of this pamphlet. It is enough here to say that they must be waged vigorously with the maximum cohesion on the strike front so as to obtain the best results in winning the economic demands.

In this new stage, revolutionaries are concerned not only with improving the workers' living conditions, which is always the case for them. The new period of the crisis of the capitalist system will not end with the present strikes. The socialist revolution will pass through new waves and new revolutionary crises. In order for these to start in the best conditions, it is not unimportant that the workers come out of the present strikes free from any feeling of failure, or of frustration, and that they end the strikes as they began them, in a very militant way.

V. Characteristics of the movement

What were the essential characteristics of the movement of May 1968? Its first characteristic, which struck everyone, was its extensiveness. Ten million strikers – France has never known such a movement. It is probable no big industrial country has experienced one like it or similar to it in proportion to population.

This movement – and this is another of its characteristics – did not include only workers. The industrial proletariat and the agricultural proletariat in the strict sense of the word, as well as most categories of white-collar workers, were encompassed by it. Besides the teachers and students who originated the movement, the participation of the high-school students, and parallel to this, of a large number of young workers, of very young people from 14 to 18 years of age, is an absolutely new phenomenon in history. Very young people have participated in revolutionary periods before, but this was always limited and never included the great bulk of adolescents. This is a phenomenon which would merit a serious sociological study. It is moreover an enormously promising development. All who closely followed the participation of these young people were struck, let me say for my part, amazed, by the seriousness and high political consciousness they exhibited above and beyond the enthusiasm of their age. This bears a promise for the movement in the coming years of an abundance of activists and cadres who will already have considerable experience at an age when recruitment to youth organizations generally used to begin.

The movement drew in a whole series of categories belonging sociologically to the petty bourgeoisie. At the side of the strikers were the greater part of the intellectuals and of the artists. Likewise, an important part of the new middle classes (technicians, etc.) joined in with the strikers. If I am not mistaken, this was the first time that the CGC took a favorable stand toward the workers demands; it even formally gave permission for its members to go to the May 13 demonstration if they wished. The liberal professions (doctors, architects, etc.) were also drawn into this movement, some of their members demonstrating against the high priests of their orders. Even the lawyers were stirred up against the archaic rules which govern them; even the judges were not left unaffected by the situation, and all the more so inasmuch as the government took a very cavalier attitude toward them during the student struggles.

Sectors as *blasé* as the journalists, as neutral as the public gardeners, as little politically concerned as the professional football players, and so on, were set in motion by this movement.

Among the peasants many demonstrators declared themselves outright for solidarity with the workers' and students' movements. I will only mention the ranks of the army. All reports agree that they followed the events with the greatest interest and that it would not have been possible to range them against the striking workers.

Even the police forces felt it necessary to address themselves through the proper hierarchical channels, to let the authorities know that it would be a test of conscience for them if they were sent against workers fighting for their demands. When cops start talking about conscience...

* * *

Another characteristic of the movement was that it bypassed bourgeois legality. May saw many street demonstrations, very strong demonstrations, for which no one had asked authorization – no more than the strikers had considered it necessary to give legal notice five days before going out on strike.

These demonstrations were not all of the same character. There were still some which proceeded calmly, quietly, and spiritlessly at the wish of their organizers and with the tacit approval of the authorities. And there were others which attained a high political level and did not shrink from confrontation with the repressive forces, giving free rein to the most varied methods of struggle.

The various demonstrations which took place in Paris expressed *in the streets* the various opposing political currents of the movement. These were the most remarkable illustration of the different orientations seeking to lead the movement toward different political objectives. Because, for all practical purposes, power was "in the street," politics was carried on in the streets. This constituted a uniquely potent school of politics.

* * *

One essential characteristic of a revolutionary period was present which cannot be overstressed. In such periods, different mass actions of greater or lesser duration and varying scope cripple the authority of the state, of the bosses, of those institutions whose basis lies in capitalist society. In Marxist terms, manifold mass actions lead to the creation of more or less prolonged dual power, that is to the creation of organs or forms, often only embryonic, which are outside the framework of capitalist society or the prevailing system, and which, as they progress could become the leading bodies of a new society. In the decomposition of capitalist society and its state, the elements of a socialist society began to form from the ground up. The balance of forces compelled the capitalist government, temporarily of course, to tolerate or accept these socialist elements. Instances of "dual power" were often produced independently of the consciousness of those who initiated them.

Here are examples: The universities and many educational institutions obviously broke most clearly with the government. They were suffering under a statute instituted by Napoleon I, and they were also the establishments in which self-government could be established with the least difficulties. It is also in this sphere that no solution has been achieved, that relations with the government have not been reestablished, and where a multiplicity of conflicts can be expected. Attempts at reorganizing the existing structures were also made by professors and high-school students; and they did not fail to run into resistance from the administration. What was attempted in the medical schools naturally carried over into hospitals linked to medical education.

I cannot go into detail here on many instances where authorities in the plants were challenged. Were there not many cases of plant managers locked in their offices or forbidden access to the plants? During the strike, the strike committees – even when they were only the old trade-union executive boards under another name – were led to confiscate plant property to assure continuation of the strike (Saclay...). In certain cases, the strike committees spread out beyond their respective plants, entered into negotiations with suppliers and laid the initial groundwork for a resumption of work without the bosses. The problems of guaranteed employment and hiring were put on the agenda (CSF) in Brest.

In services, the employees often exercised the decisive supervisory power. Postal clerks made the decisions about the texts of telegrams to determine whether or not they were urgent.

Some localities found themselves under the control of the trade unions for all practical purposes (in Nantes and Saint-Nazaire, local authorities in actuality served only as messengers between the unions and the government). In Caen, passage in and out of the city was under the control of the strikers for a whole day. In a great number of cases groups of citizens took steps with little concern for legality or bourgeois property; land and buildings were occupied and used to meet needs which had been neglected or ignored before by both the appointed and elected officials.

The printing industry merits comment. The leadership of the printing unions, by an agreement between the reformist and Stalinist leaders, permitted daily newspapers to appear and consequently the bourgeois press continued being published. True, in certain circumstances the workers demanded changes in headlines (*Figaro*) or even refused to bring out a paper (*La Nation*) when the content was directly prejudicial to the strike. In these cases, the workers amended the decision of their union organization in the right way.

But this decision held another not altogether innocent aspect. The strike was to be applied to all of the weekly press and all periodicals. The result was that the wealthy publications which wanted to could be printed abroad, while with rare exceptions, all the vanguard papers, whose financial means are limited, were unable to appear. In other words, while the bourgeois press and the reformist and Stalinist press could express itself freely, revolutionary militants were up against enormous difficulties getting their views into print.

Obviously, this was a stratagem of the reformists and Stalinists in which they conspired like thieves. Only the proofreaders' union, which was particularly sensitive to the problem, adopted the proposition in a resolution: "it [the proofreaders' union] declares itself for the freedom to publish *by the strikers themselves* all publications supporting the workers and students movement, whether daily or periodical."

One sphere where the question of relations with the government took an acute form was radio and television. On one hand, the government, which was so zealous about the "right to work," deprived the over-the-border radio and television stations (the only stations broadcasting which are not under government control) of the radio-telephones they had rented, to prevent them from broadcasting accounts of the revolutionary demonstrations and the savage repressions of the CRS and the Gardes Mobiles. On the other hand, under the pressure of events and general indignation, the radio and TV workers (ORTF) found the majority of its personnel, including journalists who were not known in the past for independence, refusing to carry on a systematic dissemination of official lying.

And finally the day came, at a heightened moment of the crisis, when Geismar [head of SNESup during the crisis], Sauvageot [head of the UNEF], and Cohn-Bendit could be heard and seen on television. And this single broadcast showed the damage that merely honest radio and television could do to the government. While the government seemed to abandon any idea of reestablishing its "order" in the universities for a while, it was at no time disposed to making any essential concessions in the political management of ORTF. A battle is being waged there which concerns all the working people. Will this office, whose financial support comes from them, remain the monopoly of the Gaullist mafia (which formed an anonymous committee calling for the dismissal of certain journalists by name)? Or will it remain open, even if not completely, to a confrontation of ideas and points of view? In the present circumstances, when even the most politically bland large formations are excluded, revolutionary organizations and militants cannot hope to be heard.

The most developed form of "dual power" is in the Sorbonne itself. Bourgeois laws stop at the perimeter of this building, which used to be a school of scholastic theology. The police do not enter. Immunity is assured there for those who break bourgeois laws. Cohn-Bendit, who was banned from France, lived there in safety. Socialist democracy is undergoing an unlimited development. The Sorbonne is self-governing. I am told that for some time the police have been checking papers of those entering and leaving. They are doing this at a time when police and customs forces on the borders of France have almost literally evaporated. At the Sorbonne, they no longer pay any attention to the government's decisions in educational matters, and not only in educational matters. Demonstrations are decided on there that really amount to attempted sorties into different countries, and not always peaceful ones. The word "foreigner" has no meaning, except insofar as men are given the means for preparing a struggle for socialism directed at their respective countries. The Sorbonne is, so to speak, the first free territory of the Socialist Republic of France.

Since the movement did not attain the end it could have, that is, the conquest of power, it is now reduced to strikes which are holding more or less to a united front. But it is obvious that before the next revolutionary wave, these islands of "dual power" will be subjected to attacks by the bourgeois government aimed at eliminating them. This is a problem I will examine further on in connection with the preparation for future revolutionary struggles.

Finally, the movement gave birth to manifold spontaneous forms of organization, with and without connections to previously existing organizations. No one could fail to be impressed by the number of leaflets from every quarter, alike from old organizations, more or less ephemeral new organizations, and individuals themselves. All of this testified to the impetus which socialist revolution gave to the liberation of man, from its first steps, even before its triumph.

Some have thought to display their wit by denigrating the Sorbonne occupation as a carnival. This is not very far removed from de Gaulle's thinking that it was a *"chienlit"* [a crude military expression meaning roughly "a shitty mess"]. In fact, neglecting a few things which weren't too serious, the Sorbonne revealed the creative power of revolution, its liberation of the creative initiative of masses and individuals alike. Life at the Sorbonne is not characterized by the "excesses" but all the creative ferment, the unquestionable liberation of the human spirit, what it would take a body of thinkers years to conceive – if then.

I will return to some of these questions in approaching the subject of the tasks of the revolutionary vanguard as it emerged in this movement. One task is to defend these gains. Only the living movement itself can sift out what it has created and eliminate what it does not find worthwhile. We must not fall into the trap which will certainly be there, of putting the spotlight on certain "excesses," shocking to petty-bourgeois opinion, in order to discredit the conquests of the revolutionary movement of May 1968, thus enabling bourgeois repression to liquidate them.

VI. The mass movement and the traditional leaderships

In studying the various stages of the movement closely, the following conclusions may be drawn. Within the "detonator" group ["detonator" is the term the students themselves used], there were several elements capable of playing a leading role: political groups and the UNEF and SNESup leaderships, which included politically educated militants independent of the traditional leaderships and opposed to their policies. Without exaggerating the forces on which these UNEF and SNESup leaders based themselves, or the strength of the politically conscious groups, it can be said that these few "dozen wildmen," in the objective conditions of the revolutionary crisis, played a considerable role in touching off the movement and later in advancing it through the various stages I have pointed out. They continued to perform this function up until the last stage, in which the "detonator" could have only worked again had exceptional circumstances developed – and this was not the case, as will be seen further on.

Once it was off the ground under the impetus of the "detonator," the workers movement itself went forward despite its traditional leaderships. These leaderships held back from demonstrating solidarity with the students when they were struggling against the police. They wanted a demonstration on May 15 only; but following the night of the barricades of May 10-11, they found themselves obliged, under the pressure of popular anger, to declare a 24-hour general strike for May 13.

Once that day was over, they thought they were back to peace and quiet, when, spontaneously, the workers – essentially the young workers – began to occupy factories without any directive from the unions. Once more, the union leaderships only recognized the de facto situation this created. They negotiated with the government and the bosses under the shock of the night of rebellions on May 24, but they did so ignoring the workers' real desires and so again found themselves outdistanced on May 27.

The leaderships of the CFDT and FO, whose respective influence in the working class was limited, can be left aside. No one expected the CFDT or FO to assume a vanguard role. The CGT leadership, however, had behind it the decisive battalions of the working class, as was seen in the demonstration of May 29. While revolutionary minorities were conscious of the pernicious role the CGT leadership could play because of its allegiance to the policy of the PCF, the large masses of the workers placed their hopes in this leadership. The CGT and PCF leadership was outdistanced by the mass movement as early as May 3 and for all the days following. It was only on May 29 – or four weeks late – that it seemed to regain the leadership of the actions by calling for a political change and the establishment of a "people's government of democratic union." While it was still being constantly outflanked to the left by the mass movement, it strove to limit the movement's advance by directing its principal blows against "ultraleftists," "provocateurs," etc. At no time did it undertake to criticize the leaderships of the other trade union federations, and with reason. However, it felt the need to denounce and even break with UNEF – and in harsh terms. This bureaucratic PCF and CGT leadership must have thought that once the "ultraleftists" were denounced and eliminated the movement would return to "order." Hadn't it been the case for many years that the CGT's "monitors" forcibly removed "ultraleftists" and other "provocateurs" from demonstrations organized by the CGT without the least altercation with the police? Hadn't it been seen how these disrupters were eliminated who threatened the "calm" and "dignity" of the CGT's demonstrations, that is, threatened to break agreements reached beforehand with the police? The enemy is on the left, that was the CGT and PCF leaders' slogan. And that meant not only the "ultraleftists," but the entire mass movement which was moving in a left direction.

* * *

It was not, however, so much its utterances which proved particularly harmful in the course of the movement. This movement had such power that it very often ignored these. What was chiefly harmful to the movement was the fragmentation which the CGT leadership maintained and fostered and in which it was followed by the leaders of the other trade-union federations. The students and teachers as well as the high-school students were first of all carefully divided from the workers. Everything was done to deepen this separation. For the universities, the CGT and PCF put forward slogans like "A Democratic and Modern University" which had nothing in common with the demands of the striking students and teachers. In practice, the factory gates were closed to the students, who the CGT leaders feared would contaminate the workers with their "ultraleft" politics. In order to facilitate this result, the leaders also did their utmost to reduce the number of strikers occupying the factories, urging the majority to stay home most of the time, so that the factories were chiefly occupied by those elements which were considered most reliable – from these leaders' standpoint.

Furthermore, their negotiations with the government – which should not have been considered a valid party to discussion in the first place – were conducted right from the start in a way that divided the workers of the private sector, those in the nationalized sectors, and salaried personnel. In other words, there was no general strike for these leaders. They refused to launch this slogan at one time apparently under the pretext that the general strike was already an accomplished fact and didn't need to be called. But the reality of this was their fear that if they had issued a general strike slogan they would have had to set political objectives because political demands alone expressed the common denominator of the movement struggle. These bureaucrats saw the movement only as an arithmetical sum of separate and distinct economic struggles in which each group was negotiating on its own account. This was their policy in the weeks preceding the Rue de Grenelle negotiations and during them; it remained the same immediately following the rejections of these agreements by the workers.

Even at the time when the CGT organized the May 29 demonstrations it did not establish any link between the immediate demands and the slogan of "a people's government." It never declared that the general strike, nonexistent in its eyes since it had not been called, had the objective of creating this "people's government." Finally, when de Gaulle, to create a red scare, accused the PCF and the CGT of conducting a political strike with the aim of changing the government in the country, both organizations rejected this accusation. At last, the PCF and CGT leaderships aligned themselves with de Gaulle's decision to hold legislative elections.

Thus, the CGT leadership, which had rejected the accusation that it was following a revolutionary policy (and certainly did not follow such a policy), which claimed that all political problems were the sole preserve of the political parties, reconciled itself to politics by floundering in parliamentarism. The CGT, which never failed to say all through the mobilizations that it was only concerned with economic demands and that governmental problems were the business of political parties, which ignored the question of government as long as it could and later rejected anything remotely approaching a revolutionary orientation, only began to show signs of political life when de Gaulle put the question on an electoral basis.

Turning to the PCF's own policy through May, first of all, like the CGT, it directed almost all its fire against the "ultraleftists." After the *l'Humanité* article by Marchais, the organizational secretary of the PCF, denouncing "the German Cohn-Bendit" on May 3 – the very day the struggle began – hardly a day passed without some more or less severe and more or less crudely expressed condemnation of "ultraleftists." The variations in this regard are not without interest. It is easy to show from the columns of *l'Humanité* that the virulent denunciation of the first days was progressively (if this adverb can be used in this instance) attenuated as the movement took rapid leaps forward and grew, that it took a sharper turn just before any possibility that the leaders would be outflanked, and that it assumed a heightened form after de Gaulle's speech and above all as soon as the back-to-work movement developed. Now that elections are the order of the day, monopolizing the PCF leaders' attention, the "ultraleftists" are increasingly becoming the target of virulent attacks[66].

Throughout May, the PCF leadership's favorite term for attacking revolutionary militants was "ultraleftist." Now it is resorting to the term "provocateur." The June 8 issue of *l'Humanité* is a choice specimen in this regard. The "provocateurs" at Flins were not the government and the Gardes Mobiles but the students along with Geismar from the SNESup, who went there to express their solidarity, with workers driven out of the factory and to fight alongside them against the forces of repression. The students there were not organized in disciplined commando groups (which would not have been a bad idea in facing the forces of "order"). However, *l'Humanité*, through its published statements, can only be said to have played the role of an informer. These are the real provocations whose infamous ends must be denounced. And the reason for the PCF's outburst can be found explicitly stated in a declaration by the CGT Railway Workers Federation, which is Seguy's own union: Incidents with the state forces, they say, could have a bad effect on the election campaign. The distance from this to condemning those who came to support strikers is not long. After all, the Stalinists are not novices in these matters.

---

[66] It should not be forgotten that the UNEF and CGT leaders could not come to an understanding because the CGT leadership refused to condemn the government's measure banning Cohn-Bendit from France. What authority will the protestations of the PCF or the CGT have tomorrow when the government expels foreign workers? Their aversion to "ultra-leftists" has taken precedence for them over solidarity with foreign militants struck by administrative measures. Of course, the Stalinists never defend oppositionists persecuted by the bourgeoisie.

Didn't one Stalinist secretary of the CGT declare in December 1945 "strikes are the weapon of monopolies?"

* * *

But the "enemy on the left" slogan is only one side of the CGT leadership's policy. How did it conduct itself toward its right, that is toward the FGDS?

The line the PCF leadership has been following for some years is well known. It wants to reach a "common program" with the FGDS to wage a joint election campaign. It was rather neatly added that this would be linked to a mass movement of "unrivaled breadth." One doesn't know whether for Waldeck Rochet this meant a revolutionary movement, which is doubtful, or whether his vision of such a movement corresponded to the one which occurred in 1968. In passing it can be remarked that he isn't known for such imagination. In any case, when this movement of "unrivaled breadth" occurred, he did not seem to recognize it or to feel any need to draw conclusions from it. From the first day and almost up until the end of May he stepped up his appeals and letters to Mitterrand to speed up the negotiations on a common program. This leadership refused to serve as an "auxiliary" (its own term) for UNEF in organizing a demonstration against the Algerian war in 1960, but pleaded day after day to the FGDS to agree to a meeting to negotiate this mysterious "common program." Moreover, no one knows what this program could be since the *Declaration of February 1968* was not to serve as the model. The PCF did not want to be an "auxiliary" of UNEF in the struggle against the Algerian war; but it was acting as if it was anxious to be an auxiliary of the FGDS, on the basis of no-one-knows-what program, at a time when the mass movement had reached an exceptional peak.

From May 3 to 27, the PCF leadership did not advance in action a single slogan on the question of the government. Its decision was, so to speak, subordinated to an agreement with the FGDS on this "joint program" which no one has yet seen. The PCF leadership thus had no political solution of its own for the crisis for more than 25 days. For it, everything depended on an agreement with the FGDS. Does this leadership, after that, still dare to claim that it is leading the party of the working class, and even that it is its vanguard?

But the PCF leadership made a turn toward the end of May, declaring itself for a "people's government of democratic unity" and calling for the constitution of "committees of action" for such a government. A few preliminary words are necessary. First of all, one cannot find any definition of the content of such a government in the CP press. "With Communist participation," PCF agitators chanted in the May 29 demonstrations. But, assuming this, who would they be "participating" with? The FGDS, one might think. There is a small difficulty in this, which I will take up right after noting one other point. The PCF leadership used the term "action committee," which refers to manifold organizations created during the May mobilization with a policy quite different from the one the CP has been following. Here, the CP duplicated the operation it carried out a few months earlier when it created "Vietnam Committees" totally different from those which for long months had been waging a real struggle for Vietnamese victory and which the CP continually fought as "ultraleftist." When it does not slander the "ultraleftists," the PCF tries to mix up political labels. It creates "action committees" whose objective in regard to real mass action is inaction.

Having said this, we can return to the question of the government itself. The formula "people's government of democratic union" did not drop out of the blue. While the PCF leadership was pleading heart and soul with the FGDS leadership to come to an understanding on the "joint program" which did not seem to be about to see the light of day, a little operation had been plotted for several days by the FGDS leadership and other forces on the left. A good many people were aware of it or in on it and it was revealed at the very moment the PCF (also on to it) presented its new formula.

The May movement itself posed the question of government. This was correctly appreciated even in Gaullist ranks. It was then that Mitterrand, having totally forgotten the existence of his "shadow government," made a declaration in favor of a "government of transition" which had little in common with a special alliance between the FGDS and the PCF and consequently with an FGDS-PCF government. Mitterrand added that he was ready to take the lead of such a government, but – oh, what rare generosity for the political world! – others were as worthy to lead it as he, for example, Mendes-France. The name which had been quietly whispered about for some days was finally pronounced publicly.

What was the meaning of this political operation? Mendes-France did not exclude participation of Communists in his government, but at the same time Lecanuet[67] himself would not have done less. Mendes-France added that such a "provisional government" should not be based on a "concoction" of different political parties. This became very clear. The operation consisted in replacing the right Bonapartist government of de Gaulle with an equally Bonapartist

---

[67] The leader of the Centrists or the party of "Progress and Modern Democracy." This party is identified with a program of bourgeois modernization and strengthening the "Atlantic Alliance." – Ed.

government, but a "left" one, with Mendes-France. This would not be a government based on a parliamentary majority but one which would continue playing the game of balancing between opposing social forces in the country. This balancing game would be more anchored to the forces on the left in distinction to that anchored to the forces of the right in de Gaulle's time. Mendes-France is no novice in this type of operation. His government in 1954 was the groundbreaker. It contained, moreover, several politicians who have since reappeared in de Gaulle's governments (among others, Fouchet [Minister of Education under de Gaulle]).

In the face of such a powerful movement de Gaulle's "strong government" might no longer be the most indicated solution for French capitalism. There was, however, no question of a return to bourgeois democracy. Another team under the leadership of a so-called man of the left would have operated in the same way as de Gaulle.

The PCF leadership saw a danger to itself in this attempt. Hadn't it served before (when Thorez was its leader) in such a government led by de Gaulle? It wanted a government, whether led by Mitterrand or someone else, in which it could bring pressure to bear – not for the victory of socialism (if it had wanted that, it would not have needed to take a detour through Mitterrand or anyone else). What it was seeking was essentially concessions in a direction favorable to what the Kremlin wants – notably in international policy. A parliamentary government of the Mitterrand type would have been more sensitive to pressure than a Bonapartist government of the Mendes-France type. In the minds of its organizers, the May 20 demonstration for "a people's government," ostensibly directed against de Gaulle was at least as much against a Mendes-France coalition.

Finally, when de Gaulle decided to turn and fight, the first response to his decision to call legislative elections came from Waldeck Rochet. De Gaulle, he said, had only adopted the PCF's own demand on this score. The PCF leadership then called on all PCF members to roll up their sleeves for the coming elections, which could only be done by draining the energy devoted to continuing strikes.

One can legitimately doubt the PCF leadership's desire to oust de Gaulle. Reading the Soviet and East European press shows that de Gaulle has the favor of the governments in these countries. He has been enthusiastically received there in recent years. A change appeared only after his recent anti-Communist statements. While this is debatable, there can be no hesitation on another point. In a pinch, the CP might replace de Gaulle's regime with another, but not on the basis of a mass movement like the one in May. It wants to do this only on the basis of an electoral success. This is less dangerous for the government which could result.

Let us sum up the May 1968 balance sheet of the Stalinist PCF and CGT leadership:

- It opposed the revolutionary struggle of the fighting students and did everything possible to prevent a political and organizational link between them and the workers.
- It divided the various categories of workers (private industry, the nationalized sectors, and white-collar workers) instead of uniting them on a common program.
- It refused to declare a general strike on the pretext that one existed in fact, but in reality so as not to have to advance the only proper slogan for a general strike – a slogan of struggle for power.
- It. negotiated in disregard of the workers' desires and accepted miserable agreements which the workers spontaneously rejected in as many seconds as the union leaders had spent hours working them out with the bosses and government.
- It never took the slightest initiative to mobilize the strikers, limiting itself either to keeping them bottled up in the plants or sending them home to twiddle their thumbs.
- It never stopped making war on and slandering the "ultra-leftists," tacitly encouraging physical violence against them as in the past, and at the same time, it never organized workers to defend themselves against reactionary bands and state repressive forces.
- It never raised the slogan of dissolution of the repressive forces (*Gardes Mobiles*, CRS) which were sent against the students and the workers.
- It betrayed the defense of "foreign" militants faced with repressive government dictates (the Cohn-Bendit affair), thus promoting its factional interests ahead of proletarian internationalism and at the expense of it.
- It never publicly denounced Mitterrand's maneuvers and never stopped chasing after the FGDS to get a "joint program" already outdistanced by the political events.
- It held an equivocal attitude on the referendum which de Gaulle decided to call at one point.
- It never sought to overturn de Gaulle and was the first to accept his decision to hold legislative elections. Thus, it betrayed 10 million strikers in the quest for five million votes.
- It did not want to utilize a movement which was leading to socialism. Seeking a "new democracy" of a bourgeois character, it assured the maintenance of de Gaulle's regime.

This betrayal of the PCF leadership equalled and surpassed the oft denounced betrayals of the Social Democracy. If this leadership has not up until now acted in the manner that the Noskes and the Eberts acted against the German revolution of 1918-19, it is because the bourgeoisie has no need of it. But its conduct toward the "ultraleftists" leaves no doubt that it is ready to do so should the need arise.

VII. The organization of the working class during the strike

A few words must be added on the organization of the working class by the PCF leadership through the CGT apparatus. For a good many years the Stalinists have stifled workers democracy in the organizations they dominate, above all in the CGT. It was almost impossible for a worker to rise to the most modest post in a union local, in a national union, or even to the position of plant delegate – no matter how devoted or how active he might be – without the endorsement of the factory cell or the trade-union apparatus in his plant. Only those who had passed through this screening were eligible to be officially entrusted with the confidence of the workers, even at the lowest level. That is, while they were not necessarily members of the Communist Party, they were not to constitute an obstacle to the policy which it conducted through the intermediary of the CGT. Only rare exceptions could be noted in recent years: For example, some union activists held PSU cards. Furthermore, criticisms in union meetings could not go beyond a certain limit. In these conditions, the opportunities for activity open to critical elements were restricted if not nonexistent. There was never any question of getting a serious hearing in trade-union congresses, or being able to openly advocate a different line than that of the leadership. Known oppositionists were barely tolerated.

In the course of the movement, "strike committees" were designated in the factories. But for the great majority of workers, the concept of a "strike committee" was not clear, for the simple reason that the union leaderships never seriously explained it – because it was not in their interest to do so. They never explained to the workers that in a strike the leadership of the struggle must be *democratically elected by all the strikers whether or not they are union members*. This occurred only in rare exceptions, in scattered plants, since workers had not been alerted to this question. Generally, the union local leaders were baptized "strike committees" during the strike. The result? These "strike committees" continued to operate in the same way they did when they were the executive boards of the union locals.

They served therefore much more as transmission belts to bring the CGT's policy down to the workers than transmission belts for bringing the aspirations and desires of the rank-and-file workers up to the union tops. This, of course, helped to keep the union leaders in the dark about the aspirations of the class and to make them think that the workers would accept the agreements which they had negotiated on the Rue de Grenelle without any problem.

But this camouflaging of the union locals leadership as "strike committees" had another consequence which was really grave. These "strike committees" were bound together only by the union apparatus. If there had been real elected strike committees it is probable that we would have seen, at least in certain places, the tendency which has always manifested itself when there were elected strike committees – that is the tendency for these committees to federate on the local, then regional, and finally national levels. Then, instead of a bureaucratic halter and brake on the movement, there would be a network of democratically elected committees from the ground up which would tend to give birth to a much more representative leadership of the class in struggle, to a leadership subordinated much more to the strikers than to a trade-union apparatus or party whose special interests ran counter to the most profound natural tendencies of the movement and notably to the revolutionary tendency which was carrying it toward the conquest of power to create a socialist society.

VIII. The revolutionary vanguard

The revolutionary vanguard in May is generally conceded to have been the youth, youth who very largely escaped control of the traditional organizations and leaderships of the workers movement.

It was the student youth who, first of all began the fight at the university. New movements emerged, like the March 22 Movement at Nanterre. There were formations claiming to base themselves on Trotsky, Che Guevara, Mao Tse-tung. In UNEF, these line formations played a leading role or acted as the motor force, instigating the taking of positions, demonstrations, etc. There was no room for doubt about the relationship of the old leaderships of the workers movement to this student youth. Hardly a word was heard about the Social Democratic students. The Communist students, led by the political bureau, had over the preceding years expelled in successive purges all elements from the Communist Student Union (UEC) inspired by political orientations different from that of Waldeck Rochet – and they were the majority. It was these expelled members precisely who were in the leadership of the "grouplets."

Banned from the peaceful and spiritless demonstrations which sometimes moved from the Place de la Republique to the Place de la Bastille, and sometimes from the Place de la Bastille to the Place de la Republique, these "ultraleftists" turned up again in the May 1968 demonstrations at the head of tens of thousands of demonstrators. And these were ardent, militant demonstrators not afraid to confront the repressive forces of the capitalist state.

In the student-occupied Sorbonne courtyard the UEC has its place – because the other groups respect workers democracy even for those who have trampled it underfoot for years. However, the authority and influence of the UEC, and through it of the PCF leadership, have been mortally damaged in the student milieu. It is not anticipating the future to say that the PCF leadership has little further chance in this milieu. Observations which it has been possible to make here and there indicate the UEC's recruitment in the most recent period has been among the most politically backward layers. This is only normal. Once a party has (capitalist) "statesmanship," as the editor of *Le Monde* described the PCF, the only ones who can turn toward it in such a period are those who still dream of leading a quiet life in the service of the state or the bosses – not those who dedicate themselves to the socialist revolution.

The university student youth were joined by the high-school youth. The participation of hundreds of thousands of 14- and 15-year-old young people in the May movement is a phenomenon absolutely unprecedented in history. The high-school movement originated in the course of actions in solidarity with the Vietnamese revolution. Some very young militants who sought to campaign for solidarity with the Vietnamese people in the high schools collided with the administration as well as many teachers attached to the old idea of the barracks-type school. In order to struggle against the regime in the high schools, these very young militants founded the high-school action committees (CAL). One of the leaders was expelled from the Lycée Condorcet[68], and this touched off a protest demonstration of several hundred high-school students outside this lycée. This movement grew during the early months of 1968. On May 9, the CAL decided to call a high-school general strike for the following day. This strike was begun in a manner rather like factory strikes. The strike (the high-school students used the same term as the workers) began in the morning; the striking students went out into the streets to go to

---

[68] The French lycées are on the order of the English "public schools" like Eton and Harrow. The Lycée Condorcet is one of the elite lycées, along with the Lycée Louis le Grand and the Lycée Henri IV. Expulsion from such a school could represent a serious threat to a student's future career. – Ed.

other high schools in order to bring them out on strike; street meetings were held. In the afternoon, a demonstration of close to 8,000 high-school students went from the Gobelins to the Place Denfert-Rochereau to join the university students and teachers' demonstration. This demonstration was to end with the night of the barricades in which a great number of high-school students participated. The strike movement extended to the technical high schools and all institutions of the same type. The CAL, democratically representing all of the strikers, initiated several street demonstrations together with UNEF and SNESup.

Politically, the active wing of the CAL shares the views of the university students; it is resolutely anti-capitalist and internationalist. Some pressure from the teachers has made itself felt in the schools, since the secondary-school teachers' union is in the hands of the Stalinists. But one can be confident that Stalinist influence will not make much headway with this section of youth either.

After May 3 the number of young workers demonstrating side by side with the students grew daily. This was also a revelation: The unions which held sway over the factory workers exercised only relative control over the youth in the factories.

In the months preceding May, on several occasions (Besançon, Caen, Le Mans, Rouen, etc.) there was a conspicuous combativity on the part of the youth in strikes; this could be particularly noted in confrontations which had already occurred in the streets. These were the advance signs of the explosion. These developments showed that the youth were exhibiting signs of a militancy and a combativity which they had not learned from their organizations. But it was still difficult to discern in these manifestations a break with the traditional leaderships and their policy. The youth were unable to assert their views against the union apparatuses because of the lack of workers democracy. It took May to reveal this break. And it came out into the open primarily because the students, by taking the lead with a different policy from the traditional leaderships, offered the young workers a pole of attraction; the young workers flocked to it en masse. Dissatisfied with the policy and methods of the traditional leaderships, they came in large numbers to the Sorbonne to get direction.

Thus, the working-class youth are also showing themselves more and more resistant to Stalinism. The CGT leadership rapidly comprehended the danger facing it. For several months, it had been preparing a "youth festival" for May 11 and 12. Two hours before it was to open it cancelled it on a phony pretext. In actuality, the CGT leaders wanted to forestall the contact which would have occurred between the youth they brought together and those who had come the evening before to fight on the barricades the night of Rue Gay-Lussac – and that was the real youth festival.

It was also the youth in most cases and notably at the Renault plants who took the initiative in the strikes and factory occupations. They did not wait for orders from the union, often violently shaking up the immobility of the trade-union organizations. During the strike, frictions multiplied between union apparatuses and young workers. An impressive picture can be drawn. The May 29 CGT demonstration was called largely to prevent the unions from being outflanked by young workers. At Renault this situation assumed important proportions.

It is necessary to go a bit more into the question of the "young hoodlums" and other youth belonging to the "gangs" in the working-class districts who for years have been a frequent subject of discussion in the press. Because they participated extremely combatively in the street battles, striking fear into the forces of repression, the most violent abuse was heaped on them from various quarters. During the events, the minister of the interior Fouchet, never sparing in his use of scare words, dared to use the word "scum" to blacken these youth. These young people have nothing in common with the real scum, the riffraff who are also the best defenders of the bourgeois order. At the time of the Ben Barka affair they were on the best terms with the highest police officials, they often operated as a kind of auxiliary police service, and they mingled with secret police agents who gravitate around the highest spheres of the Fifth Republic. It is in the gangs de Gaulle is appealing to for "civic action" that you find the scum. This scum extends from the highest rung of society to the riffraff who protect the underworld. These supporters of the Fifth Republic are in the best tradition of Napoleon III's "December 10 Society."

The "young hoodlums" and other youths who were slandered by this rabble-rousing minister are nothing more than young workers whom the neo-capitalist consumer society has reduced to more than precarious conditions of existence and employment. Lacking in vocational skills, the first to be thrown out of work by technological progress, without hope, harassed daily by a police force which considers repression the highest form of education, they have built up a ferocious hatred of the repressive forces. This was, if you will, a very elementary form of developing political opposition to capitalist society. With rare exceptions, no one has had a real dialogue with them. With an unfailing instinct they took the side of the students. Their interest was in taking their revenge for all the harassment the police had subjected them to. During the events, a radio reporter asked one of these young men what his motive was in taking part in the demonstrations. He may have expected a more or less awkward political answer. "I came to beat up cops," the youth told him. According to the press reports, very few cases of looting were noted during the struggle. This proves that these youth were not interested in appropriating this or that product of the consumer society they were deprived of, but were much more interested in attacking police stations and the stock exchange. In the days of fighting, these young people, like many others, underwent a political ripening which will have its effects in the future.

* * *

With the exception of the student milieu where there were well-developed and politically well-defined organizations representing a minority of the students and with the exception of the CAL's beginning to spring up among the high-school students, everywhere else the youth had no organization of their own. In this situation, the only solution lay in the extensive improvisation that actually occurred. Whether the bureaucrats like it or not, this improvision, giving full freedom to the development of different points of view, produced results far exceeding those which the bureaucrats obtained with all the modern means at their disposal. This was so because for the first time in a very long time the initiative of every individual was appealed to. No personality was repressed; everyone could express himself with full freedom. Not only could individual personalities express themselves without constraint but in these conditions they expanded daily.

I will not give a profile here of the youth or adult political groups which were in the vanguard of the movement. The events provided an opportunity to test each of them, their men and their politics in confrontation with developments. This question will be dealt with in separate articles. What it is important to define here is the general framework so that what these groups did at different moments of the action can be understood and judged better.

In any case, there was no team or group in the movement with sufficient authority to impose its will unchallenged. At each stage discussions developed, even at the beginning of demonstrations (at Denfert-Rochereau for example) or even during demonstrations (the Gare de Lyon for example). In a general way, the results were far from bad. No serious mistakes were committed. Moments of uneasiness or uncertainty, like May 8, were quickly overcome. Things did not deteriorate until the last. By May 29 it was necessary to determine a strategy and a tactic capable of setting the movement on the road to the conquest of power. But the vanguard as constituted did not command the objective elements necessary for such an effort. This situation must be altered because the struggles tomorrow will be much more arduous and the question of leadership will become vital.

The vanguard, which was politically heterogeneous and within which only minorities were organized, had overall a high political level. It recognized that the movement's object was the overthrow of capitalism and the establishment of a society building socialism. It recognized that the policy of "peaceful and parliamentary roads to socialism" and of "peaceful coexistence" was a betrayal of socialism. It rejected all petty-bourgeois nationalism and expressed its internationalism in the most striking fashion. It had a strongly anti-bureaucratic consciousness and a ferocious determination to assure democracy in its ranks. It accepted the existence of different political groups as normal; it feared only, because of the Stalinist experience, control of the movement by any one of these groups.

On many occasions one saw this vanguard collectively reaching decisions which revealed a high degree of political maturity. But I would fall short of my responsibility if I did not say that in some cases a still inadequate capacity in the area of strategy and political tactics could be noted. If I speak of ultra-left tendencies in this movement, it is not to indulge those militants still influenced by the Stalinists. I have no reason to concede anything to the prejudices fostered by the Stalinists. However, we find in such ultra-left tendencies a manifestation which is common to all revolutionary youth groups in every period. These tendencies are heightened at the present time in reaction to the extreme reformism and betrayal of the PCF. I am profoundly convinced that once this rebel youth gains a revolutionary response from an appreciable part of the working class, it will have no difficulty in acquiring the strategic and tactical capacity indispensable for tomorrow's extremely arduous struggles.

IX. *Tasks and perspectives*

May 1968 was, let me repeat again, the first phase of the socialist revolution in France. The crisis which would have led to the taking of power in the space of a few days has given way to a period of great strikes in which state power is no longer an immediate objective. Another revolutionary wave will follow. It is impossible to say when, but it undoubtedly will come. The objective conditions (among others the situation of the French economy in the international economic context) will play an important role in touching it off.

Already the French capitalists complain bitterly about the concessions they were compelled to make to the workers. The French economy, they say, will not be able to meet international competition. This argument has no special validity for the workers whose interests are opposed to those of the capitalists. Furthermore, it is rather exaggerated because the capitalists in other countries will soon be forced to make concessions to those they exploit for fear they will follow the French example. The French economy's difficulties lie elsewhere. On the one hand, in spite of the process of concentration which it has been undergoing, concentration in many areas is still far from the level attained in other countries. The workers' only interest in this matter is to seek ways to prevent this concentration from being effected at their expense.

The French economy is also suffering from the policy of "grandeur" inflicted on it by de Gaulle. This policy commits the French economy to the execution of immoderate projects, some of which are dangerous and useless, like the "force de frappe" [France's nuclear striking force], others of which must be realized at prices higher than would result from a rational utilization of the international division of labor. De Gaulle and the men around him are for "independence" at any price, that is at the price of the greatest sacrifices by the workers. Will May give de Gaulle and his agents pause to reflect on this score? In any case, the workers will no longer submit to the sort of thing they have been experiencing for the last 10 years.

There is still one more point which must be stressed about the economy. Haven't we been told *ad nauseam* about de Gaulle's realistic financial policy in which the franc is solidly backed by gold? On this point as on all others this great mind has proved its bankruptcy.

It is worth spending a little extra time on the subjective conditions because the vanguard has the real possibility of altering these in a favorable direction. Many political and organizational problems are posed on widely differing levels. In particular, important political questions exist: It is impossible to raise the question of the government without answering the question of what programs an alternative government would have. Problems of organizational policy arise for the vanguard at the level of the large masses and their organizations, at the level of a very broad vanguard in the more specific realm of action, and at the level of a numerically smaller but highly political vanguard. I obviously make no pretense of giving definitive answers to these questions. My aim is to provide the components which can serve as a basis for fruitful discussion. The events which have taken place are of such an importance, the richness of their lessons so great, the problems they pose so complex, that these questions cannot be resolved within a narrow circle.

* * *

Leaving aside the problems posed by the economic strikes coming in the wake of the general strike, the following problems are on the agenda for the future in the arena of the broad masses: a perspective leading to the socialist society; the preparation of the great future struggles and of a revolutionary leadership to lead them;

defense of the elements of "dual power" resulting from the May movement; the problems of universities and of education, where the conflict between the government and the interested parties – which concerns all workers – remains irreconcilable.

Defense of the students and university teachers against the bourgeois government will inevitably assume multiple forms, not all of which can be foreseen. One can be certain that the government will not long tolerate what is going on at the Sorbonne, where there is a revolutionary center, a fortress of socialism and internationalism. In order to carry out this defense, the great masses of people must be made to understand its importance. A system of ever closer ties must be established between the students and the workers. The government is trying to establish a distinction between the "good" students who want to pursue their studies, and the others who think of nothing but agitation. Developing a link between the students and the workers is not a one-day affair; it is still one of the tasks which the vanguard must work at on a day-to-day basis and for which it must step up its efforts.

This is not a secondary problem. It is not surprising that the two mutually hostile forces which have an interest in maintaining the established order, the bourgeois state and the PCF leadership, express themselves in more or less identical terms about the revolutionary movements among the students. In this sector the revolutionary socialist vanguard is politically dominant in fact and offers a valuable support for all revolutionary militants no matter what tendency they belong to.

Failure to understand the Sorbonne's exceptional position today for the cause of world socialism would show an unpardonable blindness. New positions cannot be won if you are incapable of defending positions already conquered. The defense of the Sorbonne is the prime task of all revolutionaries at the present time.

(a) A transitional program

I have pointed out the basic causes which prevented the movement from making the decisive leap to take power, that is, in the first place, the betrayal of the traditional leaderships, notably of the PCF and the CGT, which the most decisive masses follow; and, in the second place, the absence of organized forces able to constitute an alternative leadership in the eyes of the workers. This is not all. The militants who made up the revolutionary minority were handicapped by a considerable gap in their political arsenal – the lack of a transitional program.

What do I mean by that? From the moment the struggle began it was relatively easy to determine a program of the workers' essential immediate demands: All that was necessary for that was to listen to the workers. Moreover, it was easy to explain that these demands could only be guaranteed by a government representing the workers and that any government tied to the bourgeoisie would be a means by which the class enemy could gain time before setting out to reconquer the lost ground. Beyond this however, questions were also posed which the revolutionary vanguard did not answer adequately. Even our own organization, the PCI, whose program holds an answer to these questions, was deficient in this regard. Caught up in the whirlwind of the events, it primarily answered the immediate questions and did not make sufficient use of the political armament it has possessed for years.

The questions which were posed can be summed up briefly:
- How was a workers government to be established?
- Above and beyond the satisfaction of the workers' immediate demands, what would the program of such a government be, not only for the workers but for all the working masses of the country? A government must have a full program.

These questions will arise anew as the next revolutionary crises develop. They will be posed even more acutely, for the coming mobilizations will not start off from immediate demands alone with only these as their object. Already certain demands were raised in May which exceeded the limits of the workers' immediate demands.

The required program is what we have long called the transitional program; this term has been picked up by others but in a meaning we have rejected as false. To deal concretely with this question, let us start from the fact that in the course of the movement the CFDT advanced more general demands in connection with workers' participation in the management of the plants. The workers in fact do not seek merely an improvement in their immediate conditions. They do not want to be cogs in the economy like cogs in a machine, only maintained better than in the past. Nor do they want to remain the objects they are in the capitalist economy. The CGT leaders responded to these questions, in the words of Seguy, that self-management was "a vague formula" (May 10 at Renault). This was quite simply the response of a bureaucrat for whom all power in the union, the party, the plant, or the nation must be in the hands of an apparatus. The Stalinist system has been and remains his model.

But the epoch of this system – which moreover never had any justification from a Marxist point of view – is now over. It is impossible to run society, the economy, the schools, the workers organizations, etc.... unless the producers, the consumers, the participants, and the membership are democratically involved in running them. It is the bosses and the bureaucrats who are proving increasingly superfluous.

The desire for structural changes is recognized even by de Gaulle. In his recent radio interview, he tried once again to offer the same tired old nostrum – collaboration between capital and labor – as an invention by which both capitalism and communism could be disposed of. This discovery is just about as old as the first clashes between capitalism and the workers movement. De Gaulle, however, chose to specify one point of what, according to him, such collaboration would be: there must be a leader in command in the plants. This point of view is identical to his conception of society. There must be a leader – de Gaulle himself. This time he has dubbed his notion "participation." We already got a long look in May at the kind of participation we will see in the coming period, the participation of the CRS and the *Gardes Mobiles*.

If the CFDT's demands in the area of plant management are examined, it can be said that they engendered ambiguity in the arguments of those defending them. For the leadership of this union federation and a large number of its activists, these demands by no means represented a challenge to the capitalist order. Their objective, in the minds of the leadership and these activists, was to remove certain aspects in present-day capitalism carried over from the 19th century and to carry out a certain number of reforms which would enable the capitalist system to function more effectively. For other militants, these demands were meant to bring about the substitution of a socialist society for capitalism. In other words, in the minds of their promoters, these demands were intended to lead to the integration of the workers and their organizations into a capitalist state renovated on the technocratic model.

However, in our conception, the transitional program is a body of general demands which bring the masses, as they mobilize behind them, into conflict with the bourgeois state, which lead them to creating the first organs of a workers state, to seize the government and begin building a socialist society.

A transitional program must be an anti-capitalist program. And to be effective its internal logic must correspond to the logic of the mass movement. No organization can seek to establish it alone. Such a program can only be the product of confrontation in large assemblies in which not only workers, teachers, students, and intellectuals take part, as was outlined in the meetings in the Sorbonne and the universities, but also the representatives of all layers of the working population – housewives, soldiers, small businessmen, peasant-workers, etc. In regard to the universities, certain people associated the formula "student power" with that of "workers power," etc. No such "power" can be effective in the framework of a capitalist state. Self-management – in the universities, the plants, or elsewhere – is only an effective force in the context of a state freed from capitalism and in which workers democracy prevails.

For the immediate future, a confrontation between needs and articulated demands can only take place in relatively restricted circles. However, in a period of revolutionary crisis the committees produced by the upsurge (workers committees, committees of housewives and small businessmen, peasants committees, soldiers committees, etc.) at once would be a place for formulating a real transitional program and could constitute a sort of national assembly of the working masses of the country. By federating on the local, regional, and national levels these committees would become the organs of the new government which would put this transitional program into effect. They would be the bodies on which such a government could be based and by which it could be controlled. A government thus constituted would really be a government of the toilers.

I have pointed out the confusion which occurred in the strike between bureaucratized trade-union bodies and strike committees. From what I have just said it clearly follows that committees and trade unions are not mutually exclusive. They are organs with different functions and different tasks. The workers will not cease to have immediate demands under the new regime, and the unions' essential task will be to assure that these demands are defended. Although I do not deny the unions the right to have an opinion on more general problems, the committees will be the political form encompassing the broadest masses. It is there that the masses will be able to educate themselves as to the general functioning of society (planning, education, justice, international policy, etc.) through a confrontation of ideological currents and opposing programs. It is there that the masses will be able to make decisions which they will execute. These committees will thus become organs of a government which involves the masses in its functioning in a continuous manner and not in the form of the "democratic" farce of elections every four or five years. These committees – they were called Soviets in Russia in 1917 – are the organs affording the greatest flexibility for drawing in the broadest masses; they are the only way to prepare for the withering away of the state, according to the concept of Marx and Lenin.

I make no pretense of setting forth a finished transitional program here. I will limit myself to bringing out a few points which, above and beyond the demands already proposed, I think must form the basis of such a program:

A higher standard of living for the masses; reduction of the workweek, which is required by increased productivity and the need to eliminate unemployment.

Nationalization without compensation of the factories and the key industries; the elimination of trade secrets; the establishment of a monopoly in foreign trade; the establishment of workers control to prepare the way for management of the plants by those who work in them.

The establishment under democratic control by the masses of an economic plan to benefit the masses (housing, schools, roads, hospitals, urban transportation, and free medicines, etc.) which would break with the bourgeois consumption model [that is, private instead of public consumption – Ed.].

The simplification of administration, the institution of control over administration by people's committees.

The dissolution of the repressive forces; the replacement of the professional army by a system of militias and the arming of the workers.

Bold social legislation concerning young people and women.

Nationalization of the large agricultural enterprises; the establishment of model state farms; the furthering of agricultural training; many-sided aid to agricultural producers or sellers cooperatives.

Withdrawal from all military alliances; aid without political strings attached to peoples struggling for their independence and to peoples formerly colonized by French imperialism; solidarity with the revolutionary movements which are beginning to develop in Europe, with the perspective of creating a socialist federation of European countries[69].

(b) Building a revolutionary leadership

Without a rationally applied transitional program it is impossible to mobilize masses of people. But how can this program be formulated by mass committees unless there exist at the different levels mentioned above organized groups to unite the masses, to pose the problems for them, to move them to action? I am going to examine the ways it seems possible to deal with the more general problem of building a revolutionary leadership in the plants, in the neighborhoods, and on a national scale.

---

[69] On these questions, see our publications: *Apres de Gaulle?* (After de Gaulle What?); *The Death Agony of Capitalism, the Transitional Program*; and *Whither France?* by Leon Trotsky.

In the arena of the large masses, the May movement unquestionably showed that, while the students were able to play a "detonator" role on several occasions, when the time came to take the leap of seizing power, a substitute leadership, or even the organized components of a substitute leadership, was lacking in the plants. I would stress the insistence with which the union leaders emphasized the opposition in the plants to "outside interference." They had asked nothing from the workers in regard to their relating to other forces; rather they speculated on the most backward layers' fear of being maneuvered. This was an echo from the Stalinists of the bourgeois refrain about "agitators" from God knows where, from abroad most often, etc., who were supposed to be stirring up the good French workers.

How can a substitute leadership, or the organized components of such a leadership, be created? If there had been real elected strike committees responsive to the will and aspirations of the ranks in a few medium-sized factories during the decisive hours, some of these committees, for example, could have taken the step of calling all the committees, or strong minorities in such committees, which agreed with them to a conference. This is not an invention on my part but a long-standing experience which has been renewed every time real strike committees have existed. Such committees, independent of the apparatuses, could have overcome the prejudice against "outside interference" and gained a hearing that the students could not.

The components of a substitute leadership for the revolutionary wave to come which, appealing and fighting for an independent policy in the factories, would offer the same sort of challenge to the CGT leadership's reformist line there as UNEF and SNESup did during the May mobilization, cannot be created overnight. These elements of an alternative leadership can only be formed by beginning a struggle against the reformist line in the workers movement right now. This is particularly necessary in the unions. Since these are the workers' permanent organizations, they regain their primary importance in normal periods, that is, in the intervals between acute struggle. What is primarily necessary in this regard is to achieve the conditions which would make it possible for the organized workers to choose between opposing positions: workers democracy in the unions, the factories, on demonstrations – in all the organizations it was eliminated from during the Stalinist years.

Here we face a crucial problem. And there is an obvious link, moreover, between the struggle against the authoritarianism of the Gaullist regime and the struggle against the omnipotence of the union leaderships. A reflection of this appeared at the time of the demonstration in the Charlety stadium, on the same day the workers rejected the Rue de Grenelle agreements. Shouts in conjunction were heard "De Gaulle Resign!" "Seguy Resign!"

This is not the place to go into detail on such a struggle inside the unions. It will be impossible to prevent a discussion of the line followed during the May mobilization in the CGT first of all as well as in all the mass organizations. Undoubtedly the CGT and PCF leaderships want to avoid such a debate. Their denunciation of "provocateurs" made this objective clear enough, one does not debate with provocateurs. However, this debate is inevitable because many trade-union activists have voiced fundamental criticisms of the line followed in May. Debate is also inevitable in the PCF. It is possible the leadership wants to "play out the fish" by keeping the membership busy with stepped-up activism, for example in the electoral campaign, and by touching,the sensitive chord of the militants which vibrates every time the government attacks their party.

Already in May the intellectuals voiced their demands within the PCF. In the June 5 *l'Humanité* an official PCF declaration mentions the existence of a letter addressed to the party leadership by a number of intellectuals in the PCF. To find out what was in the letter, however, you had to consult the issue of *Le Monde* appearing the same day. What was discreetly described in the PCF's official statement as questioning "the application of the party's policy" was put this way in the intellectuals' letter:

"Their common revolt (of millions of workers; the youth in the factories, the universities, and the high schools; and the great majority of the intellectuals) challenges, in the guise of the Gaullist regime, the very foundations of the present social system. By seeking from the outset to put a rein on this exceptional enthusiasm, the leadership cut the party off from a great force for socialist renewal... At the Gare de Lyon... many Communists were there; but the party was not. This facilitated provocation by the government which was anxious to isolate and, in fact, crush the student movement. However, if it had not been for this movement... the factories would not have been occupied... and other opportunities would not have been opened up for struggle by the workers, whose role is decisive... We cannot shirk the debate on orientations, on the structure and future of the revolutionary movement which these events demand. A frank analysis of the reality, and bold political initiatives must at all costs enable the development of links with the new forces which have revealed themselves in the struggle for socialism and freedom."

As far as links with these new forces go, *l'Humanité*, speaking for the Stalinists who remain at the head of the PCF and the CGT, found no formula but denouncing them to the repressors, slandering the students who went to Flins as "provocateurs."

The leadership wants a "debate" in the customary fashion – that is a speedy condemnation by the party central committee, which is simply a body for recording the decisions of the political bureau. But this operation will not be so easy to carry out. Is it true that Garaudy agrees with these intellectuals? And why didn't *l'Humanité* mention that once these intellectuals had gotten a brush-off from the leadership in the June 1-3 meeting they occupied the headquarters of the Paris party federation of the Rue La Fayette for several hours? This is an example *l'Humanité* does not consider it desirable to make known...

The PCF worker-militants who hold positions in the trade-union movement and the factories have been confronted with responsibilities, questions which threaten their relations with their comrades in the shops that affect them on a day-to-day basis. A number of these Communist militants will not be able to remain indifferent to the fact that their party's policy toward the youth has gone bankrupt beyond all description. It is also known that Marchais's notorious formula, "the German, Cohn-Bendit," shocked many party members, who saw in it only a disagreeable lapse.

The elements of a major crisis have come together for the first time in the history of the PCF since its complete Stalinization: a leadership with impaired prestige; a policy repudiated by large strata of the workers; total bankruptcy in such an important area as the youth. The PCF and CGT leadership will certainly not give in without a fight. Indeed, its stubbornness in maintaining the party's regime and policy is at least as great as de Gaulle's in maintaining his authority in the state. One of the essential tasks which must be accomplished so that the next wave will not remain without a substitute leadership is to wage a struggle for discussion in the CGT without delay, and, for those who are members, in the PCF. This discussion must have as its starting point a balance sheet of the events of May 1968 and the policy pursued during this month. This struggle must be tied to the struggle for workers democracy so that the ranks will be able to choose between differing lines.

In the CGT this will clearly pose the question of the right of tendencies, that is the right of those who do not think like the leadership, to combine in order to defend nationally a common line in the various unions. At present this elementary democratic right is a monopoly and privilege of the leadership. How can anyone claim to fight for democracy in society and make a mockery of it in his own organization?

This battle for workers democracy – which clearly cannot be conducted abstractly, divorced from debate over the lines followed in May – is of crucial importance. It cannot be said with absolute certainty that the leadership's betrayal of the movement would have been averted if workers democracy had existed. However, a betrayal in this case could have only been carried out under difficult conditions for the leadership. It would not have been impossible for a sufficiently strong minority of the workers to have succeeded in carrying the movement in action beyond the point it attained by its own momentum.

* * *

Now let us move on to the level of a relatively broad vanguard. The first problem which arises is that of the action committees which sprang up spontaneously in May. These committees match their name. They have no definite program, no well-articulated hierarchical structure on a national scale. In actuality, they are groups of activists who intervene daily in the neighborhoods or factories to achieve objectives through action which cannot be obtained by legal means, or could only be so obtained at the cost of great exertion, expense, and considerable time. The existence of such action committees is obviously dependent on favorable circumstances, more specifically on more or less embryonic forms of "dual power."

It is very important to maintain and strengthen these committees as long as circumstances permit by setting goals for them, whether defense of the existing elements of "dual power," or the creation of new ones, or self-defense against the attacks of the repressive forces and the "civic action" forces evoked by de Gaulle. It is in fact inevitable now that the bourgeoisie will resort to using both repressive forces of the state and extralegal forces in order to carry out a campaign of intimidation and repression. This would be true not only if de Gaulle stays in power but also if a "government of the left" were established. It must not be ascribed to chance that among the recent workers' demands the mass leaderships of all types, trade union or political, classical reformist or Stalinist, etc.... never advocated the slogan of dissolving the repressive forces (CRS, *Gardes Mobiles*) in May when the anger at, and even hatred of, these forces by the masses was at its peak. These leaderships have bourgeois "statesmanship" and the bourgeois state cannot do without repressive forces.

It cannot be thought that a dead calm will reign in the interval between revolutionary crises. Now there are many incidents, of a greater or lesser import, of clashes between the social forces. In such conditions, a revolutionary policy must consist, among other things, in a sort of "political guerrilla warfare," a continual harassment of bourgeois society at the most diverse points. Such a struggle increases the importance of the action committees in particular. They must be able to keep the masses awake, to gain a better knowledge of their demands, and, thus, to prepare their future actions.

* * *

More complex problems exist in regard to the vanguard proper. The factors in this situation are the following: a) groups and organizations formed long ago with fully developed programs; b) militants whom the events of recent years have driven out of the PCF (Vigier and Barjonet are among the most well-known and the most recent examples). One cannot predict what tendencies or formations will emerge in the PCF and sooner or later be expelled from it. The problem of revolutionary regroupment in various forms is inevitably on the order of the day. Those who belonged to the PCF and leave it or are expelled from it cannot act in isolation if they want to remain political activists. For the most part, however, they are not inclined to enter formations organized long ago and whose program was developed without their participation. In the coming period, while the old organizations will recruit, new organizations will also develop on rather generalized political bases. These organizations will provide their members with a milieu enabling them both to gain new political experience and to clarify their positions.

The members of the French section of the Fourth International think that the definitive solution of the processes at work in the vanguard, assuring the victory of the socialist revolution, will lead to the constitution of a mass party based on the revolutionary Marxist program they have defended for long years. However, they have never thought that such a party would be created solely by individual recruitment, by people just joining the organization as it is at the present time. Parties are not created and do not develop in such a way.

The most complex problem is that created by new groupings of militants, like the "Mouvement Revolutionnaire" [Revolutionary Movement]. This organization was the first to be formed and it will certainly not be the last of its type. Such groups are not comparable to the old formations, generally filled with men of fixed centrist positions whose political labels vary periodically. These new organizations will be formed primarily by militants whose political development is being advanced by the events. The attitude of the Trotskyists toward such formations must be to assist their development toward firm revolutionary Marxist positions. There can be no question of employing prefabricated formulas or more or less sharp stratagems in dealing with them. Taking account of the dynamic character of such movements or formations, the Trotskyists' political attitude will be to support them insofar as they are correct and to criticize them where they are wrong.

Obviously, the Trotskyists want to encourage the development of the revolutionary vanguard toward Trotskyist political positions. The organizational question arises as an accessory to this. One of the obstacles on this path is the present division of the Trotskyist movement in France. With a view toward reunification of the Trotskyist movement, the PCI appealed during the May 1968 events to two other formations claiming to be Trotskyist to consider ways of altering this situation of disunity. There was no response from the OCI. This organization, along with its youth group, the FER, pursued an aberrant policy in May which cut them off from the more politically mature part of the vanguard. On the other hand, a step forward was accomplished with the founding of a coordinating committee of the PCI, the UC and the JCR. The Revolutionary Marxist Group later joined this committee.

X. The international repercussions of May 1968

It is impossible as I write this to give a complete picture of the international repercussions of the May events. Every day new signs are noted. Above and beyond the direct echoes, deeper consequences can be expected which will show up less immediately.

The French student revolt was not the earliest. Similar movements have developed in several countries in Europe and North America, born in the struggle against the Vietnam war, and advancing demands of a social nature. I am not forgetting the student movements in the so-called underdeveloped countries; great revolutionary thrusts have been developing there for a long time and the students have been associated with them. But the working masses of the West European countries in their great majority have been politically inert and the student movements have seemed to be going against the current in the general situation in these countries.

There is no doubt that the victorious Tet offensive gave considerable impetus to all the vanguard movements and to broad masses and encouraged all the enemies of capitalism and imperialism. Once Paris threw itself into the battle, the floodgates were thrown open everywhere. Paris regained the old honor of its revolutionary traditions. The student uprisings, followed by the gigantic working-class explosion, gave the signal for the start or the reinforcement of movements more or less everywhere. In Spain, first of all, the fall of Franco is on the order of the day; in Italy the students are throwing themselves furiously into repeated assaults; in West Germany – this American fortress in Europe – in Britain, Belgium, Sweden, etc.

Everywhere the clarion call of revolution rang out and was heard. Everywhere the students defied the bourgeois order; everywhere they turned to the workers; everywhere the red flag was raised. University buildings tended to become free territories outside the bourgeois state's authority. In several countries and in Paris the high-school students intervened in political and social life. The essential difference in France was that nowhere else has a working-class mobilization arisen to any degree comparable to that of May. The workers' reactions are slower in appearing, but it cannot be doubted that they will react. Several politicians, generally Social Democrats, have been the first to realize this. It could well happen here, Willy Brandt plaintively reflected; and he was not the only one saying such things.

In the underdeveloped countries, the consequences have not been long in making themselves felt. In Dakar, in Santiago de Chile, in Buenos Aires, in Rio de Janeiro, and in many other cities, the revolution has raised its head. Paris has given the best possible support to Vietnam as well as to socialist Cuba. We will soon see the consequences of May 1968 in North Africa, the Near East, in all of Asia, etc.... All the students from the colonial countries living in France and the other European countries during these events and who took part in them will transmit an added stimulus to the colonial revolution as well as a more complete Marxist education.

Once Paris and France had moved, it could be all the less doubted that the revolutionary movement would find a response in East Europe. In Czechoslovakia, the action of the students and the intellectuals had just made a decisive contribution to bringing about the fall of Novotny. Only a few days were required before the students in Belgrade formulated a body of demands which no Marxist could find anything to object to. They also threw up barricades and occupied the universities.

Reading the press often gives a deceptive impression of what is going on in a country. Is it not clear that the French press – both the bourgeois press and the press of the PCF – contributed to the self-intoxication both of the Gaullist government and the PCF leadership in regard to the situation in the country before May 1968? But what is to be said about the Soviet press in regard to the French events? *L'Humanité*, which always tail-ended the events, saw its lies printed in *Pravda* or *Izvestia* still a few days more behind the facts. We are living in the age of the transistor; and no censorship, no barrier, can limit the dissemination of the truth.

The Chinese government has sown an unexampled confusion in regard to the "cultural revolution" in the last year, and its crude accusations against the USSR have helped the Kremlin bureaucracy. This said, however, unlike Moscow, which did not hide its dismay at the idea that de Gaulle might vanish from the scene, the Chinese government organized immense demonstrations of solidarity with the May movement. The mobilization of hundreds of thousands of demonstrators – whatever the motives of the organizers – has an objective importance which no one can underestimate.

It will be forgotten by no one that in the Soviet Union, on the other hand, the government hid from the masses what was going on in France. This was not only owing to their indisputable desire to conciliate de Gaulle. During these last years, the Soviet government has been pushing a very determined campaign against the intellectuals and the university youth in that country. Everyone recalls the Daniel-Sinyavsky trial, Brodsky, Ginzburg, the Litvinov-Bogoraz protests, etc.... the movements of writers, artists, and scholars to gain freedom of expression in their fields (art, literary creation, etc.) are, in many countries as in the Soviet Union, merely the precursors of antibureaucratic workers movements aimed at reestablishing soviet democracy. The hour – I am convinced – will not be long in striking when the students and the intellectuals of Leningrad, Moscow, Kharkov, and the other big Soviet cities will move massively into struggle against the bureaucratic government. They will struggle for soviet democracy and will clear the way for the intervention of the Soviet workers.

I cannot leave the workers states without saluting the Polish students – other forerunners of these battles – and more particularly, without saluting their leaders, comrades Modzelewsky and Kuron, who have again been imprisoned for their remarkable achievement of drawing up the first antibureaucratic socialist program in the present resurgence.

* * *

The rekindling of the European workers struggle is the May 1968 mobilization's most important contribution to the world revolution. At the end of the second world war, revolutionary movements in West Europe were quickly stifled because of the class collaboration of the Stalinists who lived up to the "Big Three" wartime division of Europe into "spheres of influence." These agreements guaranteed the maintenance of capitalism in West Europe. The victory of the Chinese revolution in 1949, at the end of the revolutionary period in Europe, kicked off the advance of the colonial revolution.

At the same time, the revolutionary socialist movement in West Europe suffered a considerable setback. Social Democratic or Stalinist reformism prevailed. Apathy and stagnation characterized the European workers movement to such an extent that some thinkers drew extremely pessimistic conclusions about the potentialities of the

European proletariat and the proletariat in general. It cannot be doubted that the May mobilization of the French working class has broken the ground and set the workers throughout all of West Europe on the move. And this is true not only in the area of economic demands (properly speaking these struggles had never ceased but had remained within a narrowly reformist framework) – these struggles have been revived on a revolutionary level. The struggle for socialism is resurgent on the continent of its birth and where great revolutionary Marxist traditions exist, as May 1968 showed in France. As May 1968 showed also, these battles were renewed starting off from the heritage of the past, despite the fact that the Social Democratic or Stalinist leaderships have encased this heritage in a thick reformist shell for 20 to 30 years.

At its origin, the movement for socialism was limited for more than a half century, for understandable objective reasons, to the economically developed countries of Europe. The victory of October 1917, although situated on the periphery of Europe, was the first great success in this struggle. It gave the starting signal for revolutionary struggles in the colonized countries. For a whole series of reasons which have been set forth *in extenso* by the Trotskyist movement, Stalinism, which had triumphed in the Soviet Union and in the Communist parties, caused numerous defeats (Germany 1933, Spain 1937, for example) and the miring down of socialist revolution in Europe. In May 1968, the European workers movement first got moving again. Although the pernicious influence which the old leaderships will continue to exercise for some time yet cannot be underestimated (we have just seen this in France), it is now unquestionable that everywhere in Europe, the youth – the young workers, students and high-school students – are no longer in thrall to these old leaderships and are seeking to provide a socialist solution for these struggles. This fact gives assurance that we can hold the greatest hopes for the European socialist revolution.

Moscow was long the center of the socialist revolution, long after the Kremlin policy had lost all revolutionary character. For some years now, Moscow has no longer held any authority or prestige in the eyes of numerous young revolutionary movements. China and Cuba together have had revolutionary aspirations. Now, the advance of the socialist revolution will continue on all fronts at once (the workers revolution in the advanced capitalist states; the colonial revolution; the anti-bureaucratic political revolution in the workers states). The dangers involved in polarization around a state leadership which has given priority to the specific national interests of certain privileged layers will disappear in the face of a more even advance of the world socialist revolution.

PIERRE FRANK

* * *

A few of the initial consequences of this less lopsided advance of the world socialist revolution were quickly discernible. The theoretical problems are no less important for the revolution and socialism. In past years, aside from the old, worn-out revisionist theories picked up by the Stalinists ("peaceful and parliamentary roads" to socialism, "peaceful coexistence"), many other theories have been advanced. Here are the most well known of these:

The theories on neo-capitalism which, it seems, was supposed to have resolved the fundamental contradictions of capitalism as Marx disclosed them.

Manifold theories that the workers in the highly industrialized countries had been co-opted into capitalist society and that as a result they were incapable of serving, as the motor forces of the struggle for socialism, with this role falling to other social strata (Marcuse, Sweezy).

The theory that the role of the peasants is decisive in the underdeveloped countries where the proletariat supposedly cannot play a revolutionary role (Fanon).

The theory of revolution by an insurgent countryside encircling the cities (Mao Tse-tung, Lin Piao).

The theory of guerrilla warfare in the country, in which battles in the cities are considered impossible.

The reformist conceptions warmed over from Bernsteinism received a stinging refutation. The PCF leadership avoided drawing the conclusions of the fact that de Gaulle, who had been brought to power in 1958 by General Massu, went to visit him again 10 years later in order to maintain himself in power. Barricades did not turn out to be as old-fashioned as many claimed. It was proven yet again that reforms and demands are won, not after long years of narrow-minded reformism, but as a by-product of revolutionary struggle.

The theories that neo-capitalism had definitively assured the stability of capitalism burst like soap bubbles. Neo-capitalism, even in France, where there was a "strong state" the like of which existed nowhere else, was rotted within much more than anyone had suspected.

As for the new theories which did not renounce revolutionary socialism, they were all the products of the historical detours of the socialist revolution which I mentioned above. Each one of them based itself on one particular aspect of the situation: the fact that the students and intellectuals in the capitalist countries supported the colonial revolution, while the traditional workers movement proved derelict in this regard; powerful peasant uprisings in the colonial countries; the success of the guerrilla struggle in winning power in Cuba; the apathy of the workers movement in the European countries and its stifling bureaucratization. These experiences were overgeneralized. The common denominator of all these theories was their claim that the proletariat in the central imperialist countries was incapable and impotent. May 1968 dealt a mortal blow to all these generalizations, without, however, putting in question the validity of certain special methods such as guerrilla warfare in specific cases. It is demonstrably risky, even if you think you are proceeding in a revolutionary manner, to make revisions of fundamental features of Marxist theory, such as the role of the proletariat, based on experiences involving only a few years and in circumstances as exceptional as the period of stagnation in the European workers movement.

The May 1968 movement endowed the revolutionary Marxism which the Fourth International has ceaselessly defended against the most inclement conditions with a new luster. It verified a whole series of lessons which for 'several decades had been relegated to the theoretical realm. The real-life experience of these lessons constituted the best school of Marxism we have had in a half century. The place of the general strike in the class struggle as a stage on the road to the winning of power; the creation of real mass committees in a revolutionary period; the emergence of dual power; the fact that the question of taking of power can be resolved in a very few crucial days and that such days come into existence in a revolutionary upheaval; the decisive role of the leadership in these days; the relationship between the masses and the vanguard – all these questions came out of the books and became part of the flesh and blood of thousands upon thousands of militants who had never experienced anything like this in the past.

The mobilization of May 1968 also brought a series of enrichments which I can only mention here in this pamphlet. We witnessed in Paris a sort of overture to the great drama of the socialist revolution in the central imperialist countries. The themes of the great struggles to come were sounded. The relationship between the student and youth movements and those of the great working masses were illustrated in a striking manner. Methods of fighting in big cities were outlined. It is impossible, without smiling, to think of all the theories built on the idea that the masses were brutalized by the mass media. These theories were also one-sided, as we saw when all France lived through the barricade battles and the revolts in Paris for nights at a time. It was not brutalization but revolt that the communication media fostered.

The relationship among the various European movements, in particular among the various student movements, has underlined the need for a liaison and even coordinated activity on the international scale. As it develops, the European workers movement will be compelled to organize itself on a more international basis. The Common Market represented a defensive effort by the European capitalists in the attempt to hang on after two world wars. This miserable attempt to organize the productive forces within the capitalist system will be shattered by the exploding revolutionary struggles of the European working class, which will put the creation of a Socialist United States of Europe on its agenda.

And in regard to Europe and the Common Market, it is not unworthy of note that these champions of "European integration," the German, Italian, Belgian, Dutch, etc. reformist socialist party and trade-union leaderships did nothing – not a single appeal, not a single meeting, not a single solidarity demonstration – in support of the 10 million striking French workers. Moreover, among these striking workers were members of Force Ouvrière, the trade-union federation linked to them in this Common Market. For them, "European integration" means a share in the graft; it does not mean international solidarity of the European workers.

The necessity for a common international strategy for the struggles of the socialist revolution will make itself felt more and more imperiously. Thus, the question of the revolutionary international, which has been obscured and submerged for years by bureaucratic leaderships with special nationally limited interests, will arise with new vigor. Born in Europe more than a century ago, the mass revolutionary international will resurge more powerful than ever.

The French socialist revolution has begun; the European revolution has resumed its march forward. Fifty years after October 1917 worldwide victory looms on the horizon.

Chronology of the May Events

May 3 – UNEF meeting at the Sorbonne against Fascist attacks and government repression. Police invade Sorbonne campus and make arrests. Violent incidents in Latin Quarter lasting six hours.

May 4 – UNEF holds to its plans for demonstration Monday May 6. SNESup sets strike of university teachers for same date.

May 5 – Extraordinary session of the Court of Summary Jurisdiction to sentence demonstrators arrested Friday.

May 6 – Violent fighting in the morning and then from 2 p.m. in the afternoon to 1 a.m. the next morning on the Boulevard Saint-Michel and Saint-Germain. Grills around trees and paving stones are torn out to resist the repressive forces firing tear-gas grenades. Close to 600 students and police wounded. Student strikes spread to the provinces.

May 7 – UNEF demonstration from 6:30 p.m. to midnight, going from the Place Denfert-Rochereau to the Place de l'Etoile on the Champs-Elysees, and then from the Place de l'Etoile to the Latin Quarter. More than 25,000 demonstrate. Violent fighting after 10 a.m., from Saint-Germain-des-Pres to Montparnasse, lasting until 3 a.m.

May 8 – Debate in National Assembly. A hypocritical statement by the minister of education Peyrefitte. A meeting in the Halle aux Vins which breaks up without incident.

May 9 – The Sorbonne is still closed despite the words of the minister of education. Impromptu meetings on the Boulevard Saint-Michel. The strike continues with three primary demands: release of all those imprisoned; halt to prosecutions; withdrawal of police forces from the university campuses. A meeting continues long into the evening at the Mutualite. The CGT and CFDT project a joint demonstration with UNEF for May 15.

May 10 – A high-school student strike in Paris in the morning; a demonstration of high-school student strikers at 5 p.m. at the Gobelins to join UNEF and SNESup demonstration at the Place Denfert-Rochereau at 6:30. The united demonstration returns to Latin Quarter at 9:00. Barricades built, principally on the Rue Gay-Lussac. Violent fighting in the night from 2:15 to 6:00 in the morning. Almost 400 wounded.

May 11 – CGT, CFDT, and FEN call a 24-hour general strike for Monday May 13. Pompidou speaks at 11:15 p.m., accepts the students' three primary demands.

May 13 – General strike and monster demonstration in Paris. A minority continue the demonstration from the Place Denfert-Rochereau to the Champ de Mars and hold a meeting of about 20,000 persons. The students leave the Champ de Mars to occupy the Sorbonne.

May 14 – New debate in National Assembly which fails to came to a conclusion. Late in afternoon, workers at Sud-Aviation in Nantes occupy their factory and shut the plant manager up in his office.

May 15 – Renault plant in Cleon struck and occupied.

May 16 – Renault strike extends to Flins. Speech by Pompidou.

May 17 – Solid strike at Renault (Sanouville, Le Mans, Orleans, Billancourt). Strike at Berliet (Lyon), at Rhodiaceta-Vaise, Rhone-Poulenc (Saint-Fons). Air traffic halted.

May 18 – The CGT in the person of Seguy formulates demands and announces that there will be no "all-out general strike." Student demonstration in front of and around the Renault plant. Trade-union officials refuse to let them enter the plant. Strike in SNCF, in the PTT, airplane construction, the Creusot and Rhone-Poulenc foundries (throughout France).

May 19 – Strike at the RATP.

May 20 – The strike extends to include millions of workers, the merchant marine, banks, insurance companies, gasoline industry (refining plants and distributors). Printers union authorizes publication of the daily papers.

May 21 – New extension of the strike: textiles, the arsenals, construction, the big stores, the paper industry, Citroen, municipal services, entertainment. Declaration by Seguy: "empty formulas like self-management, reform of civilization, and other inventions..."

May 22 – Beginning of peasant demonstrations (fraternization with the striking workers at Saint-Brieuc). Expulsion decree against Cohn-Bendit. The ORTF employees broadcast the debate in parliament. Extension of the strike to all agencies, to the Atomic Energy Commission, and to the social security administration. Temporary occupation of the CNPF and CGC. Trade unions declare their readiness to negotiate with the government.

May 23 – The motion of censure is defeated. Resumption of student demonstrations on the Boulevard Saint-Germain and at the Palais-Bourbon with fighting until 4:00 a.m. The CGT breaks with UNEF. Declaration by the police unions: "Missions against striking workers would pose grave tests of conscience." The big Paris hotels, ORTF, and taxis strike.

May 24 – Peasant demonstrations throughout France. Separate CGT demonstrations in Paris and meetings in the working-class neighborhoods. De Gaulle's speech announcing a referendum. A demonstration by the Action Committees at the Gare de Lyon which continues into a night of rioting in several neighborhoods in Paris. Five hundred wounded. Fighting in several cities, including Lyon and Nantes.

May 25 – The strike encompasses 10 million workers. Opening of negotiations between the government and the unions at the Rue de Crenelle at 3:00 in the afternoon.

May 26 – Negotiations continue.

May 27 – An agreement is reached at 7:30 a.m. This agreement is immediately rejected by the workers at Renault (in the presence of Frachon and Seguy), Citroen, Rhodiaceta, Berliet, Sud-Aviation (Nantes), SNECMA, etc. Demonstration at Charlety (UNEF and SNESup), the Mendes-France maneuver comes out into the open.

Mitterrand mentions Mendes-France in a press conference. The CGT organizes meetings in Paris.

May 28 – Negotiations continue separately in many sectors.

May 29 – De Gaulle leaves for Colombey. Scheduled to report to the Council of Ministers on the following day. The Mendes-France maneuver takes clearer form. For the first time, the CGT raises the question of a "political change opening the way for social progress and democracy." The PCF calls for "a people's and democratic unity government." CGT demonstration on the main streets of Paris. Statement by Mendes-France.

May 30 – De Gaulle dissolves National Assembly and announces immediate elections. Pompidou remains premier and the government is to be reshuffled. De Gaulle appeals for "civic action." Gaullist demonstration on the Champs-Elysees.

May 31 – Change in the ministerial lineup. During his absence from Paris, de Gaulle met with the army leaders. The CGT wants to reopen negotiations and declares its desire not to disrupt the elections of June 23 and 30. The PCF expresses its satisfaction on the holding of elections.

PIERRE FRANK

Otto Bauer, Representative Theoretician of Austro-Marxism

The arguments to prove that Stalinism was the natural outgrowth of Bolshevism have been innumerable. Wasn't Stalin a member of the Political Bureau? Didn't he always identify himself with Lenin and Leninism? Weren't the methods of Stalinism "embryonic" in Lenin's "amoralism," in the centralist conception of the party, in the ban the Tenth Congress placed on factions? And so on.[70]

How many times Trotsky had to refute such arguments, to show that Stalinism had no theory of its own, that it was the political expression of a social stratum – the Soviet bureaucracy – that this bureaucracy destroyed the Bolshevik Party, which had been the political expression of the revolutionary proletariat. Trotsky did not neglect also to point up the social, political, psychological, and other affinities between the Soviet bureaucrats and the bureaucrats of the Social Democratic parties and the reformist trade unions.

This correspondence is striking in the realm of ideology. It is evident when you compare the fundamental views advocated by the Stalinists with those that have been put forward by the reformists, most especially by the left Social Democrats, who were the last in the Social Democracy to give lip service to Marxist theory – that is the Russian Mensheviks, the Austro-Marxists, the Italian Maximalists, and the Guesdists, Bracke and Zyromski, in the SFIO [Section Française de l'Internationale Ouvrière – French Section of the Workers (Second) International – the French Social Democratic party].

It is these profound ideological affinities, moreover, that explain why, when these circles have experienced crises, some left Social Democrats – and not the least prominent – capitulated to Stalin or even joined the Communist Party. This was the case of Dan for the Mensheviks; of a wing of the Italian Socialists; and of Zyromski, who joined the PCF [Parti Communiste Français – French Communist

---

[70] Otto Bauer, A Representative Theoretician of Austro-Marxism (January 1969) comes from *International Socialist Review*, Vol.30 No.3, May-June 1969, pp.36-41.

Party]. This was also the case of Otto Bauer, the dean of Austro-Marxism in the last years of its existence.

The case of Otto Bauer is by far the most illustrative because he was the most inclined to offer theoretical justifications for his positions. He did not lack culture and a certain agility in the game of ideas, which made him much more subtle that a Kautsky in this regard. The younger generations know nothing about Austro-Marxism generally, even the name of Otto Bauer.

A French writer, Yvon Bourdet, has taken up the study of Otto Bauer, along with other Austro-Marxists like Max Adler. His book *Otto Bauer et la Revolution* [*Otto Bauer and the Revolution*][71] is especially interesting because it offers a compilation of the essential body of Otto Bauer's major theoretical and political writings from 1917 to 1938. Thus this book enables us to make an instructive comparison of the Austro-Marxists' thought with that of the Stalinists or post-Stalinists[72].

Otto Bauer's idea of Marxism is characterised primarily by fatalism. For him what happens in most cases is "inevitable" and "necessary." These adjectives dropped repeatedly from his pen. I stress them in the quotations that follow in this article.

His conception was also marked by a view that socialism would develop country by country – that is fundamentally of socialism "in one country." He had no idea of *combined* development, of societies where features belonging to different epochs or modes of production are combined.

Thus in 1917, since Czarist Russia was a backward country, he drew the conclusion that the revolution, which the Russian workers carried out in alliance with the peasants, would not lead to the dictatorship of the proletariat but... bourgeois democracy:

"I consider from now on (October 1917) the transitory rule of the proletariat allied with the peasantry as a *necessary phase* of Russia's evolution in her march toward bourgeois democracy" (*"Neue Kurs" in Sowjetrussland*, p.73).

---

[71] EDI, Paris 1968.
[72] I will refrain from any criticism of the part of the book written by Y. Bourdet. On reading this book and other writings by the same author I was immediately struck by certain astonishing remarks. For example, in his articles in the journal *Autogestion [Self-Management]* (No.4, December 1967) he says: "The general attitude of the Austro-Marxists – quite like that of Rosa Luxemburg – toward the Russian revolution," "Lenin did not follow his theory but Bauer's, it is true without ever admitting it," etc. Finally, I reached the conclusion that this writer did not mean to distort deliberately or intentionally, as might be thought from a first reading. In comparing all his interpretations of writings by Lenin, Trotsky and Rosa one can only conclude that he is totally incapable of comprehending these revolutionary thinkers. He literally does not grasp the meaning of their ideas. His distorted view of the socialist revolution rather resembles a color-blind man's conception of colors.

For him, Russia had necessarily to follow the road followed by France, Britain, etc. He very frequently refers to the French revolution and the period of the Jacobin dictatorship. He adduces that this dictatorship was necessary, as well as the "illusions" of the plebeian masses on which it depended, in order to clear the way for the capitalist system. He concludes that the Bolsheviks had the "illusions" which all fighters need but that history would use them as a means of advancing to a bourgeois democracy:

"Their [the plebeian masses'] rule... cannot achieve their communist ideal. It has only been the means used by history to destroy the vestiges of feudalism and thereby create the preconditions for the development of capitalism on a new extended base" (pp.79-80).

Thus, he was one of the creators of the theory that the Soviet system constituted "state capitalism," which was to find popularity in the most diverse political circles (Eisenhower-type capitalists, Guy Mollet reformists, Bordigist ultraleftists).

When the Bolsheviks instituted NEP he considered himself fully vindicated:

"The *inevitable* results of free commerce (NEP) are the restoration of commercial and industrial capital and the reestablishment of capitalism" (p.79).

Of course, while he was for the defense of the USSR, it was in a very Austro-Marxist sense, in order to better assure the transition to bourgeois democracy:

"It is in the vital interests of the Russian proletariat and the international proletariat that the *inevitable* liquidation of the dictatorship be accomplished through a peaceful transformation and not through the violent overthrow of the Soviet regime" (p.82).

In his own country, in Austria, where he was the theoretical guide of the Social Democratic Party which embraced the very great majority of the working class, he held that there could be no question of using force in the struggle for socialism The world war victors would not permit it. In a pamphlet *The Road to Socialism* (1919), he wrote:

"Let us imagine that in a single day the workers seize the factories, kick the capitalists and the bosses out just like that, and take over the management themselves! Naturally, such an upset would be impossible without a bloody civil war... The foreign capitalists would deny us raw materials... and the indispensable credit... America and the Entente would maintain a blockade..." (p.90).

But he, Otto Bauer, had found a solution. He developed a whole program fitting into the framework of the democratic republic:

"Socialization begins with *expropriation*. The state [the bourgeois state – *PF*] declares the present owners of big industry divested of their property. *Compensation* must be paid. It would be unjust to despoil the owners of mine and foundry stock while the other capitalists remained in possession... The cost of compensation must be borne by all of the capitalists and landowners. To this end, the state will level a progressive capital tax on all capitalists and owners, the proceeds of which will be used to compensate the dispossessed owners of stock in big industry. In this way, no harm will be done to stockholders in big industry..." (p.93).

Would the reactionaries permit such a program, which has great similarities to the "transitional programs" of the Togliattis and other advocates of "renovated democracy"? What is to be done if the bourgeoisie resists? Otto Bauer's answer, while reformist, is – let us give it its due – superior to that of our contemporary post-Stalinists. He does not only say, like them, that in that case the workers must resort to force. He also advocates political propaganda in the army and aimed at the state repressive forces. Still more, he has an armed workers militia in mind, the Republikanische Schutzbund, a vestige of the aborted Austrian revolution of 1918. Listen to what he said in 1924 in a pamphlet entitled *The Struggle for Power*.

"We cannot use our soldiers' arms to take power. No, we must win power by the ballot. But our soldiers' arms can protect us from a counterrevolution, which would tear the ballot out of our hands at the precise moment it could bring us power (p.157)... If the soldiers remain in our camp, if we manage to win a part of the police and security forces, if the *Republikanische Schutzbund* remains powerful and alert, then reaction will not dare rise up against the Constitution of the republic. And then we can take power without resorting to violence and without civil war but simply by availing ourselves of the right to vote" (p.158).

We must also recognize that in 1934 Otto Bauer applied his theory of "defensive force" fully. The tragic example of the heroic but hopeless struggle of the Vienna workers implacably condemned this too subtle theory that claimed that class struggle could be won from all positions – either within the framework of bourgeois democracy, or failing that and leaving the decision up to the enemy, in armed combat.

Having taken Germany and Austria, Nazism advanced throughout Europe. In exile, Otto Bauer erected new "Marxist" theories. He had lost his illusions about bourgeois democracy but not his fatalistic interpretation of Marxism: "Bourgeois democracy *necessarily* ends in fascist counterrevolution" (p.222).

I will come back later to this proposition in examining Otto Bauer's conception of the relations between the class and the party. But the loss of his illusions in bourgeois democracy made him discover that socialism really had been achieved in the USSR. In a work entitled *Between Two Wars*, he made startling discoveries: "Socialist society is not only an abstract idea. It has become a tangible reality in the Soviet Union" (p.169).

He was even to discover that socialism "in one country" was perfectly possible:

"'Socialism in one country' is entirely possible in an immense country like Russia which has almost all the important raw materials in its soil and can absorb almost all its own products" (p.174).

Let us reserve comment on the economic views of this Marxist who abandoned the international division of labor in favor of autarchy. Let us limit ourselves to the political side of his view. When he wrote such lines, he was aware that Stalin's regime no longer corresponded to that of Lenin:

"In the first phase of its evolution, the dictatorship conformed approximately to the idea Lenin had of it before the October Revolution" (p.18).

"The dictatorship of the proletariat has become something quite different from its founders' original conception. This evolution was *inevitable*" (p.198).

Why was this evolution inevitable? Because Bauer had found that Stalinism was suited to building socialism. He expressed this in striking terms:

"The transition from the capitalist mode of production to the socialist mode of production requires many years. In order for this process to proceed undisturbed and uninterrupted, a stable state power is required. It must be stable enough to guard the process of social transformation from popular criticism midway in its development, when the masses have begun to feel acutely the temporary sacrifices it entails without yet appreciating the gains it promises. This process can be subjected to popular criticism only when the fruits of the socialist revolution have ripened.

"The dictatorship changed... its function. It enforced the needs of the future of the proletariat against the present wants of the individual proletarians. This task obviously could not be accomplished by a dictatorship of Soviets. Since their members could be recalled at any moment, they would always base their decisions on egoistic desires, on the limited conceptions and immediate wants of their constituents. This task could be mastered only by a one-party dictatorship with an all-powerful police, military, and bureaucratic apparatus. It could only be accomplished by a dictatorship setting its goals on the basis of a knowledge of the future evolution and interests of the proletariat but imposing the means necessary for the realization of these goals even on recalcitrant strata of the proletariat... Only an iron dictatorship over the party itself could guarantee that it would maintain the unwavering tenacity and perseverance necessary to attain its end" (pp.192-193).

He was opposed to terror against the bourgeoisie in the 1920s but for terror against the workers who had "egoistic desires, limited conceptions and immediate wants" in the 1930s. Thus, Otto Bauer capitulated to the Soviet bureaucracy.

But this capitulation never involved accepting Lenin's ideas on the special role of the party as the revolutionary vanguard of the working class, nor on the relations between the party and the class, nor on the failure of the Social Democracy in August 1914. Bauer made numerous criticisms of the Social Democracy without personally disassociating himself from it. But he never got to the root of its problem. According to him the main responsibility for Social Democratic reformism belonged to – the working class!

Again we find Otto Bauer citing the "inevitable and the necessary." Reformism, he says, is not the influence of bourgeois ideology on the working class nor the betrayal of the leaders of the workers parties. It is the ideology of "the Marxist who has understood that reformist ideology and tactics are a *necessary and inevitable* phase of the development of working-class consciousness in given conditions" (p.273).

"Reformism... was not, as Lenin said, 'the ideological subjection of the working class by the bourgeoisie.' It was the tactics and ideology of the working class itself in a historical situation..." (p.223).

"Reformist socialism is merely the *inevitable* ideology of the workers movement in a given stage of its development" (p. 271).

Here is the main lesson the man who swallowed Stalin's terror drew from the split resulting from the position the Social Democrats took in August 1914 – it was all the Bolsheviks' fault: "The Bolsheviks provoked splits in all countries and unleashed fratricidal struggle" (p.249). In all his oscillations Otto Bauer showed one constant – the working class had no revolutionary capacities; it was an amorphous mass preoccupied with its "egoistic desires" and "immediate wants." It was for this reason that the Socialist party leaderships appealed to the workers to fight their class brothers in 1914.

Then after the Bolshevik conquest of power, which the working class achieved because it was full of "illusions," socialism had to be constructed by means of "an all-powerful police, military, and bureaucratic apparatus setting its goals on the basis of a knowledge of the future evolution and interests of the proletariat but imposing the means necessary for the realization of these goals even on recalcitrant strata of the proletariat."

The betrayal of 1914 was "inevitable and necessary," and so not a betrayal; bourgeois democracy – "inevitable and necessary"; the victory of Hitler – "inevitable and necessary"; the Stalin regime, etc....

How right Lenin was to see in Otto Bauer's Marxism an abyss of "stupidity, pedantry, baseness and betrayal of working-class interests – and that, moreover, under the guise of 'defending' the idea of 'world revolution'." (*"Left-Wing" Communism, An Infantile Disorder*). Not a word need be changed in this judgment, which applies to the Austro-Marxists of bygone days and the post-Stalinists of today.

Find out more

Resistance Books

Resistance Books is the publishing arm of Socialist Resistance, a revolutionary Marxist organisation which is the British section of the Fourth International. We publish books jointly with the International Institute for Research and Education in Amsterdam and independently under the name of Resistance Books. Socialist Resistance also publishes a bi-monthly magazine of the same name and occasional pamphlets.

Socialist Resistance members are active in the trade union movement and in many campaigns such as against the war and in solidarity with Palestine, and with anti-capitalist movements across the globe. We work in anti-racist and anti-fascist networks, including campaigns for the rights of immigrants and asylum seekers. We have been long-standing supporters of women's liberation and the struggles of lesbians, gay people, bisexuals and transgender people. We believe those struggles must be led by those directly affected. Socialist Resistance believes that democracy is an essential component of any successful movement of resistance and struggle.

Socialist Resistance is an ecosocialist organisation as we argue that much of what is produced under capitalism is socially useless, redundant or directly harmful. Capitalism's drive for profit is creating environmental disaster – and it is the poor, the working class and the Global South that are paying the highest price for this. With Britain and the western imperialist countries moving into a long period of capitalist austerity and crisis, deeper than any since the Second World War, Socialist Resistance stands together with all those who are organising to make another world possible.

A list of current titles from Resistance Books is to be found at the end of this book. Further information about Resistance Books and Socialist Resistance can be obtained at www.socialistresistance.org.

International Viewpoint is the English language on-line magazine of the Fourth International which can be read at www.internationalviewpoint.org.

PIERRE FRANK

The International Institute for Research & Education

The International Institute for Research and Education (IIRE) is an international foundation, recognised in Belgium as an international scientific association by Royal decree of 11th June 1981. The IIRE provides activists and scholars worldwide with opportunities for research and education in three locations: Amsterdam, Islamabad and Manila.

Since 1982, when the Institute opened in Amsterdam, its main activity has been the organisation of courses in the service of progressive forces around the world. Our seminars and study groups deal with all subjects related to the emancipation of the world's oppressed and exploited. It has welcomed hundreds of participants from every inhabited continent. Most participants have come from the Third World. The IIRE has become a prominent centre for the development of critical thought and interaction, and the exchange of experiences, between people who are engaged in daily struggles on the ground. The Institute's sessions give participants a unique opportunity to step aside from the pressure of daily activism. The IIRE gives them time to study, reflect upon their involvement in a changing world and exchange ideas with people from other countries.

Our website is constantly being expanded and updated with freely downloadable publications, in several languages, and audio files. Recordings of several recent lectures given at the institute can be downloaded from www.iire.org - as can talks given by founding Fellows such as Ernest Mandel and Livio Maitan, dating back to the early 1980s.

Notebooks for Study and Research

The IIRE publishes Notebooks for Study and Research to focus on themes of contemporary debate or historical or theoretical importance. Lectures and study materials given in sessions in our Institute, located in Amsterdam, Manila and Islamabad, are made available to the public in large part through the Notebooks.

Different issues of the Notebooks have also appeared in languages besides English and French, including German, Dutch, Arabic, Spanish, Japanese, Korean, Portuguese, Turkish, Swedish Danish and Russian.

For a full list visit http://bit.ly/IIRENSR or subscribe online at: http://bit.ly/NSRsub To order, email iire@iire.org or write to International Institute for Research and Education, Lombokstraat 40, Amsterdam, NL-1094.

Also by Pierre Frank

The Long March of the Trotskyists

We live in an age where everything has been internationalised. Imperialism has brought in its wake world politics and world economics.

In this book, Pierre Frank explains how the Fourth International, founded in 1938 by Revolutionary Marxist militants, nuclei, currents and organizations, answered the problem of the construction of anti-capitalist, revolutionary political formations.

As Ernest Mandel's biographical essay explains, Frank was secretary to Leon Trotsky in 1932-1933. This book draws on Frank's experience as a central leader of the Fourth International through to 1979.

Daniel Bensaïd's appendix explains the following 30 years of the Fourth International life. Two contributions develop its perspective of establishing a new independent political representation of the working class that takes into account the diversity of the working class in defending a resolutely class-based programme: a statement by founders of the French LCR explaining its decision to dissolve into the NPA; and the key resolution adopted by the Fourth International's 2009 world congress. (168pp. €8, £6, $10)

To order, email iire@iire.org or write to International Institute for Research and Education, Lombokstraat 40, NL-1094, Amsterdam.

PIERRE FRANK
Forthcoming books

• **New Parties of the Left – Experiences from Europe**
Daniel Bensaid, Alain Krivine, Alda Sousa, Alan Thornett et al, May 2011 (€8, £7, $11).

• **Capitalism - Crisis and Alternatives**
Ozlem Onaran, Michel Husson, John Rees, Claudio Katz et al., June 2011 (€8, £7, $11).

• **Marxism and Anarchism**
Karl Marx, Frederick Engels, Leon Trotsky, June 2011 (€8, £7, $11).

• **Fascism and the far right in Europe**, June 2011

• **Introduction to Marxist Economic Theory (Third Edition)**
Ernest Mandel, Özlem Onaran, Raphie de Santos, November 2011.

• **The thought of Leon Trotsky**
Denise Avenas, Michael Löwy, Jean-Michel Krivine.

• **The united front & the Transitional Programme**
Leon Trotsky, Daniel Bensaïd, John Riddell.

• **Dangerous relationships, Marriage and divorces between Marxism and feminism**, Cinzia Arruzza.

Notebooks for Study and Research

Published by the IIRE with Resistance Books:

• **Revolution and Counter-revolution in Europe from 1918 to 1968**
Pierre Frank, June 2011 (€10, £9, $14), NSR 49

• **Women's Liberation & Socialist Revolution: Documents of the Fourth International**
Penelope Duggan ed., October 2010 (€8, £7, $11) NSR 48.

• **The Long March of the Trotskyists: Contributions to the history of the Fourth International**
Pierre Frank, Daniel Bensaïd, Ernest Mandel, October 2010 (€8, £5, $8), NSR 47.

• **October Readings: The development of the concept of Permanent Revolution**
D Rayner O'Connor Lysaght, Vladimir Ilyich Lenin. Leon Davidovich Trotsky. October 2010 (£5, €6, $8), NSR 46.

• **Building Unity Against Fascism: Classic Marxist Writings**
Leon Trotsky, Daniel Guérin, Ted Grant et al., October 2010 (€6, £5, $8), NSR 44/45.

• **Strategies of Resistance & *Who Are the Trotskyists*'**
Daniel Bensaïd, November 2009 (€8, £6, $10), NSR 42/43.

• **Living our Internationalism: the first 30 years of the International Institute for Research and Education**
Murray Smith and Joost Kircz eds., January 2011 (€5, £4, $7).

- **Socialists and the Capitalist Recession (with Ernest Mandel's *Basic Theories of Karl Marx*)**
Raphie De Santos, Michel Husson, Claudio Katz et al., March 2009 (€9, £6, $12), NSR 39/40.

- **Take the Power to Change the World: globalisation and the debate on power**
John Holloway, Daniel Bensaïd, Phil Hearse. June 2007 (€9, £6, $12), NSR 37/38.

Published by the IIRE:

- **The Porto Alegre Alternative: Direct Democracy in Action**
Iain Bruce ed. (€19, £13, $23.50), NSR 35/36.

- **The Clash of Barbarisms: September 11 & the Making of the New World Disorder**
Gilbert Achcar (€15, £10, $16), NSR 33/34.

- **Globalization: Neoliberal Challenge, Radical Responses**
Robert Went (€21, £14, $21), NSR 31/32.

- **Understanding the Nazi Genocide: Marxism after Auschwitz**
Enzo Traverso (€19.20, £13, $19.) NSR 29/30.

- **Fatherland or Mother Earth? Essays on the National Question**
Michael Löwy (€16, £10.99, $16), NSR 27/28.

Also from Resistance Books

• **Militant Years - car workers' struggles in Britain in the 60s and 70s** Alan Thornett, February 2011 (£12, €14, $19).

• **The Global Fight for Climate Justice – anti-capitalist responses to global warming and environmental destruction** Ian Angus ed., June 2009 (£10, €14, $18).

• **Ireland's Credit Crunch** Kevin Keating, Jonathan Morrison and Joe Corrigan. October 2010 (£6, €8, $10).

• **Foundations of Christianity: a study in Christian origins** Karl Kautsky (£12, €18, $25).

• **The Permanent Revolution & Results and Prospects** Leon Trotsky (£9, €15, $18).

• **My Life Under White Supremacy and in Exile** Leonard Nikani, February 2009 (£10, €12, $15).

• **Cuba at Sea** Ron Ridenour, May 2008 (£8, €12, $15).

• **Ecosocialism or Barbarism** (new expanded edition) Jane Kelly ed., February 2008 (£6, €9, $12).

• **Cuba: Beyond the Crossroads** (new expanded edition) Ron Ridenour, April 2007 (£10, €15, $20).

• **Middle East: war, imperialism, and ecology – sixty years of resistance** Roland Rance & Terry Conway eds. and Gilbert Achcar (contributor) et al., March 2007 (£12, €14, $19).

• **It's never too late to love or rebel** Celia Hart, August 2006 (£8, €15, $20).

www.ingramcontent.com/pod-product-compliance
Lightning Source LLC
Chambersburg PA
CBHW031237290426
44109CB00012B/335